A trilogy
by Yannis Andricopoulos

In Bed with Madness

The Greek Inheritance

The Future of the Past

Published in the UK by Imprint Academic
PO Box 200, Exeter EX5 5HY, UK

Published in the USA by Imprint Academic
Philosophy Documentation Center
PO Box 7147, Charlottesville, VA 22906-7147, USA

ISBN 978-1845401306

A CIP catalogue record for this book is available from the
British Library and US Library of Congress

www.imprint-academic.com

Yannis Andricopoulos

The Greek Inheritance

Ancient Greek Wisdom for the Digital Era

Contents

Part I: The Culture of Joy

1. The Amorous Gods of Greece

It all began one glorious summer morning when the Earth and Time were still young. The two ebullient lovers, Aphrodite, the gorgeous Goddess of Love, and Ares, the pugnacious God of War, were caught together in the august bed of love: they had overslept and they were spotted there by the sky charioteer, Helios, the Sun. The Goddess' extramarital affair with her Olympian colleague had been stealthily and merrily going on for three hundred years producing in its course streams of love and joy – and also three children. But the seal of secrecy had now, and so suddenly, been broken. 'The claims of the unexpected', Odysseus Elytis, the great contemporary Greek poet, uneasily reflected, 'can never be dismissed'.

The high drama began to unfold immediately. Shocked and distraught as a good friend ought to be under such circumstances, Helios rushed to pass on the dreadful news to the husband, Hephaestus, the lame blacksmith-God. The man, whom Sigmund Freud, focusing on Oedipus, has failed to misinterpret for our benefit, was naturally dismayed. At first, resigned, he managed only to mutter something to the effect that he could not have seen the flames of their passion because the nights were too dark. But soon, by his sixth pint of nectar, exasperated by his wife's impeccable disregard of him, and determined to match the splendour of his failure with something equally spectacular, he was ready to strike back.

His plan of action was, as one would expect, sensational. He was, after all, the superb craftsman who had made the first ever robots to help him with his smithy, and even created a female automaton which possessed the gift of speech.

He laboriously hammered out a bronze hunting-net which he attached to his marriage-bed. Once in it, the two lovers would have no chance of escaping. Pleased with himself, the betrayed God then told his wife that, suffering from work-related stress, he would need a short holiday in Lemnos, his favourite island, to recuperate. Needless to say, the wife would have been only too happy to accompany him, but, miserably, she could not, for she had already booked a headache. With a flat face, which, like a Rosenquist painting, was far less flat than it looked, Hephaestus packed his shorts, his suntan lotion and a Jewish novel about two characters called Adam and Eve and left, and the two lovers lusciously plunged once again into the enchantment of their concupiscence.

The euphonic sound of organic kisses, delivered by 'lips as scarlet as arbute berries, and fully fleshed', reverberated once again in the infinitude of the seventh heaven they were in. As a commercial for adultery, the image would have been as brilliant as anything Saatchi & Saatchi has ever worked out for Heineken. But at dawn, caught in the ineluctable grip of the net, they could not get out of bed. Transfixed and naked, they waited for the worst.

The deceived husband, one eye depressed and the other jubilant, instantly sent for all the other Gods to witness the dishonourable event. Only the males arrived, and their 'raucous laughter ... still rang and burned within (Aphrodite's) ears like flame', Costas Varnalis, the Greek poet, tells us. The husband then announced with visibly unconquered emotions that he no longer wanted Aphrodite to be his wife. But, first things first, he would not release her before all the valuable pay-as-you-go marriage-gifts purchased and given to Zeus, head of the Olympian Gods and her adoptive father, had been returned. I am not sure whether he did not regret the subsequent turn of events.

Zeus, who would not hear a word about returning any gifts, told him he was a fool to give such publicity to his private affairs; and Apollo, the God of manly beauty, music and the arts, glancing languorously at the divine curves of Aphrodite, was overheard asking Hermes if he would mind being caught in Ares' position. 'Not at all', the God of thieves and merchants answered, 'even if there were three times as many nets'.

Hephaestus could also have done without the sympathy of Poseidon, the God of the Seas, who with a sort of imperturbable unreserve suggested that, since Zeus refused, Ares should compensate him instead, and, if he could not, he himself would pay in order to end this unprosperous affair. If that were to happen, he expected Aphrodite would, out of gratitude, end up in his bed. Homer, the eighth century BC epic poet, tells us, that Apollo could not stop laughing at the offer. But Hephaestus, demonstrating what later became known as British pragmatism, accepted it.

The end of the story which truly is a story without an end: highly appreciative of Hermes' feelings towards her, Aphrodite spent the night with him and gave birth to Hermaphroditus, a being with both male and female sexual features. The excogitation, discerning and original, resolved at a stroke those awkward issues of sexual orientation which torment our age. Thankful to Poseidon for his friendly mediation, Aphrodite slept with him, too, and bore him two sons. Then, adhering to the standards to which she was now accustomed, she succumbed obligingly to the charms of Dionysos, the God of oenophiliac bliss, creativity and subdued inhibitions. The child she had with him, Priapus, is the fellow with that obscenely huge penis whose curved image the Athenian tourist shop-owners, naturally proud of the country's past, love to display in their windows. Expanding her sexual network, the democratic Goddess later seduced several handsome mortals with whom she was also very fruitful.

Yet Aphrodite, a 'weaver of wiles' according to Sappho, the seventh century BC lyric poet, did not embody the worst aspects

7

of the Olympian Gods. She was never as raw, selfish, greedy, quarrelsome, capricious, deceitful, lecherous or brutal as her male colleagues in particular. Zeus himself was really so base that, if subject to human laws, he would have to rot behind bars for the rest of his immortal life. Even though, unlike all those other people who have nothing to say, he never published his memoirs, it is known that he threatened Rhea, his mother, with rape if she did not stop shouting at him about his lustfulness. And as she, representing the matriarchal origins of Greek society, persisted, he eventually did so. He then forced Hera, Rhea's daughter and his twin-sister, to marry him out of shame because he had also ravished her. I only hope their wedding night on Samos was not a nightmare for her as it lasted three hundred years.

Poseidon, no less of a man, raped the Goddess Demeter, and Apollo, the 'comely bachelor', who was also considered to be a God of the 'Hyperboreans' whom Hecateus the Milesian identified with the British, seemed to have set as his life's goal, as befits the God of learning, the task of helping every nymph and every beautiful mortal woman with their piano lessons, even with their tax self-assessment forms. His tutorials were not limited to female students. His love for Hyacinthus, the handsome young Spartan prince with whom Thamyris, the poet, was also in love, was the first ever recorded homosexual love affair. It ended in tragedy.

Treacherously, Apollo managed to get rid of Thamyris, but was unable to enjoy Hyacinthus who was killed by Zephirus, the West Wind, insanely jealous of Apollo's success. From the drops of his blood sprang the hyacinth flowers.

Acts that would bring disgrace to mortals did not seem to bother the immortals. Hermes, the ex-cattle-thief whom the Olympian chief had made a winged-footed door-to-door salesman to keep him off the streets, stole a fine herd of cows from Apollo, and also appropriated the three silver talents Heracles had given him to give to the orphans of Iphitus. Ares murdered, although he claimed in self-defence, Poseidon's son Halirrhothius – his trial at Areopagus, the rock directly opposite the entrance of Athens' Acropolis, was the first ever murder case; and Apollo, unable to stand his reputation for being harmless, killed Zeus' bodyguards, the Cyclops, in revenge for the killing of Asclepius by Zeus. His punishment was a year's hard labour. Asclepius, the healer, had been thunderbolted because he tried to improve the humans' life expectancy, raising, as a result, hell in the soul of Hades, the boss of the underworld, who happened to be Zeus' brother.

The immortals, though their actions did not ooze tender feelings, had, nevertheless, a benign side too. They could be, and often were, just, gracious, generous, understanding, sympathetic and accommodating. Zeus – 'God preserve his soul', as Kazantzakis' Zorba said – in moments of compassion felt sympathy for the humans, aware that age, death and sorrow had made them the only unhappy living beings on earth. He would also never lie except, of course, in love and war, and was still capable of being a good sport: when he fell in love with beautiful and clever Sinope and promised her whatever gift her heart desired, he let her have what she chose – her virginity.

The immortals were also the only Gods in the history of humanity who had a GSOH. They laughed at Ares, the ferocious warrior God, who ran like a chicken back to Olympus when chased by Heracles, the hero who battled on mankind's behalf only to be turned by Disney into popcorn entertainment; and were able to laugh again at themselves when, the time that Gods and men first apportioned the sacrificial ox, Zeus was tricked into choosing the inedible portions of the carcase, probably more tasty than the vinyl meat offered at contemporary classy restaurants. Zeus tried subsequently to make a point about human irreverence but failed. The point did not want to be made.

To the Christian mind a religion demanding devotion to such bizarre characters is, of course, bound to look absurd and ludicrous. The Greek Gods, in their unexamined life, lacked the most essential qualities of Gods – aloofness, imperiousness, disciplinarianism, retributiveness. They did not personify 'pure good', cold and uncontaminated as the water of the Castalian Spring, and could never claim, even if they tried, to be the guarantors of a morally ordered universe or the source of moral obligations.

Unscrupulous and wretched, they often, instead, offended human decency and were severely reproached for their misdeeds by the humans. Amphitryon, his blood boiling like the juice of the grapes of Megara at the callousness of the divine order, its lack of moral discretion, shouted at Zeus, according to the fifth century BC tragic dramatist Euripides: 'your very nature lacks a sense of right and wrong'. In a fragment of another of his plays that has been lost, Euripides effectively dismissed all the Olympian Gods on moral grounds in his offhand statement 'if the Gods do anything base, they are no longer Gods'.

The amorality of divine omnipotence did not, however, bother the Greeks, for morality did not emanate from the Olympian Holy See. Man did not expect his Gods to provide the standards of moral behaviour. Standards could be provided only by man himself: 'Learn to feel shame before yourselves rather than before others', Democritus, the philosopher, advised his fellow citizens. Morality, an exclusively human affair, unbolstered by fear of punishment in the 'other world', reflected only, as Joseph Conrad, the Polish-born novelist, might say, 'the inner worth of man, the edge of his temper, and the fibre of his stuff'. Backed by a boundless faith in his own potency, man was, indeed, his own God, able even to shame his Gods if they acted shamelessly – 'I, a man, put you, a God, to shame', Amphitryon shouted at Zeus, hoping, perhaps, that Zeus, if clever enough, would learn something from human behaviour and morally improve himself over time. Morality was a purely human affair with nothing divine about it.

'Then, do not the Gods care for us?', Onesimos asked himself in *Arbitration*, a comedy by Menander, the fourth century BC comic dramatist. 'Oh, yes, they do', he answered. 'They've put a guardian in each one of us, namely his character'. When Heraclitus, the sixth to fifth century BC philosopher whose 'brevity and weight of style' were according to Diogenes Laertius 'incomparable', pronounced that 'a man's character is his daemon', he meant exactly that: one's personal destiny is determined by his character over which he has some control. Jean-Paul Sartre, the French Marxist-existentialist philosopher, who emphasised that man is what he makes of himself and that this is his freedom, or Carl Rogers, the American humanistic psychologist and writer, who, like Sartre, insisted that man chooses who to be, endeavouring to become his own unique individual self, did not say anything different.

The Greek Gods never had the powers which Christianity invested in its own lonely God. Considered to be neither the creators nor the sustainers of the universe, they were not its masters and its rulers, and they had no jurisdiction over the fate of mankind. Free from the stage-managed high dramas of Genesis, creation was, according to Greek cosmology, a long evolutionary process initiated by the happy union of *Gaia*, the Earth, with *Ouranos*, the Sky. Life on earth, Aphrodite said in *The Danaids*, an Aeschylus play of which only fragments have survived, had emerged following her impregnation by the rain falling from the amorous heaven. Being *Gaia's* spontaneous and most splendid fruits, produced as seeds produce trees, Gods and humans were, thus, brothers and sisters – 'one is the race of Gods and of men; from one mother we both drew our breath', Pindar, the fifth century BC lyric poet, informed us as confident as Orange, the mobile phone company, was of the colour of the future.

Having their own distinct place in the world independently of their Gods, humans were, thus able to move between the hidden parallels of their destiny confidently and uninhibitedly. They were, indeed, so respected by their senior brothers for their wisdom and good judgment that they were often invited to settle disputes between them. Alalcomeneus, the first man of the 'golden race' born to Gaia, rather than a pitiful figure, was employed as a marriage counsellor to help Zeus sort out his marital problems with Hera. He was not very successful, but at least he averted an expensive divorce which would have been bound to attract much adverse publicity.

The Trojan prince Paris, likewise, was brought in to decide who was the fairest of the three Goddesses, Hera, Athene or Aphrodite, and the citizens of Athens, similarly, acted as arbiters in a dispute between Athene and Poseidon. The dispute was settled democratically in a referendum won by Athene, the Goddess of wisdom, with a majority of one: all the men voted in favour of Poseidon and all the women in favour of Athene, but the city had one more woman than there were men. Unfortunately, the women paid dearly for their numerical superiority as, to appease Poseidon, the Athenians thereafter deprived them of their vote. Men were also forbidden to bear their mothers' names as they had hitherto been. According to the myth, that was how patriarchy was instituted, and women since had to look as virtuous as organically grown sprouts.

The Gods were, of course, invested with great powers, far superior to those of the mortals. But these powers were not unlimited. They were determined by *Anánke*, Necessity, the force behind the creation which controlled the actions of both men and Gods. *Anánke* had imposed limits which even the great Zeus, subject to the three Fates, the parthenogenous daughters of the Great Necessity, could not break. Zeus did, of course, deny it arguing that he controlled the Fates, instead, because he was their father. His claim was mockingly dismissed by Aeschylus, the tragic dramatist, Herodotus, the historian, and Plato, the philosopher. None of them would have such nonsense.

Anánke existed to demarcate physical and human limits that could not be crossed without punishment. As such, it was the powerful force that maintained the world's balance, ready to step in if and when this balance had been disturbed by forces beyond human control or by humans themselves. This force had nothing to do with fate which played such a prominent role in the East, and it did not negate free will.

Restricted by *Anánke*, the Gods were not, thus, the all-powerful rulers of the universe. If they were to think so, they would only be acting as self-deludingly as cockerels believing the sun rises in response to their call. They could not step over the boundaries of their role or misbehave, for humans, anything but the digital face of an extra in a Hollywood film, were ready to confront them as they often had. The giants Otus and Ephialtes, the handsome sons of Aloeus, piled up mountains in order to attack them and they even captured Ares; Sisyphus, outwitting Hades, the king of the dead, arrested and imprisoned him for a few days – as a result nobody could die; and, in the midst of the Trojan war, roisterous hero Diomedes attacked and injured Aphrodite with his sword, and then, unapologetically, told her to go and see her hairdresser as she had no business on the battlefield. Pentheus, the mythological king of Thebes, who banned the worship of Dionysos and even jailed him, did not, however, fair so well. Angry at the man, 'a fighter against God who dares to defy me', the God of physical and spiritual intoxication lured him in a Bacchic frenzy in which he was torn, like an animal, limb from limb by the maenads.

The affronts to the Olympians had, indeed, no end. Like Heraclitus and also Plato after him, Xenophanes, abandoning himself to what an American pragmatist would regard as profitless speculation, ridiculed the anthropomorphism of the Greek pantheon. If cattle and horses had hands to draw, he inferred from his endeixes, their Gods would look like cattle and horses. A monotheist who nevertheless never claimed that his views were the result of divine revelation, Xenophanes held, like an agnostic, that no man knew, or would ever know, the truth about the Gods. Even if one accidentally discovered the truth, he said, he would not know it to be the truth.

But even their existence was questioned, for as contemporary Greek poetess Zoe Karelli put it, 'nor Achilles, not even Odysseus set forth to war believing in the handsome Gods'. Protagoras, the agnostic philosopher and rhetorician, articulated the point when he said 'I can not know for certain whether they exist or not for there are many things that hinder certainty – the obscurity of the matter, and the shortness of man's life'. Critias, the philosophical poet and dramatist, on the other hand, went much further when, like a contemporary atheist, he dismissed the Gods altogether – they had been invented, he said, to keep man in subservience.

Naturally, the Olympians, as Aeschylus informs us, were getting increasingly irritated at their humiliation by their junior brothers. The latter's temerity, intellectual disrespect, their dauntless challenges to their higher status were, indeed, exasperating. But they could do nothing to curb the growth of their rebellious brothers' power or their unbounded self-confidence. They could neither 'wipe them off the face of the earth', as the Jewish God is reputed to have done once, for they depended, as Aristophanes ascertained, on the humans' good will to receive the sacrifices and the honours vital for their own survival. And they could not even threaten the humans to ensure deference to their wishes. As Euripides explained without a trace of cynicism, 'frightening stories' of divine wrath at human misdeeds were just invented tales, 'profitable for the worship of the Gods'.

The Gods, if not honoured, or when their patience, tried by mortals, seemed to lose its temper, could be as awkward as Aphrodite was when she punished saffron-robed Eosa with a constant longing for young men or when Apollo gave Midas a pair of ass' ears which later produced quite an instructive story about secrets. But the Greeks did honour them. The essence of myth, Neoplatonic philosopher Salloustios said in the fourth century, is 'what never happened, but always is'. Myth does not need to be realistic to be socially accepted. It holds us because it expresses something meaningful to us and, therefore, real.

In such a context, Greek religious rituals were not a formalised introspection in search of communion with the divine. Performed by the entire community rather than priests, they were, instead, festivities and celebrations which was what the carefree Gods, lovers of beauty, feasting and a good laugh, expected from the humans and were entitled to enjoy on account of their divinity.

Happy to oblige, the Greeks offered them what they wanted: chilling out with a delightful spiral dance performance, a fine dramatic show, poetry recitals, songs and games, chariot races, archery contests, banquets, carnival processions – in other words, decent prime-time entertainment with, perhaps, a few special effects. The popular feasts of the Greeks, Hegel, the nineteenth century German philosopher noted, were all religious feasts, yet none of them had the colour of mourning, joined in with downcast eyes; and in none of them did people put money on a plate. Instead, they wreathed themselves in flowers and dressed in the colours of rapturous joy, celebrating life in a way which people during my childhood used to celebrate the death of an uncle in the United States. Greece, a 'land of music and dance', contemporary American author Tom Cahill exclaimed, knew 'how to party'. She 'did not invent joy and youth', André Malraux, the French novelist, said before him, 'but she was the first to celebrate their glory'.

The Panathenean procession in Athens was the most splendid feast of its kind. Others, particularly in Greece's countryside, divinely curved, had elements of what scholars have termed 'ritual obscenity'. Invented a long time before modernism killed not only the great goals of humanity but also the individual's instinctual aims, these salacious, orgiastic celebrations, adored by the Gods, i.e., the males of their species, manifested a respect for the irrational in the form of Dionysian frenzy. Rationality, as it was widely accepted, is irksome as much as virtue is boring if the impulsive, instinctive and primitive in man is extirpated by civilisation and prudence kills passion.

Heraclitus called these celebrations 'paeans to penis', the penis being presumably a symbol of some cosmic energy proudly depicted in the form of huge erect penises in processions and religious celebrations to the delight of the faithful, or worn in the form of jewellery. The poor man obviously did not expect Andrea Dworkin, the American radical feminist writer, to denounce later the male organ as 'a symbol of terror' even more frightening than the gun, the knife or the bomb. Without these frenzied celebrations, Heraclitus thought, people would act most shamelessly. For the females, there were other events dedicated to the pursuit of ecstatic irresponsibility which freed them from domestic felicities and male authority – albeit temporarily.

Proud of being men, the Greeks refused, thus, to melt in ecstasy or fear like candles before extinction, to be the 'slaves of our Lord', repenting day and night for their sins and begging the Gods for forgiveness as men do in many of the great religions of the world. Rather than 'powerless, crushed, reduced to nothing before the infinitude of the divine', they had presence, will, and the determination to run their lives according to their own values. Hence they prayed to their Gods 'like men', proud, erect and unbowed. To think of Pericles, the Athenian statesman, going down on his knees and praying to Athene with clasped hands or of Socrates delivering pious sermons to his pupils would look to them as absurd as organisational systems do to modern Greeks. It might even look 'disgusting' which is what Herodotus felt about the way the Egyptians used to salute each other: 'they half-prostrate themselves to one another, and behave like dogs, lowering their hands to their knees'.

In their unbounded self-confidence, proud of being human and, thereby able to achieve the seemingly impossible, the Greeks often did not even court their Gods' favours. Ajax, a Greek hero of the Trojan war, advised by his father Telamon to conquer 'but always with the help of Gods', retorted that 'with the help of Gods any coward or fool can win glory; I trust to do so even without them'.

'The norm of human conduct', Joseph Campbell, the great American cultural anthropologist, said, 'became not the nursery norm of obedience, but a rational individual development under laws that were not supposed to be from God, but were recognised to be the products of purely human judgment'. Miserably for the Gods, the tales about them, 'playful, humorous, at once presenting and dismissing the images', were formulated, as F.M. Cornford, the English philosopher, said, not by priests nor even by prophets. They were, instead, the work of poets, philosophers and artists none of whom traded in religiosity and the mysteries of the beyond. The focus, which defined humanism for ever as man's endeavour to identify with his essence and live freely and in dignity with his humanity, was on life itself, humanly shaped and mellifluous as the whispering of the Aegean Sea.

In the Zeus of Pheidias or in the Hera and Aphrodite of Alcamenes, the beard and the dresses of the sculptures were, thus, of more interest than the Gods and the Goddesses themselves, and in the Hermes and the Cnidian Aphrodite of Praxiteles there was not a spark of anything religious except the allure of the delicately winsome nymph of the waves. The Goddesses, when compared to austere Christian images, were of course sensuous; yet the images were not erotic figures, a going concern in all their parts like Britney Spears, but, like 'La France', luminous images inseparable from their radiance.

In any conflict between Gods and the highest principles of humanity, the loyalty and sympathy of the Greeks were, thus, inevitably on the side of humankind. Rather than repent and ask for God's mercy like Job, who, addressing a God who had 'destroyed him without cause', still, pious and submissive, pleaded 'I despise myself and repent in dust and ashes', they would stand up for their human judgment. 'I defy divinity', roared Heracles, a hero of the Greeks, strepitantly enough to be heard by, and unnerve, the yet to be born Islamic, Christian, Jewish and Hindu fundamentalists. Tortured Prometheus, the demigod who became the Greeks' model, when ordered by Zeus to capitulate, did not think twice, Aeschylus tells us in his masterful style, before telling Hermes, the messenger of Zeus:

'So let the pronged locks of lightning be launched at me, let the air be roused with thunder and convulsion of wild winds, let hurricanes upheave by the roots the base of the earth, let the sea-waves' roaring savagery confound the courses of the heavenly stars;

let him lift me high and hurl me to black Tartarus on ruthless floods or irresistible doom... For great Zeus I care less than nothing'.

Prometheus, punished by Zeus for giving fire to mankind, had been chained naked to a pillar in the Caucasian mountains, where a greedy vulture tore at his liver all day, year in, year out; his torture would not end because every night his liver became whole again.

'Only the Greeks', Antonio Gramsci, the prewar Italian communist leader and a most influential Marxist, said, 'could have imagined Prometheus ... The Hebrews, producing the image of Job, were more realistic; their hero was more true to life'. But the Greeks, Isaac Newton's 'greatest people in the world', were larger than life; and their universe, a universe of free will and individual freedom, was as Karl Kerenyi, a leading Hungarian classical scholar, enthused, 'chiefly one of sunlight, though it was not the sun, but man at its centre'. Confronted with 'the dreadful destructive turmoil of so-called world history as well as ... the cruelty of nature', Nietzsche, likewise, exclaimed, rather than look for recourse in 'a Buddhist negation of the will' the Greeks said 'yes' to life and its angst. The clotted darkness of religions haunted by death were as alien to them as oriental immobility.

Euripides' 'I love not the Gods that are worshipped by night' illustrates eloquently their instinct and also their passion for the consummation of their love affair with the light before their sky's limitless blue was wrapped up in reddish bars of cloud.

2. Divine in Itself

Woven with the sunlight, playing 'among trees and flowers secure in their kindness', as Hölderlin, one of Germany's poetic giants, would sing, Greek religiosity was, evidently, worlds apart from what Hegel called 'the poverty and fear' of the Judaeo-Christian worldview. The Greek Gods had not presented themselves to mortals through revelation as on Sinai, in Christ or the words of Mohammed, and had not laid down a divine law, strict or otherwise, to which the humans had to conform. The concept of a God remote from humankind, an awesome and haughty authority inhabiting the dreadful stillness of eternity, and yet powerful enough to dictate the norm of human conduct and punish plurality and diversity, arbiter, through his representatives, of human affairs, and a disapproving force of life on earth in favour of life after death, would have been for them as credible as our own belief in dragons.

The Sermon on the Mount, in which the word 'reward' after death is mentioned nine times, the idea of reward another nineteen, and the threat of punishment a dozen times, would have, likewise, sounded both absurd and totally offensive to their sense of human dignity.

Life, a dancing tongue of flame, was for the Greeks not a preparation for eternal life and it did not demand obedience in readiness for the approaching end. In their insouciant, heliotropic world, the river Ilissus did not swell with the tears of Athene as the Nile did with the tears of Isis; and the earth, 'mother of all life' as Prometheus affirmed, was anything but the Christian 'Vale of Tears'. Their indomitable spirit never entertained such a heap of reasons for comfort in misfortune, which provoked Hegel to comment sarcastically that 'we might be sorry in the end that we cannot lose a father or a mother every week'.

The Greek religion, 'a ship loaded with Homeric myths', had no laws codified in a book, no religious teachings, no clergy, no blind dumb terror of the sacred and no religious oppression. Freedom had been sanctioned by the Gods themselves – man had been given choice, the cornerstone of the free market, as to which God to worship: the amorous Aphrodite or the ever-virginal Artemis, Dionysos, the God of ecstasy, or Athene, the Goddess of wisdom. 'Men', Euripides said, 'make their choice: one man honours one God and another one another'. Free from eschatological calculations, active members of this world rather than future 'citizens of heaven', and poles apart from Christian ethics, which, as the German theologian Günther Bornkamm said, 'does not know the idea of the good deed that has value in itself', the Greeks, Paul's 'fools', anchored their religiosity in a moral decency for its own sake. The sustaining images of the religious eternity were for them present in the earthly here-and-now, the textured face of life's pleasures and pains, the well-known caprices of fortune.

Their religion had no scope for denial and no original sin, either. Unless they had themselves committed a disgraceful act, the Greeks were pure. There was no guilt, no Judge, no need for redemption, no doctrines, no eternity in Hell or paradise, and no Satan, a projection of man's own tormented mind. 'Do not imagine', Aeschines, the fourth century BC Athenian orator and statesman, told his countrymen, 'that wrongdoing originates with Gods rather than with the vileness of man'. The fire that burns us is in ourselves rather than in the other world, he could well have added if he had anticipated the time the world's door, as the Iraqi poet Walid Khazendar put it, was 'shut against the hoary stranger claiming to be you'.

Life after death was never really an issue at any time in the Greek philosophical tradition. As Jean-Pierre Vernant, the eminent French historian, stated, the idea of individual immortality must have seemed to the Greeks 'quite strange and incongruous'. Even Plato, who in the *Phaedo* introduced the concept of the individual's immortal soul, did not see this soul connected to the individual but to the divine itself, of which the individual soul was only a small particle. Divine punishment in the other world, washing the floor of hell, would likewise be simply an absurdity.

Paradise, if there was one, was here, on earth, and the 'key' to it, as Nicos Kazantzakis, the Greek poet and novelist who was anathematised by the Greek Orthodox Church, once said, is the 'penis'. The body, the 'profound body', was not an 'it', separate from 'us'; although we are more than our body, the body was 'us', and rather than denied, it was adored and enjoyed. The plea to God by St Augustine, the major Christian philosopher, to help him overcome all temptations, the lust of the flesh, the enjoyment of food, the allurement of sweet scents, the pleasures of the ear, the lure to the eye of the various forms of beauty, and the temptation of 'knowing for knowing's sake' – the only type of knowledge to be desired was knowledge of God and the soul – would have shocked them. In St Augustine the Greeks would have seen not a sage but a man, who, having been born in his sleep and bearing a grudge against the world, had simply gone insane.

So, too, would they have regarded the fierce dedication of St Francis of Assisi to poverty, hunger and ecstatic prayer. Renunciation of the world, the Christians' 'lowest and vilest element in the scheme of things', for the benefits of the afterlife, the vegetative indolence in which those who turn their back on the world live, was not for them an option. The task, instead, was to make life more beautiful, blithesome, harmonious and just. For Aristotle, any creature to whom nothing is pleasant and everything indifferent is 'very far from being human'. If his path had crossed St Francis', he might well have told him: man 'get yourself a good woman and give up this nonsense'.

Socrates, the closest one could come to a Greek sage, would have never shared Gandhi's belief in the conservation of vital fluids as a means of deepening a man's spiritual understanding. He would have opposed, too, the Buddhist physical denial of the body, as commemorated by a skeletal sage meditating under a Bo tree. Socrates is, instead, well-remembered for his appetite for sex, 'moderate but inventive', as first century AD epigrammatist Marcus Martial might have said.

Worlds apart from the latter Christian understandings, engaged with the physical world, the Greeks did not plunge into the void of oriental mysticism, either. The Buddhist, Hindu or Jainist spiritual realities, unfrequented by passions, unable to install any desire other than becoming a component of a tenebrous nonexistence and bound only to increase the insignificance of the things people say, would have looked to them as meaningful as a die without spots. Oriental religiosity demands the annihilation of the individual as a preliminary to its absorption in the Absolute of the divinity, the creation of a human zero, which can then be propelled into infinity. 'I do not exist', Kapila, the sixth century BC sage, contentedly announced, and Taoism, a movement in opposition to Confucian despotism, explained: the extirpation of the self is the prime purpose of existence – the perfect man has no self and no essence. Becoming is hopeless. To hope is futile.

'Happy the man ... whose dreams are dead or never born', Primo Levi, that so touchingly human Italian-Jewish poet, ironically reflected; 'he fears nothing, hopes for nothing, expects nothing, but stares fixedly at the setting sun'. Perhaps, even happier is the man who is never born.

As decreed by the Buddhist, Jain and Hindu law of karma, man's first duty is to play his given role without resistance, like the sun and the moon, the rocks and the stars, ensuring the elimination of craving and the extinction of desires. 'Free will' is, in any case, according to Shri Ramakrishma, the Indian saint, 'a mere appearance'. All is an illusion, and nothing can be gained by action. It follows that the only course open is a deliberate benign indifference to the external world because the latter could be tucked into a fold of Brahma's robe. Life is apparently as exciting as the adventures of yellow.

Indeed, non-action, not-doing, is the individual's shield. Tao Te Ching advises: 'Those who have true te are like a newborn baby – and if they seem like this, they will not be stung by wasps or snakes'. To be safe, mentally humans would have to remain babies. In the fixed hierarchy of the Bronze Age cosmology out of which these oriental systems emerged, Joseph Campbell says, there is no space for either will or mind as a creative force – nothing to be gained through individual originality and effort. The world is not a process – nothing has apparently moved since humans invented the art of making sense or, at least, since Hector's farewell to Andromache.

It is, instead, a state to be understood by what the sages have taught from yore and revered.

Greece, André Malraux observed, gave the world a culture in which man based his supreme values on his loftiest ideals and concentrated his efforts on all he could do to harmonise himself with them; not on what he ought to be so as to attune himself with the eternal. The Greek nation, Karl Beloch, the German historian, explained, too, was too full of youthful vigour for the general acceptance of beliefs which deny the world and transfer real life into the darkness of the grave, mystically identified with absolute bliss and light. Full of May, free from mysticism and far from thinking that they were a mere nothing in relation to their Gods, the Greeks, this 'Godlike race' according to Schiller, had, instead, to remind themselves constantly that they were not Gods themselves. 'Never again, until the Greek spirit intoxicated Italy at the Renaissance', Professor H.D.F. Kitto, the respected twentieth century authority on the classical age, in lyrical terms revered, 'do we find such superb self-confidence in humanity'. In the Greeks, Nikolai Gogol, the Russian novelist, acknowledged, 'we recognise the divine origin of man'.

Still, although they never recited thirteen *Our Fathers* before going to bed, the Greeks were not exactly atheists. Atheism, as it emerged in the eighteenth century, could have never taken root in Greece, for the Greeks had neither religious doctrines nor an all-powerful clergy on which atheism thrives.

Their world had something divine in itself. The spark of divinity existed not in the Gods, but in the omnificent force which gives the poppy a black cross over its heart and a tuft of deep blue eyelashes. God in this sense was an immanent God, a divine presence pervading everything, in the rebirth of nature in the spring, the flow of the streams, the order of the universe and the actions of men – indeed, in the multiplicity of events and in the intertwining of all forms. 'God', Heraclitus wrote just as Thales had written before him, 'is day and night, winter and summer, war and peace, satiety and famine'.

The universe was 'itself the maker and creator of itself'. The sacred was to be found, not in an all too powerful divine absurdity, but in the songs of nightingales, in daily experiences and routines, in Heraclitus' kitchen fire on which he used to roast his chestnuts in the long winter nights, or, to use a graceful line from a Pablo Neruda poem, in 'what spring does with the cherry trees'.

Democritus, the philosopher whose voice according to second century A.D. sceptic philosopher Sextus Empiricus compared to that of Zeus himself, likewise, held Zeus to be 'all things', justice and injustice, love and hatred, beauty and ugliness. The revelation was within the miracle of nature – it did not need to come through special word – and religiousness meant experiencing the divinity in the miracle of life itself. As Zeno, the fifth century BC Stoic philosopher, explained gently but firmly, the substance of God is in our universe.

Respect for the divine demanded, thus, no reverence for the Olympian Gods, but respect for the intelligence inherent in the workings of the universe, for the cosmic *Nous*, which was identified with Necessity, Logos and its laws. Of paramount importance among the latter was *Dikaiosyne*, Justice, and *Isonomia*, Equality, between all elements of the world. *Dikaiosyne*, translated poorly as Justice, combined a cosmic sense of order, which, internalised, projected itself back in the world as fairness in externals. It meant living a life connected with the divinity within, in harmony with the eternal rhythm, tuned, as the second century AD Roman Emperor and Stoic philosopher Marcus Aurelius put it, to 'the movement of the stars as if you were turning with them'. The natural law, the laws by which the world is governed, as Baruch Spinoza, the seventeenth century philosopher, concurred later, were for the Greeks the laws of beauty.

This understanding, which was never dissolved in time, was based on respect for everything in the universe, whose creative power enables the seed to blossom in the spring or the earth to heal her own wounds. 'When shall we open our arms', Kazantzakis, author of *Zorba the Greek* wondered like his ancestors, 'to embrace everything – stones, rain, flowers and men?'

That 'everything' had a soul, but the soul of 'a glass of wine, a roast chestnut, a wretched little brazier, the sound of the sea', like the magnet which Thales thought had a soul, had nothing to do with the divine as orthodox religions understand it. God for the Greeks, the eminent German theologian Paul Tillich said, was not out there, but in 'the depth and ground of our being'. The soul of things, if acknowledged by 'a simple, frugal heart', was happiness, 'simple and frugal', in the here and now. Angelos Sikelianos, one of Greece's great twentieth century lyric poets and a man accustomed, like the ancients, 'to eat at mystic banquets with all the Gods', felt, likewise, that 'the very language' of his soul was 'the whisper of the dry grasses'.

Soul and matter were always one at least until Plato, the fourth century BC philosopher, who, reading celestial autocues, split the world into the physical world which is nothing but an illusion of the senses, and the spiritual world, the real world apprehended only by the intellect. Influenced by Eastern theologies, for which the clash between man and God looked as absurd as it did later to Christian eyes, the Gnostics in the Hellenistic and Roman times then turned Plato's intellectual construct into a set of beliefs which, though rational in origin, became mystical in orientation, exempt from intellectual influences. In empathy with the One, the soul of matter, the *anima mundi* which pervades all life, they called for full identification with the divine in preparation for life after life. The love for life had gone. Thoughts had no place in people's private lives.

The religion of the Greeks, though far superior to anything else the world has ever seen, can easily be dismissed as a farcical representation of religiosity. Even the term Greek religion may sound an oxymoron, much like American diplomacy and liberal imperialism or, to quote poet Philip Larkin, the British Kavafis, happy Christmas and family holiday.

But these Greek Gods, so dignifiedly silent since their demise, did not lock themselves, like their monotheistic competitors, into any absurd postures of seriousness, and did not force anyone to believe the unbelievable biblical stories: the tale of Adam and Eve, the ready-made humans plonked down on earth by God, or the myths of hellfire, the Virgin Mary and the resurrection. They were not tyrants calling for the unconditional mental capitulation of their subjects, nor sadists demanding from them solitude, fasting and sexual abstinence on which the religious fundamentalism of our era thrives. Zeus never excluded either as, Luke tells us, Christ did with his 'if anyone comes to me and does not hate his father and mother, wife and children, brothers and sisters, even his own life, he cannot be a disciple of mine'.

Likewise, the Greek Gods, dressed in civilian clothes rather than nationalist khaki, did not promise to drive out 'the Amorites, the Hittites, the Perizzites, the Canaanites, and the Jebusites ... little by little until your numbers have grown enough to take possession of the whole country'; they did not strike down 'every first-born in Egypt'; and they did not reward the faithful with 'flocks and herds, silver and gold, male and female slaves, camels and asses'. As opposed to Yahweh, the God of the Hebrews, they were never concerned with possessions; and, again unlike him, they never sanctioned slavery.

The Greek Gods did not, of course, have the excessively loving temper of the Christian saints. But neither, on the other hand, did they know the meaning of the zealots' crystal hatreds. In 'the gyration of centuries and the hideouts of myths', both age-old and, despite the vacillations of memory, endlessly newborn, they played, cheated, fooled about and enjoyed life to the full – childhood, adolescence, maturity and old age, though not necessarily in that order. They had a good sense of humour, far superior to that of any Christian, laughed as no other Gods have ever done, and loved the view of the world from their exquisite balcony on Olympus.

Having come to terms with human mortality, whose acceptance,

Cornelius Castoriades, the contemporary Greek philosopher, said, is a condition of living as autonomous beings in an autonomous society, blessed by the indestructible innocence of the Olympian system and liberated by their religion rather than repressed, humans were, thus, able to harmonise their existence with the order of things without the support of a religious doctrine as it is understood today. They were able to determine their course in life as they themselves thought fit with Freedom and Justice in the place of God.

As Émile Durkheim, sociology's 'father', would have said, rather than an expression of true religious feeling, the Olympian system existed as the symbolic and ritual representation of the Greeks' political and social order. This being the case, the word 'religion' did not even exist in the Greek vocabulary – *threskeía*, which in contemporary Greek means religion as we understand it today, described only religious rites. Inseparable from civic life and the focal point for civic pride, these Gods were Gods of a culture much as it is for me the Christian Greek Orthodox God and His family whose praise I sing occasionally in church. The intellectual incredulity with which they were often received did not, and could not, negate them, for their existence affirmed the Greeks' commitment to their collective and democratic ideals and provided the foundation for freedom, a freedom in diversity. The system made democracy and pluralism the values blessed by the Gods; it also guaranteed the civic rights of the citizens and the rights of the individual. Greek religion, fit for men free, proud, rational, inquisitive, principled and able to see everything every day as if for the first time, was certainly not the opium of the masses.

Hence the Olympian system, colourful as Nelson Mandela's floral shirts and substantiated by a separate moral code impressively articulated long before civilisation was proudly able to compile its first crime statistics, produced no armies of proselytising fanatics, no religious wars and no atrocities and massacres perpetrated in His name. It was never appropriated by an aggressive, expansionist state, oppressive theocracies or powerful institutions for their own private ends.

The great, and rather unamusing, antithesis between the true Yahweh believers and their enemies had not crossed the Greeks' minds – the Greeks, consequently, were never invited, as Ann Coulter, the darling of the American Right, invited her fellow Americans, to 'invade (the Arab) countries, kill their leaders, and convert them to Christianity'; they were never called, as the Muslims were by Osama bin Laden, 'to remove evil' and 'lead people to the light'; and they never commanded anyone to fight Satan by invading Iraq. Unlike the Americans, they had, thankfully, never been chosen by a higher power to defeat the forces of darkness; and again unlike them, they never claimed that 'the liberty we prize is not America's gift to the world; it is God's gift to humanity'. Messianic visions regarding rectitude and purpose were the privilege of later ages.

Jerry Falwell and Pat Robertson, the American evangelists, who chose to view the September 11 terrorist attack as God's punishment for the country's moral debasement on account of its sinful acceptance of abortion, homosexuality and secular schools, would have no place in their world. The Greeks respected, instead, the rights of humans to live their lives fully, and encouraged them to do so. Disempowering theological belief systems, gaolers of the incarcerated sunlight, rooted in mythic notions of divine appointments and political absolutism, were utterly alien to the Greeks, who democratised religion well before they democratised their polis.

Hans Küng, the Swiss theologian and one of British Prime Minister Tony Blair's religious mentors, has said that man's ethical outlook can hardly be sustained without faith in, and fear of, God. If this needs to be disproved, the Greeks' irreligious ethical outlook, their secular and also righteous society, does just that. Their *aletheia*, the truth, as Martin Heidegger, the German existentialist philosopher, commented delightedly, was humanity's 'Age of the Holy' which passed away with the triumph of the religion of the cross.

The common, André Gide, the French novelist, said, is almost destined to triumph over the exquisite.

3. Awe-inspiring Abstractions

Able to inspire without rhetoric and to rule without law, open and broad-minded, flexible and dispassionate, all-inclusive and tolerant, the Olympian system, together with a common language and shared customs, gave the Greeks their identity and homogeneity. The process, structuralist Levi-Strauss would say, shows not how men think in myths but how myths operate in men's minds without their being aware of the fact. Yet the subject, the Greeks, did not disappear as reflective, responsible and creative agents. Freed from superstition, prejudice and fear, they managed, instead, to get in touch with the intangible, move to the ultimate frontiers of intrepidity, and find, as Goethe put it, 'the courage that began to shape the world'.

Rather than let others do it for them, believing in themselves, in their ability to determine their own lives, they owned themselves. 'Wonders', the chorus in Sophocles' *Antigone* says, 'are many on earth, and the greatest of these is man'. This thrilling paean to the human spirit, with all its far-reaching consequences, was the eternal affirmation of the greatness humans can achieve. As young as the sea, the truth of the Greeks, the offspring of their brilliant faculties, the yield of their essential sanity, the divine element which enabled them to cross the horizon line in search of the square root of the unknown, filled, as Ezra Pound, the brilliant American poet, might have said, 'the four corners of (their) being'. It contained the seeds of their eternity.

The rationalism introduced as a result of this profoundly poetic experience of religiosity was an earthshaking revolution. It marked the beginning of a colossal, epochal change in the evolution of the world that contained within itself the script of the future. The revolution, the pyrrhic dance of the spirit, established knowledge as opposed to religious doctrine or supernatural and mythological explanations as the key to the world's inner reality. Knowledge became the foundation of humanity's thinking. Anything, as a result, became possible, if, Umberto Eco would say, the impossible was true. The outcome was that stupendous, incredible search for rational explanations of everything under the sun, the giant steps in time each one of which was a journey into the unthinkable. To this, according to Goethe, 'we owe our liberation from monkish barbarism'.

Capricious, yet governed by laws upon which even the Gods could not infringe, the world was presumed by the early philosophers, those 'candles of the night', to be rational, submissive to examination. Hippocrates, the father of medicine, made the point early enough, in the fifth century BC, when he tauntingly taught that if we are to call whatever we do not understand divine, then 'there would be no end of divine things'. Iris might be a goddess, Xenophanes had similarly explained in the sixth century BC, but in reality the rainbow is nothing but a multicoloured cloud. Feeling, as Isaac Newton did, like a child picking shells on the shore of the great and unexplored ocean of truth, he deduced, likewise, from seashells embedded in mountains, that the earth, subject to major geological changes, is very old, much older than our most distant memories.

Earthquakes, similarly, were not the rather inarticulate expression of the chthonian Gods' displeasure with the humans. They were caused, instead, Anaximenes, the youngest of the three Milesian philosophers, asserted without fear of being lynched by a religious mob, by movements in the earth. The assumption was that everything had a rational origin and could be rationally explained. The Aids epidemic may be for Christian fundamentalists God's punishment for our sins, but the terrible plague which hit Athens at the beginning of the Peloponnesian war and killed a third of her population was for the Athenians nothing more than a plague. In the same way, psychotic episodes, once seen by Christian moralists as the price paid by the individual for his moral debasement, were for the Greeks just symptoms of poor health.

Looking into the eye of the universe, their philosophers inquired into *physis*, 'the nature of things', the 'spring of beings', and tried to make sense of the natural world, to understand all aspects of life – physical, psychological, social, political, cultural and intellectual. In doing so, they looked for 'fundamental properties' and 'primal substances' and searched for *archai*, the principles which would enable them to bear on their shoulders the weight of the unknown. Marching beyond the outermost limits of daring, they explained the universe, Jonathan Barnes wrote, from within, in terms of its own constituent features, and also systematically, i.e., in the same rationally defined terms and by the same logically progressive method. Like modern scientists, they also explained as much as possible as economically as possible.

Their conceptual understandings, what Nietzsche called their 'awe-inspiring abstractions', were at first, as one might expect, in many instances unsound. But their achievement was not to be found in the explanations themselves, or the ontological merits of their arguments. It was, instead, in their utter belief that the world was intelligible and explainable purely by rational analysis, and in the fact that, rather than making *ex-cathedra* pronouncements, they supported their views with reasons and arguments.

The process, intellectually intoxicating, captured the imagination of the Greeks and fully engaged their brilliant intellect. It took them far beyond the limits of the age – the future was filled generously with their seed, Angelos Sikelianos, Greece's William Blake, would have said. Greece, with the eyes of time firmly set on her, was set at feverish pace on the path of discovery that turned itself into another, almost incredible myth.

The resulting advance in science was so vigorous and far-reaching, so fantastic and breathtaking that as Arthur Koestler, the Hungarian-born thinker, chillingly observed, had the Greek world not collapsed, satellites and nuclear weapons would have probably arrived on earth one thousand five hundred years earlier. The honour fell, instead, to western science, which, since the time of Copernicus and Kepler, Galileo and Descartes, has been frantically dancing to the flaming tunes set by the inquisitive minds and the fearless reasoning of the Greeks. But Europe, who, as A.N. Whitehead, the English mathematician, logician and philosopher, said, knew less in the sixteenth century AD than the Greeks in the third century BC, both fulfilled and betrayed the promise the Greeks made on science's behalf.

Science, 'value-free', a means to further modernist ends, moved forward in leaps and bounds, losing in the process its innocence as fast as pollution was being democratised. Galileo, the Italian astronomer and physicist, placed his talents at the disposal of the industrial-military complex of his time to improve the artillery's fire power and the art of fortification just as the academics of the Massachusetts Institute of Technology work with the military to arm through nanotechnology, and in an 'otherwordly' fashion, the superpower's warriors. The story has been the same ever since modernism cured the world of its humanity except that at this stage of the game the future looks much more threatening than ever before for the accelerating advance of technology far outpaces the development of social and political frameworks that act as controls and brakes.

The triumph of science and technology to which the Greeks so heavily contributed was not their fault. They armed people with an unbounded self-confidence, but sadly this self-confidence today, when displayed with bells around its neck by the military, multinational corporations and scientists engaged in research on their behalf, merely looks offensive and obscene. The great beginning ended with a world in which 'all the chill of the great futility enters inaudibly and irrevocably' through the black hole of our existence, as Tasos Leivaditis, the Greek poet, rather depressingly reflected. Prophetically, the Pythagoreans warned that the secrets of science ought to be entrusted only to those pure in body and spirit. Knowledge and wisdom, Euripides advised, are two different things; 'to know much is not to be wise'. 'Much learning', Heraclitus had said a century earlier, 'does not teach sense'.

But this wisdom, the ungraspable, is in our days a half-forgotten impression of former times or, indeed, the 'memory that you don't discuss'.

4. A Primordial Perception

Knowledge for the Greeks, essential for the development of the individual and his world, but abstracted from life, was useless, inhuman and dangerous. To be validated, it had to conform with Logos. Logos, Isocrates, the fourth century BC orator, explained, is the defining characteristic of humans, what differentiates them from animals, life aware of itself, nature rendered self-conscious. To erase it, Joseph Campbell told students of mythology and civilisation, would mean for the Greeks not a return to nature but an escape from it – from man's nature. Or, as Christopher Fry, the poet, might have facetiously put it, obliterating it would be tantamount to returning to the preconscious, the 'first prelaughing condition of existence'.

The ultimate meaning of Logos (the word), whose language has no alphabet, defies translation in any contemporary language and remains as inaccessible in our day as during the long Christian winter. In an anthropocentrically-perceived world, the concept it epitomises and represents can no longer reach us. The disclosure of the world, the creation of meaning, occurs just behind our backs. Translated at the start of St John's Gospel as the 'Word', Logos became the 'Word of God' – in American terminology, 'Manifest Destiny'. As such, it stands in opposition to the Greek Logos which, Christians hold, envisages harmony through violence, which Christ can neither understand nor accept.

For the Greeks, Logos was the *Nous* of the universe, the intelligence behind the silent immutable laws of nature, the power which ensured the smooth functioning of the world, and the imagination that gave it its singular beauty. Inherent in the movement of the planets, the regeneration of nature, the harmony of the world, it was both the logic indispensable to their function and the force that upholds it and keeps the whole together. Its silent but commanding voice, the voice of the whole as a living entity, spoke on behalf of the entire animate and inanimate world – the stars, the Gods, the streams, the humans and their very souls, the whole to which man's own life was inseparably linked like a shadow to its owner. Rather than Reason in the Hegelian sense of absolute subjectivity, Logos, Heidegger said, is 'the gathering that allows the display and appearance of everything that is, the totality of entities'.

As such, Logos was the voice of everything visible and invisible, finite and infinite, ephemeral and eternal. It embraced both the inner and the outer, the material and the spiritual, the rational and the irrational, both of which Aristotle believed are constituent parts of the human being. It also contained all oppositions, including the *alogon*, i.e., the universe's illogicality and passions which conflicted with the intelligence of Logos. The human universe, Anaxagoras, the fifth century BC philosopher, said, had to accept and embrace the opposites, the plurality which has always been and will always be. Life, viewed as a partnership, included, according to Plato, nature and, according to other philosophers such as Pythagoras, Empedocles or Diogenes, the animals too.

Like contemporary environmentalists, Thales, Greece's first philosopher, held that the whole world is a living organism, possessing, as his fellow Ionian philosopher Anaximenes said in his simple and economical style, a cosmic soul, a breath which is the air, equivalent to the life-soul of man. On this assumption, Heraclitus of Ephesus built up, according to classicists G.S. Kirk and J.E. Raven, a rationalistic psychological theory in which for the first time the structure of the soul was related not only to that of the body, but also to that of the world as a whole. The 'soul-fire', Heraclitus believed, had some kind of physical affinity with the cosmic fire outside, the objective world, and was increased by it. He refused nevertheless to name the One as God because, he said, it itself did not want 'to be called by the name of Zeus, being thereby degraded to the level of existing as one entity present among others – even if the "among'" has the character of above all other entities'.

A similar approach was taken by Empedocles, the fifth century BC philosopher and famous doctor whose theory about the four stages of evolution of life, combined with that of the survival of the fittest, was acknowledged by Charles Darwin, the English natural historian and geologist, as the forerunner of his own theory. Empedocles believed that sexual love and cosmic love are one and the same self-existent external force which acts upon the person or the things that love. This whole, unified in its diversity and wonderful in the arrangement of its parts, was bound by an ethical code to which both humans and their senior brothers, the Gods, adhered strictly by *Anánke*, Necessity. Necessity, as Thales the Milesian said, is the strongest, for it controls everything, just as Time is the wisest, for it discovers everything.

In its philosophical context, Logos meant the rational structure of meaning which accesses, articulates and externalises the equally rational structure of the physical and moral universe. In itself, Hans-Georg Gadamer, the German philosopher, explained, Logos was not a philosophy grounded in a highest principle. It was, instead, a primordial world-experience achieved through the conceptual and intuitive power of a language 'charged with meaning' in the effort to capture, as Rainer Maria Rilke, one of Germany's greatest 2oth century poets might have said, 'the silence of (its) concentrated reality'. Rooted in the subconscious, it is accessible to humans through their intellect, instinct, feelings and intuition, their wisdom in touch with the unknown, or as Emerson, the American author and philosopher, put it, through the inborn energy of manhood combined with the engaging unconsciousness of childhood. As such, it becomes the voice of both the conscious and the unconscious self, i.e., the voice of an all-inclusive entity encompassing all that exists.

Logos in this sense was access, and also intelligent response, to what Friedrich Schiller, the eighteenth century German dramatist, historian and poet, called 'the tender voice of our mother Nature'. It was human wisdom in tune with nature's silent wisdom, the immensity of the eternal order, the authentic voice of everything that exists.

Yet this beautiful concept was castigated by the religious orthodoxies for its denial of the soul, which in Sikelianos poetry 'still is, as it was, in Hell', and by the Gnostics and their descendents, the herbal tea brigade, the New Agers, for its disregard of intuition. Disfigured, Logos could no longer recognise itself in the mirror of the mortal centuries. Its new image, so ugly, convinced the Manicheans, the third century AD religious movement which spread from Persia to the entire Roman empire, that this world had, indeed, been created by an evil God. Introducing the transcendent as the underlying structure of the world, Christianity divorced life from itself, detached the shade from its owner. Its heteronomy of a universal law imposed from without swept away the previous universality without law, which was, as Foucault said, the happy privilege of antiquity. Man could no longer live in an intimate and harmonious relationship with it. The unity between everything there is was broken to pieces.

Capitalism subsequently reinterpreted the concept once again when it crudely split mind and matter and turned Logos into instrumental Reason, which reduced the full range of human needs to the level dictated by the market, heavily protected against life. The concept was further reinterpreted by the Romantics and the existentialists who denounced Reason for the banishment of feelings into the basement of our existence, and by the postmodernists and many others as the source of all contemporary evils. Carl Jung, one of them, likened it to animus, the male principle, intellectual and scientific, which, he said, is conscious in man and unconscious in woman, and which is opposed by anima, which he identified with Eros, conscious in woman and unconscious in man. The New Agers identified Logos with male analytical power as opposed to the female power of intuition. For Fritjof Capra, the physicist and system theorist, Logos started a trend of thought which led, ultimately, to the separation of spirit and matter and to a dualism which became characteristic of Western philosophy.

The Left, likewise, assailed what Max Weber and then the Frankfurt School called instrumental Reason, which is Reason that treats everything – man, nature, society, knowledge – as a means to an end, the end always being the accumulation of as much wealth and power – and status, as Alfred Adler, the Austrian psychiatrist, would be eager to add – as possible. The original understanding had gone. What remained was its horrible misapplication.

Logos can be understood only in non-anthropocentric terms in a human world, not separated from, but immersed, in nature, in tune with the cosmic order and at home with itself. The Greeks had not split nature's order, the living whole's order, from humanity's will as they had not placed their subjective realities in opposition to those of their 'home'. Today's dichotomies did not torture their minds. Nature was not the Other, something foreign to them, an enemy to be defeated, an obstacle to the identification of the soul with the divine or the limit to the modernist ambition to overcome natural barriers. She did not pose an unacceptable restriction on the individuals' freedom to pursue their preferred 'lifestyle', either. Aristotle's definition of the 'natural' as something which has the same validity everywhere and does not depend upon acceptance does not restrict. It only clarifies.

Moreover, the world did not exist by accident. Everything in it had a purpose and a function involving motion, space and time indicating a design and a rational plan. The humans had their place in it, but not as its undoers, for nature, though cruel at times, was endowed with dignity and fairness. Benevolent rather than wicked, it enabled people, Hesiod, the eighth century BC poet, held, to live at least at the beginning in harmony together like bees – feeling and acting virtuously was considered to be man's natural disposition.

Hesiod's views were echoed by Jean Jacques Rousseau, who held that man, 'naturally good' in his 'natural state', was corrupted by 'civilization' and its institutions – 'man is born free and everywhere he is in chains' as he wrote in his famous opening to the *Social Contract*. Murray Bookchin, likewise, considered that in the beginning the community valued cooperation, sharing and caring.

Believing that goodness is engendered in us neither by nor contrary to nature, Aristotle did not, however, share this view. We are constituted by nature to receive moral virtues, he held, but their full development is up to us – except that we do not always take advantage of it. As Socrates said, the ignorant, enchanted by his own ignorance, does not seek wisdom because, satisfied with himself, he does not think he is lacking it.

Yet, the dispute over the nature of nature goes almost as far back as memory. On the one hand, nature was honoured, for nature's works, compared to those of man, are still beyond what man can aspire to create. As Charles Darwin, the English naturalist, exclaimed, Nature's productions are far 'truer' than man's productions, infinitely better adapted to the most complex conditions of life, and of a far higher workmanship. Moreover, nature sets the conditions of human existence. It provides, as Robert Nisbet, the sociologist who anticipated the communitarians and the civil society theorists, put it, 'the normal, inherent constitution or manner of growth of an entity in time'. Or, as Leo Strauss, the German-born philosopher, put it, it is a restraining order by which humans have to abide.

But Greek naturalism was challenged by the first postmodernists, the fifth century BC Sophists, who argued that nature as a just, democratic, egalitarian force was nothing but a myth. Their thesis was taken to its extremes by Thomas Hobbes, who held that the lesson of nature is war of all against all. Nature, Charles Lyell, the Scottish geologist, added later, is cruel, a 'slaughterhouse' to be, of course, checked, controlled and civilised by capitalism. Society was set apart from nature which became the enemy to be confronted and defeated. Greek naturalism, bound to ethics by eternal moral laws, of which humanity's values are the humble embodiment, was further seriously challenged by the theocratic, reactionary and avaricious ethos of the later ages. 'Memory's clear unbroken lamp' had been broken.

Espousing the doctrine that the 'earth is the Lord's' and identifying the natural order with the will of God, still as a photograph, Christianity first eunuchised nature, and then later on, helped to exploit it. God had laid down the earth's deposits of coal, an English clergyman asserted in 1836, so that man could eventually burn them. Certified Christians, Wendell Berry, the American Christian naturalist said, had no difficulty in helping the destruction of the natural world, the 'Lord's world', as much as they helped the annihilation of cultural identities and the economic exploitation of peoples. They joined, he added in anger, 'the military-industrial conspiracy to murder Creation'. Miserably, even Calvinist-reared Piet Mondrian, the Dutch abstract painter, dreamt of humanity's 'detachment from the oppression of nature', the time, he said in 1942, when 'we will no longer have the need of pictures and sculpture, for we will live in realised art'.

Dualist modernism, in turn, separated nature from humanity and pitted it against man. For humanity to be liberated from compulsion to natural necessity, for man to win his freedom, nature had to be conquered. Ethically abused as being indifferent and cruel, and, thereby, subject to the civilising influences of the cultured mind, nature had to be subjugated to man's will. All obstacles to this end were, for both liberals and Marxists, harsh necessities which denied humans freedom from nature, i.e., the freedom to conquer, dominate and exploit it. The humans' 'very aim and object', John Stuart Mill, the nineteenth century English philosopher and economist, said, 'is to alter and improve nature' – perhaps by cloning humans capable of gracefully carrying out the most ravishing atrocities. Nature, Karl Marx argued, too, was 'an object for mankind, purely a matter of utility'.

Modernism was determined to prove that, rather than learn

from nature, we can teach her a lesson. Subscribing to this notion, even Nietzsche dismissed nature on the grounds that life is the very will of man to overcome the limitations of nature. His thesis echoed that which had been endorsed earlier by the German idealist philosophy for which culture, as opposed to nature, represented the realm of freedom.

Modernist science, for its part, unhappy with the Greeks' belief that human life is in harmony with nature only when individual will is directed to ends which are in accord with those of nature, and ever ready to see nature as its playfield, rejected any link between nature and philosophy. A contemporary writer, the neurologist Raymond Tallis wrote: 'there is nothing in nature itself to explain why anything in nature should be valued ... Humanity cannot be reduced to animality'. Nature's inner truth had been lost. Our natural home exists only in order to be abused for profit, the money which the stem cell companies are expected to make from cell research and cloning for reproductive purposes. The law of nature, if there is one, serves only the interests of growth and capital accumulation that turn everything into a resource. Nothing exists in its own right. Even Seléne, the moon as it appears in the sky but no longer answers to that name, and the Aeschylian 'nightly conference of stars' are now a resource for the future's space wars.

A further distortion of nature's nature was inflicted by the Romantics, who, in their hostility to its objectification by capitalism, mystified it. Nature, in Schelling's *naturphilosophie*, 'divinely willed' and in opposition to the rational, was 'the expression of the Absolute'. As a concept, this would have horrified the Greeks who never dissolved nature into a mystical 'oneness'. Postmodernist writers objected further to the Greek understanding of the 'natural' as it, presumably, excludes in our days 'unnatural', *para physin*, forms of sexuality.

Equally disputed by the later non-Greek world was the original Greek understanding of man's goodness as for both Jews and Christians man had succumbed to evil from day one. Transcending the religious sphere, the theory of the innate depravity of man became a cultural one, too. Hence Thomas Hobbes' description of the state of nature as being nothing but 'fear, and danger of violent death' and his view of the life of man as being 'solitary, poor, nasty, brutish and short'. Hence also Émile Durkheim's conviction that the individual's appetites are 'by nature boundless and insatiable', Sigmund Freud's denunciation of the belief in the innate goodness of man as 'disastrous', or even Immanuel Kant's understanding of feeling and acting virtuously as being a struggle against natural disposition.

Though in a global antagonistic relationship to the natural conditions of existence, separated from the natural world and even from our own nature, we still cannot, however, dismiss nature or force her to do what she has no intention of doing. Violating the limits she has set can only invite natural disasters, even question man's right to exist. Divorced from nature and irreconcilably opposed to her claims, a sustainable future is an impossibility. Indeed, any future, sustainable or otherwise, rests on the assumption that we live. Life will not, however, go back to its earthy roots unless it opens its eyes to see the miracle nature reveals to us day after day, recaptures its lost innocence and rejuvenates the spirit that is currently dozing under the influence of too many sitcoms.

In any case, whatever our utilitarian mind dictates, instinct drives us to clean air, organic food, natural products, traditional medical therapies, the protection of soil, flora, the wildlife and the countryside where we expect to replenish our energy and find the missing peace of mind. Rather than systems relying on experts and institutions, it also encourages us to go for natural, self-regulating systems in tune with the rhythm of Logos. But this is probably an issue living on the horizon's line which we, nearsighted, just cannot see. What we can see, instead, is the fact that nature's protection threatens property, capital, jobs, trade union power, the economic foundation of whole sectors and regions, the prosperity of nation states and the profitability of multinationals.

'What we do best is breed', said Yorkshire-born poet Donald Davie, and there are times I do not feel like arguing with him.

5. Dreaming Innocence

In the context of the whole, a world which the Greeks refused to objectify, nothing was external to themselves and nothing existed only insofar as it was represented in their thoughts. Man, correspondingly, did not exist because the world, the Other, furnished the consciousness of the individual. Humans had their place in it as much as 'it' had its place in them. Unconsciously identifying the universe, nature and the Others with the self, individuals, rather than isolated units at war with the whole, felt engaged in an intimate relationship with it, blending together in a homogeneous whole which belonged as much to the world as to the individual himself. 'I am not just me, still I am', wrote the British Rastafarian poet Benjamin Zephaniah, who in 2003 rejected the Order of the British Empire because, as he put it, the word 'Empire' made him angry. A Greek would have been only too happy to repeat his statement.

This unity of the 'I' and the Others, the time of 'dreaming innocence' as German theologian Paul Tillich, one of the foremost theologians of the twentieth century who was forced to leave Nazi Germany, called it, represents an unconscious quite distinct from the Freudian perception of it as 'the dark, the nocturnal, the demonic'. It is, instead, the primeval unconscious in which being is experienced as unity, an all-encompassing totality in time and space. If the Greeks were, as some have argued, more in touch than us with gentle unconscious drives, these drives, which Freud, in his insistence on repression, failed to highlight, might well paint a different picture of the natural man. But Freud did, perhaps, recognise it when he assumed that the so-called superego operates partly in the unconscious as the voice of conscience, the inner judge, the vehicle to the ideal struggling against the 'repressed unconscious'.

The Greeks' identification with the whole had, however, another side concerning the interaction between the two. Being part of the whole, the individual, they believed, was both affected by it and also reciprocally affected it. The sight, Aristotle said, is affected by the object, but 'it also acts upon it in a certain way' because it radiates a sort of light comparable to that of the sun. Plato, too, had talked about the light which proceeds from within to meet the light which comes from without, with the whole affecting anything it touches. Physical reality, sensory perception and mental activity, blending with each other, were, thus, viewed as a single entity which belonged to both the individual and the world.

Building on this hypothesis, Denis Diderot, a leading figure of the Enlightenment in France, in his *D'Alembert's Dream* argued further that the whole imparts directiveness to the organism and reciprocally receives directiveness from it. This holistic concept provides an interactivity between the part and its contextual whole. Thoughts, individual consciousness, from this point of view, rather than being subjective were, instead, of the world in which human existence was embedded before the split between man and the world produced the generations of discontent. The Cartesian 'I think therefore I am', which was set forth as a condition for, and a foundation of, all knowledge in a world from which the individual was ripped apart, was alien to the Greeks. Nothing, French historian Jean-Pierre Vernant stated, was further from their culture.

Thinking and being, when coming into presence as One, were for the Greeks the 'thing itself', whose definition has been the guiding question of western philosophy to this day. Nevertheless, western philosophy cannot arrive at any conclusion mainly because, as Heraclitus himself said, the 'thing itself' is elusive. It 'prefers to hide' within the indivisible unity of the 'apparent' and the 'unapparent'. Things which appear to be opposite are one and the same: the end is a beginning and the beginning is an end as on the circumference of a circle. This is the paradox of existence and its algedonic polarity. The path up and down is one and the same, the sea, most pure and most polluted, is drinkable and life-preserving for fish, and undrinkable and death-dealing for men.

Heraclitus' rather Delphic pronouncement made Socrates smile. 'What I understand is splendid', he said, 'and I think that what I don't understand is so too. But it would take a Delian diver to get to the bottom of it'. He could have said the same about Martin Heidegger, a disciple of Heraclitus, two thousand five hundred years later.

This whole, the physical and moral universe, perceived as an organic, wonderful, simple, orderly and probably symmetrical whole, a living entity that contained and transcended all opposing forces, was the source of the essential sanity of the Greek world. Its unity enhanced diversity, its purpose underpinned freedom, and its wholeness strengthened individuality. Rationality respected subjectivity, and morality liberated rather than repressed. Logos for the Greeks had armed man with a power which, intelligent rather than brutal, ensured that nothing important in life was neglected just as nothing in it was overdone. The same whole was also Europe's spring of wisdom before the Gods and heroes of Greece were consigned to oblivion by Christianity to be resurrected later by capitalism as names of financial services and consumer goods, or before, as novelist Joseph Conrad might have said, 'the shortness of memories and the length of time' placed it beyond our reach.

The limits set by Logos were, of course, subject to interpretation. But interpretation was not the business of just the rational mind, which, subject to externally imposed limits, was not in a position to comprehend all the laws and uncover all the secrets of the universe. It was, instead, subject to rational thinking, working in conjuction with all the forces that determine our existence – intuition, feelings, passions and unconscious drives, all these tools of understanding which we have currently locked up in the basement of our existence. Being all parts of the One, they welded together Reason and morality, intellect and feeling, body and spirit, inner and outer, science and intuition, individuality and the public realm, nature and culture.

Philosophically, however, the nature of the One troubled the Greeks. The Milesians took for granted man's connection with both his physical surroundings and the universe; and Heraclitus, the man whose dialectics exerted a profound influence on Hegel, Marx, Nietzsche, Heidegger, Arendt, Marcuse and many others, continued in their tradition. In spite of the apparent plurality, 'all things', Heraclitus said, 'are one', bound together in a coherent system of which men themselves are also a part. Logos for him was both the formula that kept these 'things' – as a union of opposites – intact and also its actual constituent. The union of opposites had nothing either solid or static. It was, instead, subject to perpetual change, which meant that the balance of forces either in the universe or in the city was continuously being negotiated in the unending 'strife', the war of opposites which is 'the father of all and king of all'. Maintaining that opposites imply one another, his doctrine was endorsed by Chrysippus, the third century Stoic philosopher, polymath and writer of three hundred books, who argued that good without evil is logically as impossible as a week without Tuesdays.

According to Heraclitus' doctrine, alarming to all conservatives ever since the collapse of the Greek world, reality has, therefore, nothing stable. Its essence is its continuous change and development. Being is an ever-unfolding becoming – 'the creation of the world', Marcel Proust said accordingly, 'is taking place every day'. All this was summed up in Heraclitus' famous image of the river into which one could step only once. Far from being an evil, conflict was the dynamic tension which kept things together, and, as sociologist Georg Simmel put it, the very essence of social life, an ineradicable component of social living, a creative force rather than a force of destruction. Should it end, according to the Greeks, and one extreme secure victory over the other, the world would come to an end.

Miserably, as Murray Bookchin, a major voice of North America's Green Left, commented, Heraclitus' dialectics, rarefied by Hegel into a cosmological system, verged on the theological, and intermingled with the laws of natural science by Engels a generation later, produced a crude dialectical materialism which marginalised people as beings with consciousness and values.

The understanding of the One by Parmenides, the fifth century BC philosopher, was the opposite of Heraclitus'. Working on his own maps of the unknown, Parmenides held that the One, defined by Reason unaided by the senses, was just One, homogeneous, indivisible, material, unchangeable and indestructible – 'substance' is indestructible. His dogma on the indestructibility of 'substance' became and remains one of the fundamental concepts of philosophy and physics ever since. This One also had to be motionless because there could be no motion without a void, and by definition void does not exist. Logically speaking, if a void does exist, it would not be nothing, and therefore it would not be void.

This paradox, which tormented minds for over two millennia and had famously perplexed Newton, Copernicus, Descartes and others, was not resolved until the time of Einstein when it was decided that space is a system of relations which became known as the 'time-space continuum'.

The Parmenidian One was scorned by the Pythagoreans and defended by both Zeno of Elea, Parmenides' lover, and Melissus of Samos. The latter did, however, modify the dogma by arguing that if there was a plurality, things would have to be of just the same nature as the One – this was essentially the view of the atomists. For Empedocles, on the other hand, there was no such thing as an original unity, but eternally distinct elements, which, as he said in a manner reminiscent of Heraclitus's dogma, are united by Love and divided by Strife, the twin causal powers in the universe. Change was, thus, only a rearrangement dictated by the two ultimate realities, the moral and psychological forces of Love and Strife. Unity and peace prevail under the sway of Aphrodite, and plurality and war when Strife is on the ascendant. The outcome is nevertheless a new unity which is one, but which derives from the plural.

In the same irreligious tradition of the Milesians, Anaxagoras, the man who discovered that the moon reflects the sun's brightness, taught that the primary sources, which included the opposites and also the 'things with like parts', *omoiomere*, were all parts of the 'one world-order' controlled by the separate, single intellectual force of Mind, the *Nous*. The *Nous*, an original, abstract and subtle principle, was 'the finest of all things and the purest'; 'although mixed with nothing', it was nonetheless present 'there, where everything else is, in the surrounding mass, and in what has been united and separated off'. His description of 'there' was an incorporeal entity, yet his *Nous*, as a primary cause of physical change, was, in the rationalist, scientific tradition, like matter, corporeal.

For Anaxagoras, a card-carrying atheist, a wealthy individual who generously ceded his inheritance to his friends, and a thinker, Aristotle said, so great that he appeared as a sober man among drunks, the world arose from a universal mixture of every single thing that is, was and will be. Things that emerge do not, therefore, come into being – they are composed out of what is there already; and things that disappear do not perish – they only dissolve into the previous singleness.

Confirming the Milesian material monism by rejecting the Parmenidian One, Democritus, whose *Megas Diakosmos*, the Great World System, postulated the existence of many galaxies, advanced a theory which viewed the whole in a state of eternal motion in empty space, with a constant interaction between Being and non-Being. Being, the *atomon* (uncuttable), was thought to be compact and full, and non-Being void and rare – on this Democritus built his theory of atoms. Form was, thus, created when atoms were driven by Necessity, *Anánke*, rather than purpose into the void in which, by collision, they produced vortices which generated bodies and ultimately worlds. The atoms, homogeneous and fully corporeal, were so small as to be indivisible, and, although different in shape, arrangement and material composition, they moved in a way corresponding to rhythm, touching and tuning. Atomism postulated that there is not just one but innumerable worlds coming-to-be and passing-away, worlds which even have their own moons and sun.

Although challenged by Plato, material monism survived well into the age of the Stoics, the last philosophers of the ancient world. But its understanding had been modified – it involved 'faith' in the unity of all Being. 'All things are woven into one another', the second century A.D. Roman Emperor and Stoic philosopher Marcus Aurelius said in his *Meditations*, written in Greek, 'for there is one universe, consisting of all things, and one essence, and one law, one divine reason, and one truth'.

This would, of course, have been too much for the earlier Greeks, who had never appealed to 'faith', never spoken of 'divine reason', 'one essence' and 'one law', and never claimed to speak on behalf of 'the truth'. The maunderings in the caliginous fields of the one Truth, which gave goodness a bad name, were about to begin.

The Greek sense of the whole was challenged through the centuries by both modernism and religion, and it is still being challenged. But at the same time it did, and it still does, have some powerful advocates. From Plethon, Spinoza, Hegel, Goethe and Kant to Coleridge, Carlyle, Burke, Ruskin, John Stuart Mill and William Morris the doctrine of separateness has been resolutely rejected. Society is a 'whole organism', Mill said, 'the simultaneous state of all the greater social facts or phenomena' – philosopher Karl Popper, disapprovingly, thought this typical of holistic or utopian social engineering such as the idea of 'blueprints for a new order', or of 'centralised planning'. Peter Kropotkin, the anarchist, saw man as 'a part of an immense whole', and G.E. Moore argued that a thing does not exist by itself. Properties in isolation, he said, 'have not nearly so much value as has the whole of which they are part'.

John Ruskin, the nineteenth century English social critic whose writings profoundly influenced the British Labour movement, emphasised that a good society ought to promote 'wholeness of being', and regulate itself by attention to intrinsic, rather than exchange values. The concept of an organic and holistic community, which coexists in harmony with nature and cultivates the whole person, was also taken up by William Morris, an ethical socialist, who, as a Greek classicist and translator of Homer's *Odyssey* into English, disentangled it from all its mysticism. Holism, as a set of values, became the image of 'Athenian' socialism.

Young Marx, likewise, asserted that 'the truth is the whole', for, as Nietzsche said after him, 'all things are chained and entwined together'. The aim, Marx held, is the meeting of the expectations of the whole, the all-rounded, the fully developed man, the 'integral' individual which the specialisation of labour and the general atomization of society has broken into pieces and separate entities with no intrinsic connections. To free themselves, the oppressed, also Georg Lukács, the Hungarian existentialist Marxist, explained, have to adopt the standpoint of the whole and question whether the parts are as objective and immovable as they seem to be.

Goethe fought 'the mutual extraneousness of Reason, sense, feeling, and will', and so did André Chénier, Stéphane Mallarmé or Hegel, for whom 'Godlike activity is the re-establishment and representation of unity'. Friedrich von Schiller, despairing at the fragmentation of modern man, caused, as he said, by the separation of the senses from Reason, sought a return to the wholeness and integration that marked the life of the Greek individual. The Greek Reason, he said, 'never mutilated what it touched'.

Salvation, Jean-Paul Sartre also insisted, must be won upon this earth for the whole man by the whole man. With a rather disagreeable anthropocentrism, he then added: 'Without the world there is no selfhood, no person; and without selfhood, without the person, there is no world'. E.P. Thompson, likewise, stressed that quality of life needs to be assessed by 'the total life experience, the manifold satisfactions or deprivations, cultural as well as material', the factors of concern to normal people rather than statisticians.

Ludwig Wittgenstein talked of a 'new ' conception of the human being 'in which body and mind, and body and soul are more immediately and intimately related than we have realised'. T.S. Eliot, the American-born British poet and dramatist, argued in favour of 'a whole way of life' embodying the principles of Christianity, and pragmatist William James emphasised that 'the whole is in each and every part, and welds it with the rest into an absolute unity'. Carl Rogers held that the more aware one is of the whole system, or perhaps context, the more hope there is that one would live a balanced human life, and Murray Bookchin called for an ecological thinking which would place its emphasis 'on the organic, holistic and developmental'. The 'total history' of Lucien Febvre, the founder of the *Annales* group of French historians, is another form of holism – you cannot say 'here the events, there the beliefs', he explained. 'Man cannot be carved into slices. He is a whole'.

Raymond Williams developed his theory of culture as a theory of relations between elements in 'a whole way of life, material, intellectual, and spiritual'. Human nature itself, he said, is the product of a 'whole way of life', of a 'culture'; and Jürgen Habermas placed his analyses of communication in a holistic context.

Whatever the arguments, the songs of innocence seem, however, to be a thing of the far distant past, when one could tell the original from its echo.

6. Noblest is the Justest

The assumed rationality of the world was a manifestation of its intelligence, the chief feature of which was respect for *Dikaiosyne*, Justice, and *Isonomia*, Equality. Justice, the universal Justice, associated with *Anánke*, the Great Necessity, ensured that the balance in the union of opposites is not to be disturbed. *Avghi*, the Dawn, was there to prevent *Nykta*, the Night, from exceeding its limits. With Zeus' permission, Ovid says, *Avghi* was absent only once, the day she mourned the killing of her son by Achilles. No element in Greek cosmogony was allowed to steal the lunch money of another or achieve complete victory over the other. Eternally fixed bounds could not be crossed.

For Anaximander, the sixth century BC Milesian philosopher, who argued that the world was not created but evolved, and man developed from fish as, indeed, the three fossils discovered in the Canadian Arctic in 2004 confirmed, *apeiron*, the infinite, contains oppositions each one of which is perpetually attempting to enlarge its empire at the expense of the others. They are prevented, however, from doing so by the cosmic rule of law, the cosmic Balance of Forces which ensures that no injustice is committed by the victory of one element over its opposite. As Poseidon told the great Zeus, the world 'is common to us all'. The just distribution of resources could not, therefore, be unsettled. No power could encroach upon another. Should that ever happen, Anaximenes, the third Milesian philosopher, said, the injustice committed would be punished, and Justice, as Hesiod, the seventh century BC poet had proclaimed, would prevail. The eternal moral law, 'the moral law of nature' in Shakespeare's *Troilus and Cressida*, made sure of it.

Law-governed and permeated by ethics, the universe, Heraclitus held, had a moral structure irrespective of human purpose. *Cosmos* was infused with a moral meaning and empowered with a moral force that answered to the name of *Anánke*, Necessity, the arbiter between extremes. *Anánke* acknowledged limits and interdependencies that transcend us all, protected the natural rights of its subjects, and ensured that in its world that enjoyed acres of sunshine, there was space for everything provided that everything moved within the limits set by the cosmic intelligence. The implications of this poetic and visionary assumption in the field of political theory were monumental. Cosmic intelligence nurtured no hierarchies, no despotic institutions, and no structured subordination and domination. It espoused no 'natural order' on whose back inexorable social and political 'laws' were subsequently built. In this intelligent universe's web of relations, everything, the 'invisible, visible, our horses, the gods and the air we breathe in the same cool crystal sphere', as poet Angelos Sikelianos put it, had its rightful place that no arbitrary act could deny. This 'everything' included the individual, not yet menaced by what Søren Kierkegaard, the Danish philosopher, called 'levelling'.

The Greeks knew, of course, that this was not conclusively demonstrable – Aristotle, the fourth century BC philosopher, did not even think that everything that happened in the world was natural. But, on the other hand, they explicitly recognised it, respected it, and saluted it as the moral foundation of their world.

Cosmic Justice was the revelation of the eternal into the temporary and of the universal into the particular both of which set the parameters of life and limits which humans had to respect. This cosmic morality was their community's moral guiding force and the philosophical foundation of their cities which were believed to owe their origin to the desire for Justice. Grounded in nature, human conduct was philosophically the embodiment of the same cosmic morality believed to be applicable in the field of human relations, too, determining the norm of conduct for both the individual and the city-state. Human laws, according to Heraclitus, the man whose 'steps devoured the way in mighty chunks', as Rilke might have put it, are nourished by the universal law of Justice which nobody could undermine. This law, the sovereign nomos, Pindar, the poet, reiterated, 'reigns over all, mortals and immortals alike'. In such a context, arbitrary action could not be excused.

Its violation was hybris, an act of aggression against the natural moral order, its arrogant defiance; and hybris was bound to be punished. He who, in his proud success, forgets the laws of righteousness, Aeschylus further explained, will face the counter-blow of the dark Furies who will crush his strength and cloud his brightness, 'till the dim pit of oblivion swallows him'. What Parmenides, the fifth century BC philosopher, called the 'all-avenging *Dike*', or what the modern Greeks call *Theia Dike*, Divine Justice administered here on earth, would make sure of it.

If the Greeks were right, greenhouse gas emissions cannot be allowed to spiral out of control, for the punishment is global warming and grievous climate changes; the escalating and enormous losses of biodiversity cannot go on indefinitely, for the damage to the biosphere will make our own survival impossible; and the foaming desperation and hatred, the Force 12 rage of the disempowered at the world's obscene inequalities cannot continue, for the price the West will pay one day may cross the line of everything currently conceivable. A criminal might, of course, escape 'death's scythe'. He would not, however, escape punishment altogether. Failing anything else, he might well expect to find 'poison in marital kisses', as Andreas Kalvos, the nineteenth century Greek poet, rather humorously reconfirmed. Wisdom, and virtue on which it is based, consists, as the Stoics in particular held, in a will which is in agreement with nature.

True, forced by superior power, the whole, as Plato said, has often no option but to enter into a kind 'of civil war between the same elements'. But in the long run superior power in the hands of a part cannot win against the power of the whole, as the Americans have discovered in Iraq. In the worst possible scenario, the whole and the dominating part will find themselves together in the flames of self-destruction. Rather than a dogma, Justice was, thus, a lesson given by the physical world; and humans did not have to remember it, for it remembered itself.

Hence a natural mode of being for the Greeks was grounded in Justice and *isonomia*, the equality between all the elements, their blending and rotation, on which harmony rested. Nature was the embodiment of *aletheia*, the truth, which encouraged plurality and diversity. In this moral system, which existed irrespective of human motivation and was irrevocably attached to all great themes of the time, from Being and Form to Motion and Causality, everything had its rightful place. All things were inalienable parts of a democratically constituted and autonomous cosmos. They had, therefore, to be respected.

In the human realm this egalitarianism meant that democracy

was the natural system of government, and fairness a universal imperative. 'Everything that is unfair', Aristotle wrote, 'is unlawful'. Equality had been sanctioned by nature. Women and slaves were, of course, excluded from the benefits of Greece's high moral order. But, as equality between all the rest was guaranteed by the social order of the city and its democratic institutions, the step forward made was so stupendous that the world did not witness its equal in the next two millennia.

The physical macrocosm ran in parallel with the individual microcosm. As Isocrates said, Logos, the *Nous* which produces a subjective presence, conforms 'to law and justice' with which the individual has to harmonise his existence. Justice, understood as fairness, was underpinned by unwritten cosmic laws infused with moral meaning. This ethical commonality between the cosmic and the human, adjusted to political life, meant that the polis, the city-state, had to be as diverse, unhierarchical, harmonious and just. The ecosystem, Murray Bookchin said, is 'the image of unity in diversity, spontaneity, and complementary relationships, free of all hierarchy and domination' which means a society free of 'gerontocracies, patriarchies, class relationships, élites of all kinds, and finally the State, particularly in its most parasitic form of state capitalism'. Kirkpatrick Sale, the American writer and two-wheeled environmental activist, likewise urged humanity to model itself on nature, recalling that 'in the natural world... nothing is more striking than the absence of any centralised control, any interspeciate domination'. Nature's eloquence lies exactly in this absence.

Arbitrary acts were a violation of natural law, an attack on its basic tenet, the principle of equality. Nature's diversity, and also respect for all parties' rights and obligations, was, indeed, an inspiration for the development of the city's democratic institutions. Its distinctiveness underpinned individuality, its self-directedness boosted self-empowerment, and its developmental nature nurtured human growth. Incidentally, nature in English, deriving from the Latin word *natus*, born, and meaning that basic attributes are inborn, does not have the same meaning as the Greek word *physis*. The latter, coming from the verb *phyein*, means both born and grown out of. Man is born but then develops towards the fulfilment of his potentials. In its original and primary essence, the word has, thus, meaning not only as nature's name but also as a poetic and noetic experience relating to human destiny.

The affinity the Greeks saw between nature and the human realm guided young Marx in the vision of his own ideal future society. Communism, he said well before socialist thinking took voluntary retirement and withdrew into the safety of a blissful lethargy, is the mode of life which is appropriate to human nature. Only in communism, he wrote, 'has man's natural existence become his human existence... Society is the perfected unity in essence of man with nature, the true resurrection of nature, the realised naturalism of man and the realised humanism of nature'. Considering, however, that nature cannot be endlessly subjected to exploitation, Marx's later failure to appreciate it in non-human terms opened the way to the so-called scientific socialism which took over the machinery of domination from capitalism in order to 'improve' it. Its contempt for nature, naturalism and natural rights prompted Castoriades, the contemporary Greek philosopher, to write pointedly: 'the continuation of Marx requires the destruction of Marxism which had become, through its triumph, a reactionary ideology'. The young Marx's utopianism concerning the reconciliation of humanity and nature was, however, taken up directly in the German Green's first economic programme. Others argued in favour of 'a rational, humane, environmentally unalienated social order'.

Greek ethical morality, recognised by 'generations of myrtles', as Elytis would have said, or this 'elegant tissue of assumptions', as the Greek-born philosopher Gregory Vlastos called the parallels between society and nature, produced the concept of natural law, believed to be inherent in human nature. Natural law, deduced from the state of nature, Rousseau, the main champion of the doctrine, held later, is the voice of nature, which, David Hume, the Scottish sceptic and empiricist philosopher, said, 'has determin'd to judge as well as to breathe and feel'. For Spinoza, natural law is, indeed, divine law.

Inherent in this understanding of natural law was the concept of universal natural rights, today called human rights, possessed even in the absence of political and legal institutions. These rights, which Britain and the US have so disinterestedly offered to protect globally with a world police force, the ultimate aspiration of imperialism, were considered to be in conformity with the infinite and the eternal. When, thus, Oedipus' child descended into 'the loveless dust', as Irish poet W. B. Yeats might say, and Cleon, the tyrant of Thebes, acting with extreme prejudice, banned his burial, the august virgin Antigone, Oedipus' eldest daughter, buried her brother and was killed for it. Her action, she said, was in conformity with 'the unwritten unalterable laws (which) are not of yesterday or today, but everlasting'. Cleon's decree contravened the supreme moral law and thereby the spirit in which the affairs of the polis were expected to be conducted.

This doctrine, which was articulated by the Stoics, acquired a political force from the seventeenth century onwards in Europe's struggle against despotism. But it was challenged, initially by the Sophists. The law of nature, they had argued, is the law of the stronger, and Justice could, therefore, be defined only as convention. Historicism, likewise, endorsing the view that the local and the temporal is of higher value than the universal, has questioned the legitimacy of ahistorical claims about 'justice', 'human nature' or 'human rights'. Such rights, it has also been argued, do not satisfy the minimum condition necessary for them to be recognised as rights, for they have neither been given by God nor can they appeal to positive law. Jeremy Bentham, the eighteenth to nineteenth century English philosopher, in particular, opposed them as they have no reference independent of their claims in any particular context. They are, he said, a 'nonsense of stilts'.

His nonsense, riding in nature's name on the back of a traditional essentialism, has nevertheless been instrumental in reducing women, blacks and homosexuals to second rate humans. John Locke, the seventeenth century English philosopher, founder of empiricism and political liberalism, further argued that slavery, too, is moral under certain circumstances because it is in nature's system. As conveniently, capitalism's claim that 'all free subjects are born inheritable' was based, its philosophers held, on 'natural law'. All this was, of course, too much for some. One of them, Jean-Jacques Rousseau, the Swiss-born French radical philosopher, disgusted by hypocrisy, retorted bluntly: 'that which is good and comfortable to order is so by the nature of things'. His views were echoed by many other nature philosophers, including Marxist Ernst Bloch and anarchist Gustave Landauer.

Notwithstanding their misappropriation and abuse by the leader of the world's most God-fearing nation, natural rights in the form of human rights are, however, the flag of humanity's better part. Except that often this flag is hoisted over a void.

7. A Semantic Field

Greek ethical assumptions did not emanate from God – the Koran, the Bible or the Torah on whose literal reading fundamentalism thrives. But they were not, either, as in Kant, the product of an abstraction, that of a metaphysical conception of the moral agent, the 'noumenal' self, and they did not involve duties and obligations imposed upon the individual by some universal 'categorical imperative'. Right and wrong for the Greeks had to conform with some kind of eternal norm, but this norm was determined by the individual in a rational way. The power of the ethical was the power of Reason – there can be no ethical life without a rational life, Murray

Bookchin reiterated more than two millennia later. This, as Aristotle explained, means only that the standards by which man judges his own actions are rational – not that he always acts rationally.

The intention, more sophisticated than anything religion has produced, was not to show how an ethical life would be good for the person, but how a proper understanding of the self included living life in an ethical way. Rationality, both Plato and Aristotle believed, dictated that virtue, being part of human good, could not be external to the happiness of mankind. A life of Justice, Plato explained, was not a good external to the self but an internalised rational objective, or, as Aristotle put it, an intelligent disposition involving the exercise of judgment.

Justice demanded basically only one virtue, good judgment, delivered by the individual's rationality. The substantive ethical dispositions were the content of the self, the person's character, or, in the current jargon, God within. Goodness, in this sense, was not the consolation prize for lack of worldly success or the price to be paid for a reward in heaven. It was, instead, the way to live one's life. The good life was the life of the good, rational person. Armed with the power of Reason, Democritus explained, a man does what ethically needs to be done. Optimistically, the Greeks placed their trust in the full development of human potentiality – every human being, Aristotle held, has a kind of inner drive towards a life of at least civic virtue, and also a tendency towards the perfection of his life. Life was a harmonious culmination of human potentialities. But, of course, as Euripides put it, 'everybody loves himself more than his neighbour'.

Though a moral imperative, Justice was also the mark of nobility – 'most noble is that which is justest', read the epigram at the entrance of the temple of Leto at Delos. Even more than that, it was the foundation of personal happiness, for those, as poet Kalvos put it, who lack the 'sweet serenity of the just', or, as Democritus said long before him, pay no heed to Justice and do not do what they ought, find joy in nothing. 'The glory of Justice is confidence in judgment and imperturbability. The price of injustice is fear of disaster'. Democritus' ethics, together with his scientific theories, were probably the crown of Greek philosophical achievement. Yet Democritus, though highly regarded by Aristotle but not mentioned by Plato, never achieved the status of Plato or Aristotle that he deserved. From his fifty books only fragments have survived.

Justice, Theognis and Phocylides, the sixth century BC poets, said, 'sums up the whole of virtue in man' – whole, because it involves its active exercise rather than its possession, and also because its possessor exercises it in relation to other people and not only by himself. Injustice, on the other hand, 'sums up the whole of vice'. Justice, an order above challenge, was, thus, the content of the self, associated with the kind of life that is worth living, the kind of things that it is worth having, caring about or fighting for, and the individual's performance in the public realm. As opposed to the seven deadly sins of the Christian tradition, which illustrate the essential triviality of its morals, and the attention paid to the destiny of the individual's soul, the focus was far more, as in our days, on our mutual responsibilities to one another. No distinction between public morals and private pursuits could interfere with this basic understanding of morality; and no pressures from within could undermine its democratic nature underlined by its distributive spirit as dictated by the natural moral order. For Aristotle, who articulated this concept of Justice to perfection, what is unjust is unequal, and what is just is equal.

Theognis and Phocylides had already explained that equality meant 'rendering to each man what is due'. These words, incidentally, were repeated later, in the opening sentence of Justinian's sixth century AD legal code which read 'Justice is an abiding and permanent intention of according to each his due'. This understanding, which relates to the perennial issue of distribution of wealth and power, burdens and benefits, means that, though the weak need to be supported, everyone receives his or her due, neither more nor less. A man's due for the early Greeks was not, however, determined by accountants, and was not confined to 'resources'. It went far beyond it. Distributive Justice, Aristotle said, includes the distribution of everything, 'money, honours and other divisible assets among the members of the community'. It embraced the whole spectrum of human activities and covered the whole range of human needs, liberties, rights and interests – from dignity and honour to fortune and fate.

As L.R. Palmer remarked, Justice for the Greeks was a 'semantic field'. It included boundaries, limits of time and place, marks as characteristics and marks as aims, and it related to everything, from measuring to doing things at the right time. A temperate man, Aristotle said, desires the right thing in the right way and at the right time. Transferred to politics, this belief meant that goods and power had to be more or less equally distributed among the citizens if the status quo were not to be short-lived by a planned obsolence. Cities of injustice, tyrannies that enraged everything that had blood in its veins, the Greeks knew, defeated the purpose of their creation. Hence Theseus' pride in telling Creon, the tyrant of Thebes, that Athens was not 'a city of slaves, or a city of emptiness. Ours is a land that lives in justice, knows no rule but law'. This striking commitment to civic virtue was based totally on Reason. It was also backed by the Olympians – the Goddess Artemis was prepared to use her silver bow to force culprits back into line.

Dikaiosyne, Justice, and *eunomia*, the good application of the laws of Justice, were, as it was stated again and again, the reason for the establishment of the city-states, and their 'chiefest price'. The rule of law, rather than a commitment made in the interests of the status quo, was the insurance policy the citizens had taken against threats to their rights; and it had to be observed whatever the circumstances. Even if not true, the story of Diokles, the sixth century BC lawgiver of the Syracusans, shows how seriously obligations under the law were taken. He had forbidden, under pain of death, the entry of any person carrying arms in the city's agora, the marketplace, except that once he accidentally did so himself. When reproached for breaking his own law, he answered that, indeed, he upheld it, and he killed himself.

Justice, as Plato put it so neatly, meant 'doing the right thing'; and the 'right thing', Aeschylus in *Seven Against Thebes* said long before the media felt they had to reinforce the negative in the pursuit of profit, demanded 'to be and not to seem good'.

This did not, of course, mean that particularly in its distributive sense, Justice was subject to a single interpretation. For the democrats, it meant distribution according to the laws of fairness. The conservatives, on the other hand, emphasised the claims of both good birth and wealth. For Aristotle, the philosopher of the Athenian middle class, it was neither. Those who should benefit from the distribution of goods, he said, are men of superior virtue, those whose lives are in tune with the aims of their community. In the latter's moral code, those favoured by Tyche, the Goddess of fortune, and particularly the rich, had to alleviate the poverty of their fellow-citizens. Parents, guests or hosts, heralds and suppliants, and also the dead, had to be honoured and protected; so too had the truth, particularly when offered under oath.

Failure to do so would bring in Nemesis, the Goddess of retribution and vengeance. The Goddess had emerged as a moral force, ever present as the sky, and ready to ensure that moral obligations were duly met.

Justice, not only distributive but also remedial, involved an agonising search which is expressed with unalloyed beauty in the work of Aeschylus, the radical dramatist who, like all other playwrights of his time and a few of ours, remained critically engaged with moral and philosophical questions. For Aeschylus the only law is the ancient moral law which makes sure that punishment follows hybris as night follows day. In *The Oresteian Trilogy*, his masterpiece, Agamemnon, the King of Mycenae, returns from the Trojan war only to be murdered in his bathroom by his wife Clytaemnestra and her lover Aegisthus. Orestes, their son, then decides to punish the guilty because otherwise society would be shaken to its foundations, and to avenge his father by killing his mother. He assumed, Sartre said in his *Les Mouches*, full responsibility as a free human being and used his freedom effectively.

But matricide outrages the deepest human instincts, and Erinyes, the Furies, who have no interest in social order, demand the punishment of Orestes. The latter had escaped to Athens where the goddess Athene arranged his trial by a jury of the noblest Athenian citizens. The public prosecutor is one of the Erinyes. The votes on either side are, however, equal and Orestes as an act of mercy is acquitted. The Erinyes then threaten Athens with destruction. At this stage, matters obviously had to be negotiated, and the Greeks with generosity of spirit did just that. Athene persuaded the Furies that it was in their interest to take up residence in Athens, instead, for the Athenians, she said, would bestow them with 'honours which no other land could equal'. The Erinyes, graciously, accepted the kickback, to be renamed, in turn, by the Athenians Eumenides, the benevolent ones. Aeschylus' view was that retributive justice inflicted in plain revenge leads to chaos.

Remarkably, Justice in the case of Orestes had been administered by humans, the polis, formed to run the affairs of the community in Justice and defend its shared values. For the same reason, in Aristophanes' *Acharnians* the chorus appeals for help, not to the Gods, but to the audience, the 'whole polis'. A just state of affairs maintained by the polis was, of course, impossible without freedom. That was the freedom the citizens had, as Michel Foucault, following Nietzsche, said, to align their own rules with a universe presumed by them to be ordered and also elegant. This universe did not command the stoning of those who had uttered the name of the Lord, worked on the Sabbath, or taken both a woman and her mother. It took no interest in the way the young did their hair and coped with their beards.

Without ever moralising, the morality of the Greeks, founded on ethical grounds, reflected their rationality. Virtue, Democritus said, is a matter of self-interest, which, nevertheless was never understood as buying a thing for a dollar to sell it for two. It demanded courage, Justice, *sophrosyne*, which means restrained, temperate thinking, and *sophia*, wisdom. It also counted, as Kenneth Dover, that excellent classicist, said, on 'self-sacrifice, self-subordination to the community, meticulous observance of the law, distaste for violence and puritanical disapproval of consumption and promiscuity'. As Zeus, who had never made profound statements on matters of no importance, had made clear, virtue demanded responsibility for everyone's actions, personal, social and political. He himself was, of course, excused.

Greek morality did not require compassion, the virtue which is cultivated by conquerors after they have crushed the opposition, and which is for the Buddhists the most priceless treasure. Compassion, as Milan Kundera, the Czech novelist, wrote, 'designates what is considered to be an inferior, second-rate sentiment that has little to do with love. To love someone out of compassion means not really to love'. But Greek tradition did acknowledge the human capacity for suffering – in Euripides' play *Trojan Women*, for example, Hecabe, the queen of Troy, invites the Athenian audience to share the grief of her bleeding heart for Troy's ragged women whose homes had been burnt by the victorious Greeks, whose husbands and sons had died in battle or been murdered, whose daughters were raped while they themselves were bound for slavery. Her plea gave the Athenians, whose behaviour during the Peloponnesian war had at times been atrocious, something to work on. Incidentally, using this play as a departure point, Martha Nussbaum, an American left-wing Aristotelian academic, reminded the Americans that, rather than set as their task to defeat, abase and humiliate their demonised enemies following the September 11 disaster, they should, instead, try to see and confront their painful realities. Pain and suffering do not discriminate between 'us' and 'them'.

Greek morality did not require, either, the Christian virtues of patience, repentance, meekness, humility, thrift or duty which characterise the puritan work ethic. The sense of duty was there, but it was duty only towards one's own self; and it had no use for the theological virtue of charity insofar as it excused exploitation. 'Pity', William Blake, the eighteenth to nineteenth century English poet and artist, said in *The Human Abstract*, 'would be no more if we did not make someone poor; and mercy no more could it be if all were as happy as we'. Indeed, there was no Greek word for charity – the word *philanthropia* was a later addition. Likewise, the Greeks were as unfamiliar with the New Testament's virtues of faith, hope and love, all of which deserve one's trust as much as tombstone inscriptions.

Rather than a pious man, the good man for the Greeks was the temperate man who had courage, valued Justice and treasured wisdom, was simple and straightforward in his behaviour and modest in the way he presented himself, told the truth, took responsibility for his actions, and knew the meaning of, and exercised, self-restraint. A most valued quality was *megalopsychia*, which can be very inadequately translated as 'greatness of spirit'. It describes a man's soul that is larger than life, able when it has the power to punish, Pittacus, one of the seven wise men of Greece and ruler of Mytilene in the seventh century BC, said, to forgive rather than seek revenge because forgiveness shows gentleness and revenge savagery. The good man was also a good citizen and a man true to his friends. Friendship, rather than efficient networking and online connections designed to increase what Professor Robert Putnam called 'social capital', was based on mutual trust and respect. It was also treasured. The man who thinks that wealth or power is greater than a good friend, Euripides said on various occasions, is mad. 'When joy comes it is good to have a friend to share it; and if sorrow comes – which God forbid – the deepest comfort is to see it reflected in the eyes of a friend'. For Socrates, a good friend, a 'soulmate', was worth more than all the gold of King Darius.

Friendship for a purpose, which is the meaning of camaraderie, as opposed to friendship for pleasure or its usefulness, expressed the moral unity of the polis and was one of its political foundations.

Friends and purpose were, indeed, inseparable. Hence the Greeks would have been overwhelmed with pity if they could hear English novelist E.M. Forster's dilemma – 'if I have to choose between betraying my country or my friends, I hope I would have the courage to betray my country'. 'Anyone who can formulate such a contrast', Alasdair MacIntyre, the British-born philosopher, pointed out, 'is a citizen of nowhere, an internal exile wherever he lives'. Such a dilemma for the Greeks would have only underlined the depth of human misery. Citizenship was not a burden but an honour conferred upon a person. In gratitude, in one instance it was conferred even upon the wind, when in 379 BC three hundred warships sent by Dionysius, the tyrant of Syracuse, to destroy Thouria, a city in southern Italy where Herodotus eventually settled, never reached their destination. The north wind destroyed them. Appreciatively, the Thourians made the north wind a citizen of their city. Another culture would have deified it.

Morality for the Greeks, as it is obvious, had nothing to do with submission to the will of God and everything with Justice. It was Justice. It was also totally disconnected from one's sexual preferences or habits. From Sappho, the seventh century poet, to the first century BC Roman poet Lucretius, the Greeks were, thus, able to enjoy life in blessed freedom from sexual shame or guilt. If Freud, who had reckoned that 'where there is no repression ... our therapeutics has no business', had been in Greece, he would probably have been living on social security whilst awaiting the arrival of Christianity.

This understanding of morality was banned by Christianity to the outer suburbs of consciousness, the land of the mute sun. Morality was turned into a miserable affair of the knickers. The new Christian era, as Friedrich Hölderlin, the German poet, said, could not 'grasp a life lived nobly', the life of the Greeks.

8. Nothing in Excess

Proportion, balance and symmetry were for the Greeks the ruling principles of all aspects of life, from religion, architecture, prose, health or mathematics to what Fernand Braudel, the French cultural historian, called *les structures du quotidien*. Thrift and fasting are good, Democritus contentedly acknowledged, perhaps after some splendid cakes enjoyed on couches of myrtle and bryony, but so is extravagance on occasion, for 'a life without feasts is a long road without inns'. All human things, Alcmaeon, the philosopher-physician active in the first half of the fifth century, explained for his part, come in pairs such as black and white, good and bad, great and small, and all have their place in life. Health, for him, is conserved by equality among the elements – wet and dry, hot and cold, bitter and sweet, by the proportionate blending of the qualities. The dominance of any one of them produces illness. Harmony, Heraclitus before him had insisted, is achieved 'through the blending of the most opposite principles'.

Passion for symmetry forced Herodotus, the first historian, into the mistaken belief that the river Nile, which has its mouth opposite to that of the Danube, must also have its sources opposite to it. In Homer, too, there is this beautiful balance between the fierce, masculine, heroic world of the *Iliad* and the graceful, feminine, splendid world of the *Odyssey*, or between Achilles, the hero, and Achilles, the young man who is tearfully telling his mother about his lost love. Plato disapproved of the latter; Sophocles, the fifth century tragic dramatist, did not mind it, for love, he said, is like a piece of ice held in the fist of a child.

Balance, proportion and symmetry, to which the Greeks had made a doctrinal commitment, called for moderation. Everything, from exercise, food, drink and sleep to sexual relations, needed to come in 'the right measure' and at 'the right time'. Immoderate appetites such as gluttony, drunkenness, lust and ambition, all manifestations of egotism, were despised – a man who respected himself had to control himself. The English poet Coleridge's serious illness during his trip to Malta, caused, according to his biographer, by opium doses which 'had completely blocked his bowels', would have made the Greeks roll their eyes up in disbelief. The Greeks were, in fact, obsessed with self-control. Only slaves, they believed, consumed immoderately, slaves to their appetites. The true man is able to manage his cravings, exert, as Xenophon put it, self-mastery and restraint. Moderation was advocated by Socrates, too, though he did not always practise it himself. He would not care about anything, Phaidros said, so long as he could have 'someone to converse with, especially someone beautiful'.

Unlike Timarchus, enslaved to vices to which 'no free or noble man should ever submit', or vulgar Cleon who wolfed his food and downed his wine in one, the man of refinement had to take time to eat as he had to mix his wine with water and conversation – the Greeks had unmixed wine, heated up and taken with bread, only for breakfast. The same man should accept public office, as Socrates said, only 'with reluctance or under pressure'. Ambition had to be self-restrained.

The pleasures of food, drink and sex were anything but renounced. Sexuality, as Rufus of Ephesus pointed out, has nothing of vice about it, for it is deeply and harmoniously grounded in nature. Socrates, whose married life with his much younger Xanthippe might well have forced him to the conclusion that the only thing worse than not having a wife was having a wife, rather than denounce the pleasures of sex, actually acknowledged that there is no 'greater and sharper pleasure than the sexual'. Associated with a force, an *energeia*, which is liable to be excessive, sexuality had, however, to be controlled. *Akolasia*, self-indulgence, was considered shameful, as shameful as everything a free man might do as a passive, obliging sexual object. But, likewise, sexual abstinence was viewed as being as abnormal as its opposite, *akolasia*.

Pleasures had, however, to be controlled and mastered by

Reason. He who is incapable of mastering his own passions, Aristotle said, applying this axiom to politics, is always prone to abuse his power. The capacity to rule one's own self was the supreme criterion of fitness to rule others. Personal needs whose satisfaction is beyond one's means, Aeschines, the fourth century BC Athenian statesman, pointed out, open the door to political corruption. Self-control ruled out excessive love even for one's own life, for such an excessive love was a politician's sure sign of slavishness. Freedom and excellence demanded courage, not Yeats' courage in 'entering the abyss of himself' which his verse, better than its sentiments, recommends, but the courage always to do the just and honourable thing. Achilles, the hero of the Trojan war, did just that when he had to choose either an early death and glory or a long but inglorious life. He chose glory – the right decision for the Greeks. Contempt for death was an ethical imperative of the higher form of a man's existence.

Sophrosyne, a man's restrained, temperate thinking, did not demand the suppression of desires, but their control. Nietzsche made the same point when he said that the highest type of man is the passionate man who is the master of his passions. The question raised was not 'which desires, which acts, which pleasures' one could enjoy, but 'with what force is one transported by pleasures and desires'.

As Aristotle wrote in his *Nicomachean Ethics*, the criterion was quantitative in nature – moral virtue is a mean between two vices, one of excess and the other of deficiency. That quantitative border had not to be crossed. This border was not, of course, the only one, for some things were wrong regardless of circumstances. Whether a man, Aristotle added, commits adultery with the right woman, at the right time or in the right way is irrelevant as adultery is wrong. But rather than establish a compulsory set of rules with universal applicability, as Judaism and Christianity did, classical Greece, free-minded and anti-authoritarian, did not seek a single universal sense of 'good' common to all cases.

This sense of balance enabled the Greeks to avoid either the voluptuousness of Sardanapalus, king of Nineveh and Assyria, the debauchery of Heliogabalus, the Roman Emperor, the lasciviousness and cruelty of Messalina, or the hysterics of Origen, the Christian theologist of towering grandeur, who it is said cut off his private parts *ad gloriam dei*. Balance, proportion and symmetry in their lives enabled them further to escape both the religious excesses of the Middle Ages and the crude materialism of the industrial revolution and beyond to our own days. Their passion for moderation, Hölderlin thought, was, perhaps, necessary to counterbalance their passionate national temper, as much as 'Apollonian fire' is necessary to the Germans to counterbalance their own innate rationality.

Moderation had the blessing even of Greece's roguish and immoderate Gods. Apollo himself advised visitors of his temple in Delphi *Medhen agan*, 'nothing in excess' and *Gnothi sauton*, 'know thyself', an axiom explicitly restated by Freud. One had indeed to know himself in order to know his limits and exert the required self-control.

Yet the Greeks, Bertrand Russell, the British philosopher, said, ended up being 'excessive in everything' – in pure thought, in science, in art, in poetry, in religion, and in sin. They combined the cheerful, empirical, intellectual, material and rationalistic with the passionate, spiritual, mystical and otherwordly; the outer with the inner, the light with the shadow. The Gods were ready to give the lead in this respect. Apollo, the God of the intellect, was happy to let Dionysos, the God of the senses and his rival, take his place in 'the centre of the earth', Delphi, for three months a year; and all the Gods accepted that the faithful had to spread their favours equally between all of them. Euripides, in fact, considered Hippolytus a tragic misfit for worshipping the virgin Goddess Artemis but paying no honour to the love-goddess Aphrodite.

This wonderful Greek sense of balance maintained by self-control was, however, destroyed by Christianity's inhuman spirituality, the focus on the 'soul'. Christ himself had taken the lead in this respect, for he never lived with a woman. 'Surely living with a woman', James Joyce impishly remarked, 'is one of the most difficult things a man has to do, and He never did'. Sexuality, an evil of fixed address, inside us, was suppressed, quelled like pain. Together with it went the Greek sense of morality founded on Justice. Splitting morality from Justice, Christianity, and its sexual abstinence campaigns, did, indeed, end up destroying both, morality and Justice.

Free from commodity-induced and expensively maintained seductive illusions, which, as de Tocqueville wrote much later when capitalism was in full swing, make people neglect their chief business 'which is to remain their own masters', the aim was the satisfaction of all human needs – physical and intellectual, social and moral, spiritual and practical, aesthetic and sensual – in the spirit of balance, proportion and symmetry. The aim of production for the Greeks, Marx observed, was the human being rather than the creation of wealth – humans had not as yet turned into a commodity, objects, passive spectators of a process that structures their lives and denies them. The question, he wrote, was only 'which mode of property creates the best citizens'.

The Greeks were not interested in acquisitiveness, 'the worst individual and social evil', as Socrates chose to put it. Unlike our own consumption-besotted society, happiness did not depend on customer choice, the mantra of the 21st century, which grants us the absolute and inalienable right to choose the toppings on our pizza. It did not look forward, as Marcus Martial, the poet and epigrammatist, said, to 'money inherited, with no need to work' or by investing in 'get rich quick' stocks; it was not a subject to be taught at schools like history or maths, as a British government adviser has recommended, and it did not relate to 'having fun', this mindless preoccupation with the trivial.

Fun, incidentally, understood in our days as going out to buy some fun in the form of a film, a meal or a CD, was dismissed rather contemptuously by the Greeks. The use of professional entertainers to shortcut the way to a 'good time' was beneath a well-developed, self-respecting, civilised person, expected, as Plato made clear, to create together with his mates the means to his own entertainment.

The same sense of balance dictated the Greeks' refusal to divide concepts into categories – the intellectual, the physical, the moral, the political, the religious, the aesthetic and so on. Rather than mutually exclusive, the personal and the political, the spiritual and the mundane, the aesthetic and the practical, the moral and the expedient, the austere and the sensual, they all blended into a happy union, fused completely and indivisibly. They were all parts of the one world, in which, as Hölderlin said, man was 'one with all', crucial elements of a materially and spiritually, emotionally and physically, and intellectually and morally rewarding life, the confirmation of the laws of Justice. The perfection of the senses in unity with man's spiritual nature, Emerson, the American author, poet and philosopher, said, gave the sculptor the 'incorrupt, sharply-defined and symmetrical features' of the human forms which have nothing to do with the confused blurred features of people abounding in the streets of modern cities.

A man *kalos k'agathos*, a good man, was not a thinker, a citizen, an athlete or a man of virtue, but a man 'beautiful and honourable', good in all realms of human activity. Action was judged only by the criterion of greatness and not the passion for the ordinary – silk knickers or quality time in front of the TV. But the pursuit of excellence, indeed, the passion for it, was never perceived in terms of trying to be just a superb athlete, scientist or artist. The Greeks despised efficiency if that meant excellence in one or another department of life. Individual excellence, *areté*, had to be in life itself. Hence the gymnasia, constantly used by men of all ages, as childhood and old age had not been wrenched away from the rest of human life, were places of physical as well as mental exercise and cultural activities. Hence also the programme of the Olympic Games which included, alongside the athletic contests, music competitions, prayers and rituals, communal singing, orations by distinguished philosophers and recitals by poets and historians.

Rather than gloat over the agony of a gladiator, as the Romans did, the Greeks, Schiller observed in his 'Letters upon the aesthetic education of man', delighted in the bloodless athletic contest of boxing, racing, and intellectual rivalry at Olympia. And rather than live the life of a fragment of themselves, the life of the marginal who watches life as it unfolds on his digital television screen, they, likewise, relished every moment they could live life to the full. The context, holistic, brought together the physical, intellectual, spiritual and moral dimension of their being. It was what opened the way to happiness, which 'men of substance' try in vain in our days to achieve through mergers and acquisitions.

But this, as a concept, is probably today as fascinating as Sulpicius Severus' lifelong silence.

9. Her Lean, Boyish Body

A*reté*, who like Bertolt Brecht's Evelyn Roe 'wore no gold or ornament except her wondrous hair', is as a concept beyond the reach of our language and of our culture. Translated as 'Virtue' in the absence of a more appropriate word, it becomes almost entirely a moral word when all it means is simply excellence. But as such, it does not relate to a man's specific function such as a father, a professional, a friend, a citizen or a thinker, or to the social role one inhabits, but to his function as a human being. It denotes personal human qualities embracing the whole of a man's existence and not tradable against other goods such as wealth. The exercise of the virtues embodied in this single word, *areté*, was a crucial component of a man's good life, and demanded the presence of all of them at once, for they related intimately to each other. Hence there was not a single criterion of goodness of the kind Christianity advanced later, the pure soul, which Greece never had the pleasure of understanding. The criterion was, instead, a rather complex one involving all aspects of a man's life.

Incidentally, *areté* in the Greek language has a female quality. Odysseus Elytis, the Greek poet who won the Nobel prize for Literature in 1979, envisaged her as a young lady with 'a lean, boyish body', who labours all day in those places 'where the earth has rotted out of ignorance, and where men inexplicably have committed their dark iniquities'. At night, she flies 'for refuge there high in the embrace of the mountain as on a man's hairy chest'. In Greek many other agreeable concepts have a female quality such as Peace, Justice or Democracy, and emotions, forces and conditions whether agreeable or not such as Hope, Kindness or Madness.

The compartmentalisation of life we take for granted in our own days did not exist for the Greeks even as a concept. The privatisation of human interest in areas such as religion, sports or science by professional bodies was not even thought of; and specialisation was abhorred – 'I used to be nice and innocent', satirist Hector Hugh Munro, known as Saki, penned. 'Now I am only nice. One must specialise these days'. The demands of 'real life', the reality, which Theodor Adorno said, becomes its own ideology through the spell cast by its faithful duplication, has a different set of priorities. But the Greeks refused to live only a small fraction of their being, to divide themselves into parts at war with each other.

People, Aristotle said, should practise athletics but not in order to acquire professional skills, acquaint themselves with music, singing and the arts but not in order to become skilled performers, familiarise themselves with philosophy but not in order to profit from it. Education, or in its more appropriate Greek term *paideia*, had to meet the needs of the whole person, and aim at all-round development, human perfection. Hence Heracles was instructed in weapons drill, in cavalry and infantry tactics and in the rudiments of strategy, but he was also taught to sing and play the lyre and was introduced to literature, astronomy and philosophy. This was the idea which inspired, among many others, young Marx, who in his *Paris Manuscripts* and also later in *The German Ideology* extolled the virtues of the 'all-round individual', the goal of his Utopia. 'Touching in its idyllic *naiveté*', as contemporary Greek philosopher Costas Axelos put it, Marx's communist society had 'no painters but only people who engage in painting among other activities'.

Professional perfection, viewed, as Proust might have said, with 'that little smile of contempt with which we greet an impropriety', was undesirable because it demanded a commitment incompatible with the proper life of a man and a citizen. The skills professionals demonstrate in our days would have certainly been admired. The price, in terms of time, the individual pays to acquire these skills was, however, for the Greeks too high, incompatible with the need of a man and a citizen to live his life fully. Hence the professional was given as little scope as possible; indeed, the expert was usually a public slave. The concept of specialisation, which as Carl Rogers, one of the 'fathers' of humanistic psychology, said, leaves no place for the whole person in conventional education but only for his intellect, was introduced by Plato later, in the PostSocratic era.

Youngsters were, therefore, not taught standardised skills leading to qualifications with an exchange value in the marketplace. *Paideia* was not a means to an end – a better job, a more attractive mate or the creation of still greater material wealth, i.e., an investment in the future as in shares, which the American economist and Nobel prize winner Gary Becker, obviously unaware of the concept's inherent vulgarity, euphemistically called 'human capital'. It was an end in itself. The ideal was the attainment of the qualities on which character is built – independent judgment, courage, personal responsibility, self-command and commitment to their world. The criterion of a man's success was not his popularity, an insurance policy against uncertainty in interpersonal relations, but moral consistency, the mastery of his life rather than of his subject, character. As for Nietzsche, Weber and Simmel who valued a man not by what he does, but by what he is, the qualities were within the person. This kind of heuristic education, formalised by the state, was, as Democritus said, an ornament for the fortunate, a refuge for the unfortunate. It was also the state's best foundation, for the hopes of the educated are better than the wealth of the ignorant.

The Greek approach to education, fundamentally aristocratic in spirit, produced what was dismissively described by mass culture later as a 'gentlemen's world'. The Greeks had not, obviously, thought out the school's huge potential to provide industry, commerce, the established professions and the state with workers, consumers, patients, and clients willing to accept the roles assigned to them. Like Hölderlin in the nineteenth century, they 'wanted to be something rather than learn' – Hölderlin was dismissed by the utilitarians as too airy-fairy, too refined for them. Yet, as Rudolf Bahro, the German Green philosopher, said, the Greeks rightly did not want to abandon 'the tasks of social synthesis' to bureaucracies and specialists; and they certainly did not want to end up with a culture like ours, denounced by Ron Miller, editor of the American *Holistic Review*, because it 'does not nourish that which is best or noblest in the human spirit. It does not cultivate vision, imagination, or aesthetic or spiritual sensitivity. It does not encourage gentleness, generosity, caring, or compassion'. The economic-technocratic-statist worldview, Miller held, has become 'a monstrous destroyer of what is loving and life-affirming in the human soul'.

Hence the inspiration in matters of education the Greeks provided, Professor Marrou of the Sorbonne School suggested, retains a permanent value. It is the 'education of culture which has as its goal the training of man, of man as such, of the whole man, and not a mere producer-consumer, a mere cog in the industrial economy'. As the agency of culture, Raymond Williams, the British Marxist, likewise pointed out, this can only aim at 'the harmonious development of those qualities and faculties that characterise our humanity'. The task was to create 'man', to mould within the ethical parameters of a democratic culture human character. This approach, which ensured moral primacy over other purposes of education, trained the mind of man to see his interests as closely connected with, rather than apart from, those of his community, and meet responsibly the demands of his role as a citizen.

The thinking behind it, which determines even contemporary humanistic thinking in opposition to modernism's depressingly utilitarian and also sterile educational doctrines, is for many the Greeks' greatest work of art. It underlines Aristotle's emphatic view that democracy can never be better than its citizens as society cannot do better than its members. Rather than systems it is the people's *areté* that give any social and political institutions the desired qualities, and *areté* is cultivated and then realised, not in isolation, but through social and political interaction.

Paideia also cultivated the Greek passion for distinction. Distinction had nevertheless nothing to do with the contemporary notion of the creative genius, whose work, commercialised, is essentially greater than the creator himself. It related, instead, to the individual's nobility, the personal greatness involving sensuousness and spirituality, profound feeling and a penetrating intellect. It demanded character which, as Aristotle said, 'appreciates what is noble and objects to what is base', honourable action and words regardless of actual achievements or motivation. As Democritus insisted before him, 'for beasts, good breeding consists in bodily strength, for men in grace of character'. Victory or defeat, and their consequences, were not important even in death, an honourable death faced unflinchingly by man. Life was not sacrosanct – the deeds of the individual were.

Yet, amazingly enough, man had to strive, not just for the realisation of all his potentials, but also for excellence. After all, it was believed, the measure of a man's worth is only the time in which he would be remembered by future generations – hence Kavafis' 'when I am dead, I hope it may be said: "His sins were scarlet, but his books were read"'. Those content with daily pleasures and fated like Tantrabolus, the grand vizier who was strangled in 1695 by order of Mustapha II, to live till they die leaving behind not a single trace of their existence, those who, as Strates Myrivilis, the Greek novelist, said, 'pass their lives and die completely unaware of it', encountered nothing but contempt at least until the age of Socrates. So did those who sought happiness in external goods, rather than, as Solon put it, in the finest deeds; or those who, 'like beasts', as Heraclitus said, were hostages of the pleasures of 'the belly and the genitals and the most shameful parts in us'.

Excellence – *aien aristevein* – demanded 'ever to excel'. The Olympics' motto 'faster, higher, stronger' was the goal of each individual life applicable to the whole person, not just the body. Action as well as thought demanded distinction, a greatness far removed from the common, the ordinary, the effortless. 'Go for the great and radiant' things in life, Democritus advised; and in their pursuit, Aristotle added, 'be afraid of nothing, not even of an earthquake or inundation, as they say of the Celts'. The free man, the true human being, the *aristos* had to go for immortal fame rather than mortal things. Men, for Heraclitus, choose only one thing in return for everything they do: immortal fame. Hence Heraclitus' appearance, as novelist Jane Austen might have said if she were to use again her superb satirical wit, was not greatly in his favour. The Greeks, certainly, had no desire to outrage the world with their ordinariness as did Leopold Bloom, Joyce's character.

From this point of view, the means were the ends – under certain circumstances, they were even more important than the ends. The telos, end, was in the activity itself. The qualities were within the person, in his character measured by the yardstick of moral consistency, sincerity and unity of purpose. This had nothing to do with social class and everything to do with individual quality, the only quality which empowered the individual to win, even if 'not master of land and sea', his own distinctive place in society and live his life with honour. This was what, Thackeray would say, 'thrilled through every fibre of (their) body, and made it tingle with pleasure'. Nothing, including a man's own life or the products of his work, was greater than the man himself.

The Greeks' criterion of greatness, Hannah Arendt in particular explained, was in the innermost meaning of each person's action, in the performance itself, the self-actualisation of the individual in the context of the polis. This was the measure of a man's worth which would earn him the honour of being a man *kalos k'agathos*. Failure to do so, to do less than what was socially expected, could bring only shame. In tune with his world's repertoire of interpretive mechanisms and value systems, 'cultured people', Aristotle said, 'identify with honour'. That was, of course, the case before the word 'cultured' obtained sinister connotations – 'I need only to talk with any of the "cultured people"', Nietzsche exploded in his *Ecce Homo*, 'to convince myself that I am not alive'; and also before honour became the prized asset of those who have next to nothing. It was also before vulgar utilitarianism legitimised the use of all means in the pursuit of privately set ends disguised as noble ends.

Honour, an indispensable element of personal refinement as real as the white Pentelic marble, was rooted in the heroic age when Electra sought 'victory with honour or honourable death'. Its culture, the culture of shame and honour instead of blame and duty or guilt and obligation, demanded strict adherence to the virtues of the Greeks: Justice, *sophrosyne*, courage and *sophia*. It was, as the poet Simonides said, what separated a decent human being from a beast. A man was entitled to honour if he performed well, and had to confer it upon others as an expression of his regard for deeds meriting honour. In their face-to-face relationships, this code of honour, today an endangered quality, made even the issue of receipts uncommon, for a man, an honourable man, was as good as his word.

Such a man, generalising, Aristotle explained, is the one who does not court danger but takes great risks when circumstances make life not worth living, confers benefits but is ashamed to accept them, helps others but never complains or makes a request for help, and is haughty towards the powerful but moderate towards the weak. The same man never talks about himself nor about others, does not pay compliments but is not abusive, either, does not flatter anyone, does not nurse resentment and is open in his likes and dislikes because he cares more about the truth. He also prefers beautiful and unprofitable possessions to profitable and useful ones.

Honour in the Middle Ages was what separated the aristocrats, those 'gilded flies' as Shelley called them, from ordinary human beings, i.e., those without any special oddities. In our times it is probably what separates the 'naive' from the streetwise. Still, in its Greek sense, the concept is not quite dead. 'Shame and pride', Israeli novelist Amos Oz, the 'Zionist Orwell', asserted, 'are generally stronger than other famous urges that figure prominently in literature'. They are often the discernible motivation of individuals in politics, too, as British prime minister Margaret Thatcher demonstrated when she decided to launch the Falklands war.

The Greek understanding of excellence was deconstructed by Christianity, which, predisposed in favour of mediocrity, or, as Nietzsche said, of downright baseness, banned its pursuit. Knowledge, Christianity claimed, was not essential in life – nothing should, therefore, tamper with natural ignorance. Essential was, instead, a pure heart. The Greeks, incidentally, never contrasted intelligence with goodness by putting down, as is done in our days, the 'so-called intellectuals', those individuals so clearly 'pretentious' at best, 'useless' as a rule, and 'dangerous' at worst. They just did not need to reassure ardent consumers that they had something good enough to compensate for their lack of intelligence.

As deconstructed in our days is the Greek understanding of manhood. What we value is personality rather than character, often acquired through the possession of products with personality, i.e., consumer icons. Character, as an ideal, was nevertheless not easy to attain even in Greece at her best. However high one may aim, desires, Socrates said in an attempt to appropriate Freud's glory, 'wake up while we sleep ... and our fierce bestial nature ... does not shrink from attempting intercourse with a ... man, beast or God, or from murder. There is, in fact, no folly nor shamelessness man will not commit'. But as Heraclitus said, nothing exists without its opposite.

The world of beauty beyond necessity, Marcuse's world of 'happiness and enjoyment', the good life demanded, as Aristotle said, enjoyment of the pleasures of the body, engagement with the affairs of the polis, and devotion to philosophy. This world, according to Heidegger, into whose philosophy people are still trying, as in the Barbican, to find their way, belongs to a different realm and rank of spiritual existence. It shares this order only with poetry, the art which transforms people's aspirations into words which fight the battle for the realisation of the holy, the great and the brave. Poetry, as Aristotle held, is more philosophical, and higher than history, for poetry tends to express the universal, whilst history deals with the particular. Informed by the insurmountable human spirit and as unselfconscious as nature itself, this world was not 'about something' other than itself and the truth.

But, of course, as Algernon said in Oscar Wilde's *The Importance of Being Earnest*, the truth is rarely pure and never simple.

10. Like a Tuned String

A just life was thought to be in tune with the just natural order which, like the stars in the sky, represented the eternal in Greek thinking. As such, it had to respect boundaries and limits imposed by the morality embedded in that order, go with the grain of natural evolution and, thereby, avoid excesses whether in private or public life. A virtuous life was, therefore, a life lived in terms of balance, proportion and symmetry in everything, and involved choices made by the rational mind in accordance, as Aristotle put it, with a mean. When Aristotle spoke of the mean, Professor Kitto explained, the thought of the tuned string was never very far from his mind. The mean did not imply the absence of tension and lack of passion, but the correct tension which gives out a true and clear note, key to man's happiness. Virtue had, indeed, to lead to *eudaemonia*, for, if not, it lacked a *telos*, a human end. The Kantian axiom 'do not seek to be happy, seek to be deserving of happiness' would have made as much sense to the Greeks as a shop with nothing to sell.

Like so many others, *eudaemonia* is a term which is, unfortunately, impossible to translate. It indicates a state of being higher than happiness, which, identified with pleasure is, according to Aristotle, just what a cow is after, or, as Marcel Proust put it, just what the 'really stupid people' are after. It is also more important than good fortune which depends on chance. Without any religious connotations, the word literally means the reign of the good daemons in a man's life. Metaphorically, it signifies a man's whistling, when in that state, in tune with the harp within and in harmony with the band without. *Eudaemonia* is, therefore, the fine attunement of man with his spirit and his nature, his community and his sense of purpose, the harmonisation of his existence with everything visible and invisible. As such, it is the application of the fundamental Greek concept of Logos to the life of the individual, open nevertheless to interpretation by one's instinctual understanding of it as much as Logos itself.

Eudaemonia, though the telos itself of human activity, was not separate from the means to its achievement, external to virtuous activity. It was, instead, inherent in man's actions, present in the inner meaning of any activity, a crucial component of the good life. Life, as psychologists Alfred Adler and Edward Chace Tolman also held early in the twentieth century, has intentionality – the intentionality which was denied by Husserl and several existentialists. It serves a purpose. Being the purpose, *eudaemonia* required action in the pursuit of excellence in both public and private life because to seek to excel was to seek to enjoy as in the case of a game in which one is thoroughly involved and which is thoroughly enjoyed. Pleasure in its Aristotelian sense comes then, as Aristotle himself said, 'like the bloom on the cheek of youth'. It glows, Ritsos would have said, 'like the waters of the Bosphorus in olden times'. Hegel used the same concept to define freedom – its 'very idea', he said, is not something which men have but 'something which they are'.

Yet happiness was desired but not as such. It was, instead, for the reasons that generated it, the force that produced it, the meaning of its associations. The virtues which enabled a person to live a life at its best had to be good in themselves, stand their ground without any reference to ends. The state of *eudaemonia* could not be reached unless achievement in any field was closely associated with an ethical set of principles. From the Homerean days down to the most confusing times when, following Alexander's campaign, the world of the Greeks expanded to what seemed at that time to be its limits, leading a just and honourable life remained the ideal pursued relentlessly and passionately. An unethical life was beyond the realm of a man and a citizen.

Fulfilment was not sought in self-actualisation, often associated in our days with the selfish pursuit of private gains and pleasures divorced from any sense of purpose and self-help books about secretaries bagging rich husbands and mutes turning into Cicerons. It was seen, instead, in terms of self-transcendence, the identification with something that is bigger than one's own self, which, as Freud said, is what makes a man strong. The point was taken by Abraham Maslow, one of the 'fathers' of humanistic psychology, and placed at the very top of his pyramid of needs although later, in 1970, cognitive and aesthetic needs took priority, and by California psychology professor Mihály Csikszentrnihályi, who developed it in his own way by introducing the notion of flow, a state of total oneness with the activity at hand and the situation.

Rather than the fulfilment of the self, the Greek ideal was, thus, the fulfilment of meaning in the world out there. Self-actualisation, Victor E. Frankl, an Auschwitz survivor and another of the 'fathers' of humanistic psychology, argued likewise, is not man's ultimate destination, not even his primary intention. A man is intent on it only if he has missed his mission and if his search for meaning has been frustrated.

This eudaemonist, non-instrumentalist foundation of ethical philosophy established by Socrates, Gregory Vlastos, the philosopher heralded as one of the most celebrated twentieth century scholars of classical philosophy held, was shared not only by Platonists but also Aristotelians, Cynics and Stoics, i.e., all Greek moral philosophers except the Epicureans.

The unfolding of truth was sought, as Plato clarified, in the thing itself rather than the meanings attached to it by religious, economic, commercial or ideological pursuits and concerns. Nature and life could, thus, be appreciated for their intrinsic rather than their use value which, incidentally, packaging and advertising has replaced in our days with an image. Free from commercialism which de Tocqueville, the French political writer, warned nineteenth century Americans about by drawing their attention to the Greek understandings, the countryside was the countryside rather than a resource, and a religious event was a religious event rather than a demonstration of ecclesiastical control and power. Or, to use Plato's own example, the wind had to be understood in its own right as a natural force rather than as a means exclusively serving human needs. Unlike a contemporary styrofoam, which Martin Heidegger, the German existentialist philosopher, said, is dissociated from customs, history, tradition and social meanings, a chalice was its chaliceness, i.e., only the meanings associated with it.

'We love the things we love for what they are', American poet Robert Frost put it beautifully; not for their benefits – hence Frost abandoned a rather unsuccessful career as a poultry farmer and devoted himself to poetry. The Olympics in this sense ought to be the Olympics rather than a commercial orgy on TV, a walk a pleasure rather than a fitness exercise, and golf a game rather than a way of making new contacts.

Time, likewise, was not money – time was not reified, turned into just another commodity, and philosophy and science were enjoyed for the intellectual challenges they presented rather than the practical benefits which they might bring. They were all an end in themselves rather than a means to an end, loved for what they were rather than for what they could be used. Learning, Aristotle said in his *Poetics*, gives the liveliest pleasure, not only to philosophers but to men in general. Hence when a student of Euclid made the mistake of asking the great third century BC mathematician what was the practical use of what they were learning, Euclid dismissively gave him a drachma so he would be earning something from his learning.

In the same spirit, William Morris rejected what he called 'utilitarian socialism' in favour of a community-based, 'ethical socialism' that coexisted in harmony with nature, cultivated the whole person, and restored the dignity and creativity of labour as craft; and D.H. Lawrence, commenting upon the advice offered by Benjamin Franklin, the American eighteenth century utilitarian statesman, to his fellow-countrymen to 'rarely use venery but for health or offspring', retorted 'never *use* venery'. Sexual gratification is not something to be used like an aspirin. Franklin, incidentally, a hypocrite, had himself a barely disciplined sexual appetite, often consorting with disreputable women.

Form and function did, thus, merge and produce a mode of being, Martin Heidegger's *Dasein*, the being-there, which means being-in-the-world as opposed to being essentially a consciousness to be hooked onto the world, and which embraced the aesthetic and the social, the sacrificial and the communal, culture and nature, the particular and the general. The merge of them all, including the sensually unperceivable, encompassing life's primordial meaning, home of an earthly divinity and a divine earthliness, was, however, demolished by the Enlightenment's instrumental rationality. The latter, as critical theorists Adorno and Horkheimer said, disregarded the intrinsic properties of things, those which give them their sensuous, social and historical particularity, and things rather than the means to the satisfaction of human ends became their own ends. The 'thing itself', which, uncontaminated by the system of meanings and values generated by modernism, and detached from transcendentalism and also from instrumentalism and utilitarianism which obliterate the 'unconcealedness' of things, became a memory. So did the human values associated with it.

The latter were, and still are, beyond the understandings of positivism. 'We have no knowledge of anything but phaenomena (whose) essential nature, and ultimate causes, either efficient or final, are unknown and inscrutable', John Stuart Mill stated clearly enough for any city banker to understand. Apparently, things desired in and for themselves, drawing upon unverifiable experiences, are, like human nature, beyond human comprehension. The desire for certainties has replaced the desire for meaning.

The Greek understandings, Alasdair MacIntyre, one of the philosophers of the 'Third Way', sadly reflected, have been expelled from our culture. Happiness is exclusively linked to external objects of competition in which there must be winners and losers; and freedom became John Locke's freedom of the individual to act solely on the strength of his desire to ensure his own happiness or pleasure, or John Stuart Mill's freedom to pursue happiness by setting his own goals and achieving them in his own way, as he sees fit. Democracy, linked to 'limited government' which is the fundamental premise of liberalism, was associated with the abandonment of both a substantive and unique vision of the common good and of *eudaemonia* as an ethical goal.

The winners, meanwhile, are never satisfied. 'With little sleep and much reading', like Miguel de Cervantes' Don Quixote, their 'brains dried up and (their) intellect deranged', whilst competition, fear, which Aeschylus called 'the enemy of sleep', envy and unhappiness have increased in line with increases in their income.

The Greeks were aware, in any case, that the pursuit of happiness is self-defeating, for it is the pursuit itself, the target of intention, that thwarts it. Happiness, whenever we try to visit her, is then never home. But again, home in our days is only a place to receive the mail.

The relationship between the two, virtue and happiness, was, of course, anything but easy or self-evident. But its existence was a fundamental assumption of Greek political theory from Thales down to Seneca. Hence the agonising concern, articulated more than anybody else by Socrates, about 'how one should live' as a human being and a citizen of the Republic. Incidentally, Greek philosophy would have dismissed as meaningless the retreat of Western philosophy into its own private garden in which the rise of meaninglessness is discussed in numerous publications in order to advance their writers' career prospects. Epicurus made the point early enough when he said that philosophical argument that is not concerned with human suffering is empty, trivial and self-indulging, as useless as medicine unconcerned about the illness of the body.

Wealth and power, the Greeks were convinced, do not make a man happy, even if, Anaxagoras said, judging by outward appearances which is all they can see, people may believe that he is. Whatever the circumstances, happiness could not in any case be taken for granted. Pre-empting the twentieth century existentialists, the chorus in Sophocles' *King Oedipus* demands, thus, what is evidently unanswerable. 'Show me the man', it calls, 'whose happiness is something more than illusion'. Tragedy, the ultimate consequence of man's vulnerability, is never too far away.

11. A Culture of Honour

In the pursuit of the thing itself, means and ends were for the Greeks identical. The means were in effect the telos itself, for goodness was embedded in the thing, the activity itself. As Aristotle made clear, flute-playing, healing or an athletic contest were not means to ends but ends in themselves worth pursuing for their own sake. The two were identical. The means were the ends. The end, telos, the activity itself, exhausted its meaning in the performance itself because of the dignity with which it was carried out, the greatness and honour it conferred upon the individual, and the fulfilment of a meaning in the course of a life dedicated to the achievement of excellence. Should the ends become the means, it was thought, something objectively given would have been eliminated – in the world of information, the truth. Things, turning from what they are into commodities, the means for our gratification, are lost to human experience. As opposed to distant ends, means were also important as ends in themselves because it is through means that we relate to each other.

No means could, therefore, become an end which would then become means to another end, for no attainment was higher than the thing itself. Humanity is not a means to an end, the enrichment of the few, but an end in itself. No noble ends can justify the use of dishonourable means if action is not to be self-defeating. 'National defence' can never sanction the massacre of civilians with all the ardour technological barbarism can inspire. And 'freedom of the press' cannot excuse the massive misinformation of Americans by Fox News, America's premier 24-hour TV news channel, which convinced them that Weapons of Mass Destruction were found in Iraq.

Whether the axiom 'the ends do not excuse the means' precludes the removal of a tyrant by assassination or mass violence, which Marx said is 'the midwife of every old society pregnant with a new one', is open to interpretation. The Greeks themselves condoned the killing of tyrants – Harmodius and Aristogeiton were celebrated after they killed tyrant Hipparchus in 514. But in general this kind of ends, just like Odysseus, whose legs were shorter in proportion to his body, sometimes look nobler sitting rather than standing.

The Greek identification of ends and means was ruthlessly suppressed by Christianity. In its static hypocrisy that rests on an absence, the latter actually invented instrumentalism, albeit in a spiritual form, inherent in the doctrine that good deeds done here on earth are a means to win a place in the kingdom of heaven.

Capitalism just continued in the same tradition except that it substituted profits for heaven. Everything, from nature and humans to time, relations and processes, has since been valued, not for its intrinsic worth, but for the benefits it provides. Means, any means, including blatant lies, provided they are effective, become permissible and justified for whatever is defined as an end. Vulgar utilitarianism, designed with cost-effectiveness in mind, cannot, nevertheless, articulate any principle on the strength of which means and ends can be defined. Utility, an end in itself with an inner meaning which renders meaning meaningless, is unable to explain the reason for which it is good. Even so, utilitarianism has orchestrated immoderate violence not only at the expense of nature, as the Greens, from the days of Plato onwards have argued, but also at the expense of man.

The philosophical understandings of the Greeks underpinned their unwritten ethical code, their civilisation of honour. The latter could not be violated without bringing shame upon the offender. 'When I consider I am doing wrong', Agathon, the tragic dramatist, acknowledged, 'I am ashamed to look my friends in the face'; and wrong was not just the criminal or even the unethical but also the indecorous. Plato illustrated the point when, for example, he reminded future generations that 'it is considered improper to accept authority except with reluctance or under pressure'.

Man was a mere nothing without the reputation which a just and honourable life was expected to confer upon him. Hence, to preserve it, to avoid being reproached for doing something ethically and morally wrong that was bound to lead to humiliation, the Greek would disregard even the calls of his rationality. Always willing and forever happy, he would sacrifice everything for it, from property, money and interests to health and even life itself. Letting others down, fellow soldiers, fellow citizens, the political refugees who sought a safe haven in his city or the dead who needed to be honoured by the living, was so contemptible that it was worse than death. Perhaps one may say that the Greeks, just like ourselves, lived on the image of themselves they projected. But the socially accepted image was that of commitment to the community rather than to one's own self. The former has blood in its veins, the latter, yellow, chlorinated body fluids.

As a Greek myself, I can relate to the ancient pride which is still honoured in Greece, though, unfortunately, in connection mostly with the wrong things. *Philoxenia*, hospitality, is one of the surviving good ones as is the contempt for those who resort to force against an adversary much weaker than themselves which partly explains the Greek antipathy to the Iraq war. As dishonourable is turning one's back on one's parents, particularly when they are in need, or on old people. The time when old age, viewed in the West as an immoral, if not an illegal, state of being, had not as yet come to Greece. One does not, however, have to be a Greek to recognise echoes of this old culture of honour in the entire world. Parents feel shame for their children's misdeeds, relations feel shame if a person close to them has been imprisoned for wrongdoings, women, both poor women with nothing but a husband and a cow and rich women with everything but a family and love, are ashamed to admit that they are physically abused by their male partners. Professionals, such as lawyers, accountants or doctors, who fail to abide by an ethical code, shame, likewise, not just themselves but their entire profession. Even an entire country can feel shame if, for example, English football hooligans abroad riot to the embarrassment of their own country.

Not everybody has, of course, this kind of inkling. As Bernard Shaw's Bentley, the son of Lord Summerhays, said, 'if I started being ashamed of myself, I shouldn't have time for anything else all my life.' The up-to-dateness of the statement can hardly be missed.

The same sense of honour often makes people ready to defend, if they can, an unknown person subject to an unprovoked attack, or to refuse to take money for something they recognise is their duty as human beings to do. The instances in which people simply do the honourable thing are numerous particularly in times of trial. I read, for example, that the Fuji Bank's senior management in New York's Trade Centre died following the fateful attack because they stayed behind to ensure the evacuation of the building by all members of their staff rather than run for their lives. This, the newspaper's reporter said, reflects a code of conduct common in Japanese companies requiring that senior managers protect the office as a whole in an emergency.

This culture of shame and honour has nothing to do with social structures or institutional arrangements. It makes no room for the simplistic belief that people will act decently only if the social system has eradicated all social inequalities and, thereby, the reasons individuals act unethically or break the common law. People can act honourably in the way they relate to themselves and others whatever the circumstances. In doing so, they may act instinctively, they may follow a habit which has become second nature or a hobby like Louis de Bernières' 'first hobby', which, he says, was saying good morning, or they may even do what they do out of pleasure. Whatever the reason, the noble and generous side of human nature always makes itself felt even in times as morally dumb as ours, which is why, I think, Charles Taylor, the communitarian, is not right when he argues that honour 'is intrinsically linked to inequalities'.

Taylor, like Axel Honneth, the German sociologist, considers, incidentally, that honour, an 'aristocratic' concept, has been replaced in the modern identity-formation process by 'the politics of recognition', i.e., the need of the individual to be 'recognised' by total strangers as something uniquely unique in the world. As a reference to our well sustained culture of celebrity and its idols of consumption, this is, of course, a valid point, but the other, the honourable side has not disappeared altogether from our daily life – at least, not as yet.

For, shaming those who violate the common trust, disregard their obligations to the community and let down their fellow human beings, those, in other words, who, though they do nothing illegal, betray the human spirit, is the very essence of ethics. This is, at least, the way the Greeks, who did not believe in rewards and punishments in another life, saw it, and this is also our ethical inheritance which, disparaged by the Judaeo-Christian tradition, has almost vanished from modern political theory. The Judaeo-Christian tradition placed, instead, the emphasis on guilt so consistently assailed by Nietzsche.

The differences between guilt and shame are nevertheless profound. Guilt is a private affair, an emotion experienced by the individual following self-scrutiny and self-blame for wrongdoings. Shame, on the contrary, is a social emotion, the revulsion felt by the community at iniquitous acts committed by an individual in violation of his or her moral code of behaviour. In the case of guilt, the individual has to deal with his own emotions, but in the case of shame on the other side stands, not the self, but the community, which, unfortunately, in our days will only rush to turn the book written by the shamed into a bestseller.

This is the reason the word 'conscience' did not figure high in the pre-Christian Greek vocabulary. Conscience for the Greeks was not the property of the individual but that of his polis, the *conscience collective* whose code of shame and honour determined behaviour more effectively than the commands of either the law or of the unfathomable inner self. There was, however, one more reason that conscience did not figure high on the Greeks' agenda. It had to do with their sense of realism, i.e. the imputation of a person's multiple motivation in any action. A single cause of one's motivation can be there but only on the rarest of occasions. Orestes, determined to avenge his father's murder by his mother, was certainly motivated, as Aeschylus tells us, by his sense of Justice. But along with it went his grief at his father's loss, fear of disobeying Apollo's command to act, the need to regain his patrimony, and shame that Argos would still be ruled, if he did not act, by the murderess Clytaemnestra and her villainous lover.

Multiple positive motivation often included reasons provided by the rational mind. Jealousy, according to Isocrates, should better be avoided because it does more harm to the person who experiences it than to the person against whom it is directed; and greed, Menander said, is undesirable for it is likely to lead to grief rather than happiness because it is so often associated with misfortune. Other and often unacknowledged motives relate, of course, to hopes and fears – hopes, for example that one's loving and generous behaviour would benefit the giver by increasing his esteem in society, and fears of disgrace, ridicule, contempt or punishment in the case of wrongdoing. The Greeks nevertheless accepted that there could be motivation relating exclusively to one's own inner self, if, for example, one had to act in a certain way to preserve his self-respect or to avoid self-loathing.

The culture of shaming encounters fierce opposition in our days, for it is considered to be limiting the freedoms of the individual. In a sense, this opposition is well grounded, for shaming, as understood by the *News of the World* and a moral hysteria which thrives on titillating sexual details, invades the individuals' privacy, imposes the outlook of its crusaders on society, and restricts individual choice, relating, as it happens, as a rule, to sexuality. In the same sense, shaming can lead to an intolerant society in which a so-called moral majority represses, and even terrorises, those who, adhering to a different value system, refuse to conform with social norms, its mode of being.

But still shame is at the heart of an ethics which gives a voice to those whom the law cannot protect and confronts injustice in a manner that is beyond the legal system's ability. It is, indeed, on the strength of this principle that the turn of the century has been witnessing the gradual rehabilitation of shame as a force which questions policies of the rich West and practices of multinational corporations: the ruthless exploitation of the environment, the transformation of both humans and the non-human world as a resource, the destruction of cultures by the homogenising drive of the major metropolitan centres of the West and so on. Its outlines are fuzzy and its proclamations stammering, but the principle is there.

Shaming the wrongdoers is, however, one side of the coin. The other is honouring, not just the absence of indifference, callousness or malice, but a person's positive contribution to society. The Greeks did just that. And the pride of those contributing handsomely to the welfare of their community was the source of great pleasure, and dramatically increased when, despite their semi-detached commitment to modesty, they could boast for giving, when they did, more than their fair share. 'Performing my public services', the Athenian statesman and great orator Demosthenes said still at a time, late in the fourth century, when traditional ethics were being eroded, 'is a joy'. The closer a thing comes to perfection, Virgil said, the more keen will be its pleasure or its pain.

Love of money was considered to be in the nature of an inferior man. An intelligent and good man, the man our own system would suspiciously treat as a potentially subversive individual, was superior to money. He would not allow himself, as Euripides put it, to be 'enslaved by money'. Wealth, as Aristotle emphasised, too, is not an end but a means for getting something else which was never consumer goods. The Greeks were simply contemptuous of consumption as they were of what capitalism values most, 'gain' and 'profit' won ideally overnight. This contempt was so deep-rooted that self-made people, as those who manage to build a fortune from nothing are called in our days, had to justify their riches and prove that this fortune benefited the community itself.

The same culture of honour admired those who chose to remain poor rather than act dishonestly, valued kindness to all those who were in need, and expected a wealthy man to invite his less fortunate friends to share his good fortune with him. These were criteria which, obviously, do not figure in the drawing of the honours' list compiled annually by the British government. The honoured individual's attitude was, of course, not entirely free of calculation, for man, never certain of what the future had in store for him, had better do all the right things in good time.

With this kind of understanding, no good was good enough if it did not enhance the welfare of the whole, and no personal goal could be set without the common goal which would enable the personal goal to be realised. The connection between the goods desired and the world within which they would be enjoyed could not be broken without damaging the goods desired. A good Greek citizen was, thus, expected to put public interest above his private interests but only because he was honour-bound rather than because he was given no choice by law. In exceptional circumstances we do just the same. In war, for example, there is nothing unusual about self-sacrifice if it saves the lives of comrades in the trenches or of civilians. The Greeks, in their heroic age, took the same concept a step further, when, for example, Euripides in *Erechtheus* has Praxithea expressing contempt for any woman who would rather see her son safe without honour than honourably dead. But this is only a difference in emphasis.

The individual could claim no rights if these rights trespassed on the rights of the community. Life, as Xenophon put it, is 'not to live for oneself alone'; 'men', Marcus Aurelius wrote later in his Memoirs, 'exist for the sake of one another'. This sense of belonging to a entity larger than oneself, encouraged by a culture based on positive ethical reinforcements, i.e., the pursuit of the ideal rather than the avoidance of wrongdoing and the individuals' personal commitment to the political and moral foundations of their city-state, has been denounced by postmodernist thinkers as the denial of individuality.

But as opposed to our culture which thrives on individualism, for the Greeks the supreme principle was that of social utility in tune with the rules of their unwritten ethical code. This approach did not repress individuality, that self-defining, self-differentiation process which Carl Jung thought is the ultimate goal of psychospiritual growth. On the contrary, it enhanced it by placing it in a different, and more meaningful, context, one that today's mass consumption society is unable to provide: that of human needs which require for their satisfaction personally significant communication with others within a responsible and influenceable society. Individuality finds its proper meaning, which individualism, often associated with a crude and self-serving opportunism, has destroyed, only when human beings are engaged with their world rather than disengaged, find life's purpose within the community rather than apart from it, and support what supports life rather than what denies it.

Respect for the rights of fellow-citizens, family members, neighbours, employees, pedestrians or customers takes nothing away from our individuality. The community context only helps the choices made by the conscious human being. To recognise this requires, however, not just goodness but also wisdom, which is the happy child of the marriage between intelligence and ethics that is so missing from a culture hooked on individualism. Socialism, incidentally, was originally coined as the antithesis not of capitalism but of individualism, a characteristic which develops, de Tocqueville said, from erroneous judgment and originates as much in deficiencies of mind as in perversity of heart.

This life-enhancing, creative and honourable culture was nevertheless quelled by what Byron called the 'barbarous hands' of the ages that succeeded it.

12. The Science of Beauty

Love, 'a word least used today', as José Saramago, the Portuguese novelist, stated rather sorrowfully, is something you do not mention in polite mixed company. It could hardly be otherwise in a cynical world which has transformed the 'I-Thou' relationship into an 'I-It' relationship, treating everything, including often our closest associates, even our own self whom we often regard as worthless and despise, as an object. Yet love is universally acknowledged as the language of the heart, the dancing flame of life, the power that turns any person into a poet carrying 'happy flowers from the mountains, bluebells, dark hazels, and rustic baskets of kisses'. In Julia Kristeva's psychoanalytic theory it is the indispensable basis of identity formation which she associates with the notion of care as the alternative to the romantic notion of love. Yet the Greeks did not have much to say about it.

Paris fell in love instantly with Helen and expressed his passion for her in the words 'I love you', traced in wine on the table top, and young and beautiful Alcestis, in love with her husband Admetus, volunteered to die, as she did, in his place. Orpheus, also in love with his wife Eurydice, whose tenure in life ended when she was bitten on the foot by a snake, descended to the Stygian realm hoping to persuade the deities of the underworld to let her back among the living. His song, just like *Orfeo ed Euridice*, Gluck's opera, was so moving that 'Tantalus, in spite of his thirst, stopped for a moment his efforts for water; Ixion's wheel stood still; the vulture ceased to tear the giant's liver; the daughters of Danaus rested from their task of drawing water in a sieve; and Sisyphus sat on his rock to listen. Then for the first time, it is said, the cheeks of the Furies were wet with tears'.

Peleus' story was happier: he fell for Thetis whom he seduced in a cave on the shores of an islet where she had arrived naked on a harnessed dolphin. Their wedding, just outside Cheiron's cave on mount Pelion, surpassed in glamour even Michael Douglas and Catherina Zeta-Jones'. It was attended by all twelve Olympian Gods as well as the Fates and Muses, who sang beautiful songs, fifty Nereids, who performed spiral dances on the white sand, and hundreds of Centaurs, who had dressed up for the occasion. Wine was served personally by Ganymedes, Zeus' beloved youngster.

Eros, the handsome little devil mentioned in Hesiod's *Theogony* (c.750 BC), is credited with the ability to overpower the intelligence and the shrewd planning of both mortals and immortals. But he does not appear at all in Homer's rhapsodies, the Bible of the Greeks. The world of the Greeks had no patience for immortal love stories and no liking for the excess and violence of the pleasures, Cleopatra's love of men's lusting after her. That was the privilege of 'common lovers', 'base men'. In a normal love affair the ethics of Eros focused, however, not only on self-mastery but also on reciprocity. Men, Martha Nussbaum and Juha Shivola wrote in *The Sleep of Reason* published in 2002, displayed their power through the act of penetration but they also worried about 'being decent and kind, and about being loved for themselves'.

As Eryximachos, the physician mentioned by Plato, complained, not a single poet out of thousands who had lived until his time had ever composed a hymn or a paean exclusively in Eros' honour. Classical literature, too, ignored him or confined him entirely to the background. Though in love with each other in a way that was crucial to the development of the story, Antigone and Creon's son Haemon do not even appear on stage together in Sophocles' play. Antigone was not even praised by Sophocles for her 'sweet decorum and such gentle grace', as Beatrice, Dante's love was. Love stories took the central stage only later, in the third century BC, when Apollonius' epic poem *Argonautica* for the first time placed love, Medea's love for Jason, at the foreground of the action, and lamented: 'Wicked Eros, great plague, great curse to humans, from you come destructive strife and mourning and groans, and countless pains are stirred up by you'.

Love was, of course, central in the theory of philosopher Empedocles. But for him love was the force of creation rather than destruction and of unity rather than disintegration. As the centripetal force which creates life's building blocks out of natural substances, it was confronted by its antithesis, strife, a centrifugal dialytic force. At a much later period, the Stoics preached the virtues of love in an almost Christian sense with Marcus Aurelius committing himself to 'love mankind and follow God'. But the Greeks really had no interest in the kind of love preached by the Christian saints just as they had no interest in other Christian virtues such as humility or modesty. Further, their understanding of love provided no space for the divine law to 'love God', which religion has turned into a false and perverted moral doctrine. Even less space was given to naked hatred which becomes the driving force when love, in despair, has given up hope.

The youthful Greeks were, instead, ferociously committed to beauty, the beauty found 'in everything there is', except that love and beauty were for them one and the same. 'There is no greater joy than Beauty and Love, and the two of them are one', Yannis Ritsos, the poet, wrote in our own time reflecting both the sense of the bygone age and his own colourful thoughts. Love was not beautiful, but an innate desire for the beautiful, beauty shedding light over every corner of their existence, embracing all aspects of life, 'what grows in the earth'. This love for the world in all its infinitude could not easily be defined. Beauty, like a spark flashing momentarily and then disappearing, or, as Paul Valéry, the French poet, essayist and critic, said, indefinable like music, is hostile to all definition. But at the core of this love was the satisfaction of all human needs and the pursuit of human perfection, happiness which instrumental rationality has managed to tame by suppressing the hankering after the primitive and the instinctive in human nature. The objective, aristocratic by our standards, was to live life in the realm of beauty, to 'be beautiful in our practices', as Thales said.

The criterion was aesthetic rather than moral. Life, sculptured to form by Pheidias, with windows on all four sides facing the sun, had to be lived gracefully and elegantly. This necessitated love for gracefulness and perfection, harmony and rhythm in all possible terms: artistic and moral, intellectual and physical. Not content to distinguish himself by one quality, Epicrates, in Demosthenes' Erotic Essay, combined 'all the qualities of which a man might justly feel proud'. That was the concept of *areté*, so valued that those who possessed it, the chorus in Euripides' *Heracles* suggested, should be awarded a second youth.

The drive was towards the full emancipation of the aesthetic, for, in Plato's inward looking words, 'the most beautiful is the most lovable'. Beauty sustained the order of gratification, and defined Reason in its own terms. Indeed, perpetuating its order on a higher scale, extended to consciousness, it enabled Reason and happiness to converge. This led to the freedom of the individual from the repressive controls that the Christian era imposed on sensuousness, the liberation of sensuousness, which, as Schiller said, brought about the liberation of the human being. Freud explained that civilised morality is the morality of repressed instincts whose liberation would bring about the 'debasement' of civilisation. For Jung, the result would be even worse. A 'depreciation of the hitherto highest values', he said, would end in the 'catastrophe of culture ' – in a word 'barbarism'. But the 'debasement' of the higher values may, as Marcuse argued, just take them back into the organic structure of the human existence from which they were separated, and the reunion may transform the structure itself.

Inspired by the Greeks, Schiller had, likewise, argued that in a genuine, humane civilisation 'man shall only play with beauty'. The liberation of the sensuous impulse, he added, must conform with the universal order of freedom which, nevertheless, must itself be 'an operation of freedom'. For, in a truly free civilisation, 'the will of the whole' fulfils itself only 'through the nature of the individual'.

Physique had its own claims to rank: nothing was more beautiful than the body of a young, healthy, nude human being. This might well be expected in a country of physically beautiful people. 'A nation of ugly people', Jacob Burckhardt, the Swiss historian of art and culture, observed, 'would not have been able to produce this beauty merely by longing for it'. And, if Wittgenstein was right, the human body is the best picture of the human soul.

Public nudity was the norm, not just at the gymnasia – the word comes from *gymnos*, nude – and in athletic competitions, including the Olympic Games, but also in civic ceremonies. Nude male and female dancers entertained guests at parties and festivities, and statues and paintings of beautiful young men and women in the nude decorated private houses, public places and temples. A beautiful body was adored to such an extent that in Xenophon's *Symposium*, Critobulus insisted he would not exchange his for the power of a Persian king. In another instance, when the Persian general Masistius was killed in a skirmish before the battle of Plataea, the Greeks carried his body about so that everybody could see his beautiful corpse.

Nudity, as it was explicitly recognised particularly in art, was linked to sexuality, the guiltless and cheerful enjoyment of life banned by Christianity. To deny one's own sexual gratification, which, incidentally, never seemed to require the satisfaction of bizarre sadomasochistic needs, would be a symptom of madness, a futile gesture or, even worse, a sacrilegious act.

Yet the emphasis was on the whole, 'the beautiful way of being' as Thales put it, the noble, the honourable way of life. Love between two people was important but not as important as beauty itself embedded in the pursuit of immortality through one's honourable actions. 'Do you think Alcestis would have died for Admetus, or Achilles for Patroclus or Codros (the legendary king of Athens) would have died for the royalty of his sons', Diotima asked young Socrates, 'if they had not thought the immortal memory of *areté* would be theirs, which we still keep?' In Plato's vision, beauty and its Apollonian appreciation by the Greeks, demanded nothing less than brilliance, that of the mind, the soul and the body, excellence which could rest only on love, love of beauty.

This love, the love of beauty, decoded the immaculate, touched the intangible and authorised every hope. It enabled the Greeks to enjoy the beautiful rather than the useful, love their friends, as Aristotle put it, for what they were rather than any incidental quality, and appreciate the river for its riverness just like, as Marx said when talking about Milton's *Paradise Lost*, 'a silkworm produces silk'. Not as a means to some further end, but as an end in itself, not a mere means to good, but good in itself, this kind of love rooted the

Greeks in the world and the world in them in a way which was not destined to be subsumed from the outset by capital. It unlocked their creative powers, and allowed them to lead a life, in Kavafis' verse, 'rich in pleasures, perfectly elegant in every way'.

As opposed to the Jews, for whom what is holy is beautiful, for the Greeks what was beautiful was holy. The concept of *agape* – based on what might be termed the third form of love after Eros and *Philia*, and implying a paternal love for all mankind – was appropriated by Christianity as love of God. Yet the difference remained. As a Plato commentator, quoted by Anthony Gottlieb in his *The Dream of Reason*, remarked, for the Christian 'God is Love', but for the Greek 'Love is God'. This, Viennese-born Martin Buber, the Israeli theologian, said, implied a kind of relation between 'I and thou', 'thou' being 'connected to everything', to goodness and joy, freedom and pleasure, or 'purposiveness without purpose' and 'lawfulness without law' according to the Kantian tale unfortunately recorded on a segment of achromatic void. As such, it precluded the instrumentalisation of life, its objectification and commodification, the transformation of human ends into means for the acquisition of wealth, power or status, the degradation of the world in line with the laws of utility. It was in tune with rationality itself, the Reason which Christianity abandoned and modernism betrayed, the Logos of the Greeks.

This beauty can still be found beyond anything that satisfies physical desires. It is in unpurchased things, a starlight smile on the face of a child rather than the glee in the eye of a profiteer, the chirping of a sparrow rather than the roaring of a car-engine, the playful rays of the sun rather than the floodlight of fluorescent tubes. Like all precious things in life, they all take such little space. It is also in the city built for humans rather than vehicles, a business which satisfies human rather than commercial needs, a culture which encourages individuals to maximise their human qualities rather than consume or a foreign policy exercised in the interests of Justice rather than those of self-interest. Beauty means people living their life creatively rather than 'having fun' as pathetic spectators in gala shows, and a society that extends the philosophy of democracy, as Carl Rogers said, down to individual life. This is the beauty of a unique, socially articulated image of a future society, in which, Ivan Illich, the radical Catholic thinker, hoped, the aesthetic and ethical example will replace the competition of economic indicators.

It can also manifest itself in a person's character, the harmonious relationship between our mind, body and spirit, the spiritual connection with all things larger than ourselves, our community, the world and our physical environment, the respectful interaction with everything that is not 'us'. Beauty, too, is in an education which helps people to gain wisdom rather than knowledge, in political institutions which enable them to run their own affairs as they see fit, in the social and political will which will eliminate the ugly side of life, or the policy which respects nature and all its creations. Doing Justice to all our needs – emotional, physical, spiritual, aesthetic, intellectual or political – creates harmony, and harmony is beauty. Indeed, Pythagoras argued, art, psychology, ritual, mathematics and even athletics are all aspects of a single science of harmony. 'Political power, glory, immortality, and beauty', Michel Foucault said in our time, are, thus, 'linked together' in what becomes 'a beautiful existence'.

Love for a world of beauty implied also love for one's own self. Self-love was, indeed, the first condition for higher forms of love. The point was made by Aristotle when he said that good people love themselves, while wicked ones hate themselves. As Joseph Campbell, the American cultural anthropologist, observed, no one achieves excellence in his life task without love for it, in himself without love for himself, or in his family without love for his home. Love brings everything to flower, each in terms of its own potential, and in this way it becomes the true pedagogue of an open, free society.

Love of beauty, Socrates, a lover of all intellectual refinements, taught, passes from the concrete to the abstract, from the individual to the universal, from the universal to a universe of truth and beauty. This mystical bridge of love is abstract as a concept, but as Kazimir Malevich, the Russian painter and art theoretician, pointed out, anyone can understand abstraction provided he has a soul. He might have added, that this 'anyone' must not be a native of a culture dominated by the pragmatism which turns humans, particularly if they happen to be French or Germans, into 'intellectuals'.

Love was of the beautiful, the beauty of everything, including the morality of public and private life, the beauty of the mind which is more honourable than the beauty of the outward form, and the beauty of institutions, laws and the sciences. They are all, as Diodima told young Socrates, part of this 'vast sea of beauty', the secret language of the inner, which creates fair and noble thoughts in boundless wisdom until the vision is revealed as the single science of beauty, existing by itself, with itself, 'marvellous in its nature', simple, unborn, undying and 'everlasting'. That was when the inner, 'not as something we think or feel but as something we are', as the old woman says in a Lawrence Durrell story, was able to include 'love' in a way which gives meaning to the word – before, in other words, it was trained to prohibit and select.

Life was, therefore, considered worth living only in contemplation of beauty itself, in touch with perfect beauty that, as John Keats, the English poet, understood so well, carries with it the ideas of eternal law, divine Justice and transcendent happiness. This is the touch of infinitude, the source of eternal spring, for, as Elytis attested in his crisply-articulated language, 'whatever I love is born unceasingly. Whatever I love is always at its beginning'.

Love of beauty in this sense is Justice as much as Justice is love of beauty. Tragic dramatist Agathon made the point in the symposium when he said that 'as the lords which are the lords of the city say, where there is love ... there is Justice'. Love is, thus, the love affair with the fair, right and sane as opposed to the unfair, wrong and insane, balanced priorities and aims including the adventurous freedom of thought which liberates the individual from forms enclosed in things destined to be forgotten. If this implies knowledge, then love is also, as Martha Nussbaum argued, the bridge to knowledge, because there are some kinds of knowledge which are accessible only when we experience emotions such as love.

However, in the turn of the centuries the power of religion and utility put what Henry Miller called the Greek 'unappeasable lust for beauty, passion, love' under overwhelming pressure. For the Christians as well as the Gnostics, beauty and all its pleasures were of the Devil. Despite Plotinus' commitment to the beauty of this world – 'the supreme ... is heralded by some ineffable beauty', he wrote – for the Christians all that mattered was moral perfection to be rewarded in heaven. The Greek approach also hit the rocks of Hindu religiousness which dismisses love as hopeless on the natural plane, for it rests on illusions, and endorses it on the eternal plane for it rests on renunciation through which one could merge with Brahman. The Buddha, likewise, recommends love as the point of departure but not the end to which it leads – as Max Scheler, the German philosopher, observed, 'it is only the self-detachment, the self denial, which love implies, that he approves'.

The Greek love as love of beauty was recaptured only by the Renaissance, which, like snow, 'play'd and melted in all her prime', as William Blake could have put it. But the point was picked up by Kant, who, in his famous paragraph 59 of the *Critique of Judgment*, saw 'beauty as the symbol of morality'. Friedrich Schiller likewise sought beauty in the liberation of sensuousness, in freedom unconstrained either by law or need, for, as the chorus of angels tells Faust, 'love sets you free'.

In England, John Ruskin associated the 'ideal, essential beauty', the 'Vital Beauty', with 'moral goodness', while William Morris, a thinker well-acquainted with the Greek culture, called for 'a life to which the perception and creation of beauty ... shall be felt to be as necessary to man as his daily bread'. Horkheimer, Adorno and Marcuse called, likewise, for a new harmonisation of our rational faculties and our sensuous nature. Aesthetic needs, Herbert Marcuse, the German-born American philosopher, said, are central in a philosophy of culture and also a force subversive of modernity's interpretation of Reason. This is what he saw in the events of May '68 in which he was well pleased.

The Greek understanding of love connects us with our better selves and the unseen order of the universe, our nature, our body, the desires of the heart, the longings of the spirit. It is the way to find ourselves, communicate selflessly with the world and connect to people in the pursuit of human rather than inhuman ends, wisdom rather than financial assets, Justice rather than injustice. It follows that the opposite of beauty, ugliness, is badness, hatred and destruction, the degradation of all forms of life, the terrible injustice we do to ourselves, our fellow human beings and the world we live in when driven, as we so often are, by ambition, greed, aggressiveness and hatred, or just indifference.

Unphilosophical people, Plato said, confuse beautiful objects, the new film by Steven Spielberg, an Alpha Romeo Spider 3.0 V6 24V, chrome and crystal toilet brushes selling for $400 a piece, with beauty itself. But it is only opinion which is concerned with particular beautiful things. Knowledge is concerned with actual beauty. Good is not what meets desire. It is, instead, what would satisfy us once our rational thought made the ascent of abstraction, from the love of the particular to the love of beauty itself, that eternal presence which transcends all visible realities. The concept is poetic, but poetry, to recall Martin Heidegger, articulates and also transforms a people's understanding of reality, brings to realisation what is definitive of a people's form of life, and reaches towards the reconfiguration of the world. Hence, he believed, our world is looking for a new poet to poeticise the new beginning just as the earliest Greek poets and thinkers, who set the measure for what was to come, did in the very first beginning.

Love, as Iris Murdoch put it, is 'the extremely difficult realisation that something other than oneself is real'. Hence, she concluded all our current failures 'are ultimately failures in love'. But for the

Greeks the world was 'real' and trustworthy. Rather than perceive their relation to it like two china dogs facing each other mutely on the mantelpiece, they engaged in an active relationship with it that involved both giving and receiving. Manifested in action and made visible in their art, rhapsodically sung about for its 'noble simplicity and quiet grandeur', this reciprocity filled them with buoyancy, energy and optimism. Narcissus, who, in love with himself, the insubstantial image of his reflection, was denied the consummation of his love, in despair, plunged a dagger in his breast. From his blood, according to myth, sprang the white narcissus flower with its red corollary.

The optimistic attitude of the Greeks reflected their conviction that they were only at the very beginning of the long march towards human perfection. Human potential was accordingly expected only to develop. Development did, indeed, occur but not in the way they believed it would.

Looking for beauty now, at a time when, as poet George Seferis put it, 'bodies no longer know how to love', is like looking for a needle lost in a maize field without even St Anthony's help. In its place we have, instead, a world with 'no green leaves, but rather black in colour, no smooth branches, but twisted and entangled, no fruit, but thorns of poison'. The Greeks had miserably 'misunderestimated', as President George W. Bush would say, the force of the law of self-destruction as powerful, perhaps, in human affairs as the law of self-preservation. They failed to foresee that rather than the free spirit of man, it would be Microsoft, instead, who would set as its task, 'to help people and business throughout the world realise their full potential', and the Bank of America who would 'help make communities stronger and people achieve their dreams'.

The Greeks' relationship with their world, their love affair with it and with its beauty, the beauty of ennobling words and acts all of which were the ingredients of a good life, a life of beauty, the only life worth living, underlined their unique individuality. The criterion was aesthetic, yet it was the only criterion on the strength of which life, not as something burdened with necessities, but as art, could be judged. Beauty was the yardstick by which everything had to be measured, from the way they lived their lives to the way they ran their government's business. Its appreciation had, indeed, turned into a science since forgotten by the world, for memories of its youth are no longer themselves.

In all their innocence, the Greeks had not, of course, realised that love of beauty cannot even pay the listening rates which, I have heard, some husbands charge their wives in our days.

13. Man's, Well, Free!

Freedom was the very soul of the Greeks long before Marathon became, as Byron said, 'a magic word'. Nothing was good enough for them if the price paid for it was their freedom. Aesop, the sixth century storyteller, made the point when the wolf of his story chose to live with dry crust and liberty than with all the luxury of a chained dog. Democritus, so humble that when he went to Athens 'no-one knew me' as he himself wrote, dwelled on the same theme – 'poverty in a democracy', he said, 'is preferable to what is called prosperity among tyrants'; and Heraclitus, 'the mocker, the reviler of the mob', called the people to be always ready to 'fight on behalf of the law as though for the city wall'.

The law of the city was, however, neither its laws nor its prohibitions, the Thou Shall Nots of the Decalogue. It was, instead, the enhancement of the life of its community. Hence the laws of the polis, a free association of individuals who shared the same goals and norms, could never be arbitrary. They were nourished by, and had to conform to, the universal laws of Equality and Justice. This, as a commitment to human values and civic virtue, made without the support of American lawyers eager to make a fortune out of it, turned the Greek world into a monument of unageing wisdom. It grounded, as Herbert Marcuse pointed out and the ghost of Aristotle raised a glass, 'politics' and 'ethics' in each other. In the midst of their great wanderings, the Greeks were, thus, able to maintain their unity and purpose, both of which were buttressed by pride in belonging to a free city, adherence to a respected set of moral laws of which they were the authors, and loyalty to their political community. It is what underpinned common action without which there are people – consumers, employees or traders – but no social body.

Absolute, uncontested rule and the political realm were concepts incompatible, mutually exclusive. To force obeyance by violence, to command rather than persuade was a prepolitical, unsophisticated way to run the affairs of the city, a feature of life outside the culture of the polis. The oriental custom of obeisance was in the eyes of the Greeks an affront to human dignity, and empires, like the Persian, were thought of as offensive, suitable only for barbarians. Hence when Atossa, the mother of Xerxes, asked what master did the Greek ranks obey, the Persian chorus, in Aeschylus' proud words, answered: 'Master? They are not called servants to any man'.

Ruled by despots, the Asiatic people, Hippocrates, the father of medicine, said, serve to aggrandise and raise up their lords, reaping for themselves only a harvest of danger and death, which explained why, in his view, they were 'feeble'. The Athenians, on the other hand, 'as long as they were under tyrants were no better in warfare than their neighbours, but once they had thrown off the yoke of tyranny they became by far the best fighters in the world'. As Sosicles of Corinth, speaking for all Greeks, said, 'nothing is wickeder or bloodier in the world than despotism'. Hence tyrannies, as if willed by a higher power, were destined to die. Absolute power no one was allowed to possess. 'Divinity', the Delphic oracle knew, 'does not allow tyrannies to reach a third generation' as the political heirs of Franco in Spain, Hitler in Germany and Stalin in Russia have discovered.

State affairs were public affairs, and even monarchs held power in trust by the grace of Logos. Agamemnon was the leader of the campaign against Troy – which fell to the Greeks in 1184 BC – but not a despot ruling like a God. Once he abused his power, Achilles, waving his youthful anger, did not hesitate to denounce his 'wicked arrogance', calling him an 'unscrupulous man', 'greedy and shameless through and through'. Despotism according to Homer cripples the soul of the people, for 'Zeus takes away from a man half of his manhood if the day of enslavement lays hold of him'. Freedom was the essence of man – 'what 's a man', like his ancestors Kazantzakis' Zorba wonders before answering his own question himself: 'man's, well, free'.

This freedom, as Adam Smith pointed out in his *Wealth of Nations*, extended to the Greek colonies established in far away places. Rather than plantations, which is what the Latin word *colonia* signifies, *apoikia*, the Greek word, signifies a departure from home, which means the expatriates were as free to settle their own form of government, enact their own laws, elect their own magistrates and make peace or war as free citizens of an independent state.

The polis, whether the mother city or its colony, provided the citizens with the framework into which they were able to integrate work and pleasure, learning and socialisation, community and family, art and spirituality. The city, Alcaeus, the sixth century lyric poet, wrote, is not well-roofed houses or well-built stone walls or canals and dockyards, an abstract entity standing above its citizens; it is, instead, 'men'. 'Men', Thucydides, the historian, repeated more than a century later, 'make the polis'. As the eminent historian Moses Finley, whom McCarthyist America blacklisted and Britain knighted, noted, it was never Athens, Corinth or Sparta that decided, for example, to declare war. With the community having an identity of its own separate from abstract legal notions, it was, instead, the Athenians, the Corinthians or the Spartans who did so. This exclusively Greek phenomenon, which embodied the disciplined, collective ideal, sustained the Greeks long after it had become an anachronism.

Bastion of a free community in which beauty and the pursuit of excellence were the cherished ends, the polis, a living entity based on kinship, real or assumed, was the extended family, holding together in its arms the poor and the rich, the weak and the strong, the ordinary and the famous. Identity politics had to wait for two and a half thousand years before it could denounce the polis as the bastion of repression. The polis never claimed, of course, to have ironed out social divisions – inequality was not felt to be incompatible with the concept of community. 'Capitalist acts between consenting adults', as Robert Nozick, the American philosopher might have said again, were anything but forbidden. But as only a few citizens were regularly employed by others, Greece experienced neither the massive inequalities in income and wealth which capitalism creates and on which it depends for its development and growth nor the social polarisation of industrialism. Social splits did not, consequently, play a significant role in political affairs; and class, according to Moses Finley, is not an appropriate tool to analyse Greece. Finley's *The World of Odysseus*, first published in New York in 1954, is largely responsible for the anthropological turn in Anglo-American Classical scholarship.

The rich, the poor and the era's middle class, Kenneth Dover, the distinguished British scholar, pointed out, did not differ in their values and assumptions. They were all bound together by their commitment to Justice, viewed as the foundation of the free city, and to democracy, the polis' natural political system. After all, as E.P. Thompson pointed out, class is not a 'thing' but a relationship defined by men as they live their own history or, in the case of Greece, by their civil society, the web of relations the individuals established amongst themselves within the context of their polis. Rather than on law or judicial obligation, these relations were founded upon reciprocity and voluntarism and did not depend on mediation by an institutional authority.

As an active, formative organism training the minds and the

characters of its members, the polis existed for the purpose of *entelecheia*, the full realisation of its own and the individual's potentials. Performativity, which Niklas Luhmann, the German social systems theorist, said, is the best criterion of the efficiency of a system of which humans are a part, controlled and empowered by knowledge, had, thankfully, not as yet entered its thinking. As such, the polis was the focus of a man's moral, intellectual, aesthetic, social and practical concerns and interests, including those of the less well-off. Benefits, which turned Greece into the forerunner of the twentieth century's social-democracies, included dowries for the daughters of, and funeral expenses for, impoverished citizens, a variety of loans and gifts for the needy, free meals for those experiencing hardship or free theatre tickets. Theatres, schools of civic education, often had an audience of as many as 14,000 people – playwrights, incidentally, did not always profit from their success: when Phrynichus presented in Athens *The Capture of Miletus* by the Persians, with the audience bursting into tears as a result, the author was fined a thousand drachmae for reminding them of a disaster which touched their hearts.

For free-marketeers, the state's withdrawal from the social scene is the indispensable condition for the citizens' liberty. Athenian society flourished, however, on active, affirmative social action which ensured that all its citizens, as free men rather than subjects to a ruler, were able to live a fully human life with the dignity they were entitled to expect. Society's support, a condition of freedom, gave everyone the capacity to engage with the multiplicity of life's functions and develop their potential as individuals – hence the Oxfordian left-wing Liberal T.H. Green's call in the second half of the nineteenth century for a return to the Greeks to get adequate concepts for the contemporary world. In utilitarian terms, the benefit of this social solidarity was what Democritus called social harmony. The latter made the citizens feel respected members of their community and parties to its running, ennobled by its trust and proud of their individual achievements within its context. The polis was theirs, and this rather than a three-bedroom apartment in Phaleron Bay gave them dignity and pride.

Participating in its life and attending its business was, indeed, the ultimate justification of man's existence, the only framework, as Aristotle said, within which man could meaningfully live, the only context in which a man could conduct his search for fulfilment and seek his self-actualisation. It was also a duty a man owed to himself – hence the aversion to employing civil servants, professionals who would do what a man was only too honoured to do himself.

This, for the Greeks, was nature's intention. For, man, as Aristotle explained, is by nature *zoon politikon*, a political animal – Thomas Aquinas, the thirteen century Italian theologian, translated it inaccurately as 'social animal' which was the term used by second century AD Stoic philosopher Marcus Aurelius to describe man. The polis was, in turn, the summit of man's achievements, where Justice was expected to be done and to be seen to be done, and its democracy simply harmonised human life with nature. To such a world, Demosthenes, the fourth century BC orator, said, only 'wild beasts' would not respond. To be democratic was to be human, and to be human was to be an active member of the community, concerned about the common good. Indifference to the affairs of the polis, Democritus pointed out, was bound to give a man 'a bad reputation, even if he steals nothing and commits no injustice'. The Buddha would have certainly not agreed with him. Talk about 'kings, thieves, ministers, armies, famine and war' or about 'ancestors and the origins of the world and the sea', he said as quoted by Nyanaponika Thera in *The Heart of Buddhist Meditation*,'is vulgar, wordly and unprofitable'. But the Greeks would not care about such pronouncements as the life of a monk had never really charmed them.

Nothing could replace the constituent elements of this realm – neither education and beauty, nor ingenuity and talent. The public realm, constituted of one's own peers in whose presence life was validated, was the complex arena allowing for both integration with entities beyond the self and also differentiation aiming at personal uniqueness. This was what gave meaning to the life of the individual but also underlined the meaning of existence in terms of its general significance. Indispensable to a truly human life, participation in *ta koina*, the affairs of their polis, gave the Greeks a sense of belonging to something larger than themselves, purpose in life, direction, safety and self-esteem, the motivation for lifetime accomplishments, which, in Maslow's model of a 'hierarchy of needs' gives a person the highest satisfaction.

An individual sunk 'in the details of his own life', as Fyodor Dostoevsky, the Russian prose writer, put it, feeding on crumbs of faith in his own uniqueness, this laughable conceit, worshipping his 'I', and steering clear of commitments was for the Greeks a man deprived of all things essential to a good life. Removed as far as possible from the public realm, as Christianity advocated later, life could only be on the Procrustean bed of a colourless existence in which, in Kavafis' lanceolated verse, ravishing and economical as mini skirts, 'the morrow ends by not resembling a morrow'. Privacy meant deprivation, unhappiness dripping in the daily life's living room, and boredom which, as Strates Myrivilis said in his great antiwar book *Life in the Tomb*, is 'like a spiritual tuberculosis' which 'consumes the soul little by little'. It can easily lead to feelings of emptiness, loneliness, worthlessness and depression, the psychological nausea experienced by the chief character in Sartre's novel *La Nausée*.

An escape from the public realm into the solitude of a life quiet enough for one to hear the breathing of his income, was, of course, always possible. This would, however, be the route taken by those who fail to understand that people's lives are woven together, the fools, the 'idiots' – the word 'idiot' derives from the word *idiotes* which describes a person leading a private life. Withdrawal from the public realm was evidence of a poor ethical attitude badly in need of self-improvement. Jean-Jacques Rousseau, the French Romantic philosopher, later, in the eighteenth century, associated privacy with the intimate in human nature. His view was developed, however, not in opposition to the public realm, but to the tawdry nature of industrial society.

The polis was the citizens' shield against the futility of a private life, indeed, the guarantee of an elegant and yet not ostentatious existence, the good life, which, central to Greek thought, connected personal happiness with involvement in the affairs of the city. Building on this, Leo Strauss, the German-born historian of political philosophy, redefined the release from modernity as a release from the self-interpreting self and the search for authenticity. He called, instead, for a re-engagement with the moral and political life that connects citizens to civic life, the structure of human excellence, i.e., for 'a return to the ancients' which he nevertheless saw as a trip to Plato's creepy ideal state. In the same spirit, Laurence Durrell, an Englishman 'despite himself' as Henry Miller decided, and a man who, in love with Greece, wanted to enlist in the Greek army for service on the Albanian frontier, held that happiness will continue to elude men as long as they continue to elude themselves and each other.

Individualism was an unattractive proposition. Hence the disdain for the Greek anti-individualist, 'repressive' culture displayed by several postmodernists. The concept of community is for them unattractive as it defines, Theodor Adorno wrote in an article on Aldous Huxley's *Brave New World*, 'a collectivity in which each individual is unconditionally subordinated to the functioning of the whole'. As objectionable is the concept of identity, which means 'the elimination of individual differences', and of stability, which signals 'the end of all social dynamics'.

But Greece was not Huxley's *Brave New World*, and individualism is different from individuality, which, fiery and explosive, flourished within the polis as in no other time. The Greeks, history professor Donald R. Kelley, stated in 1990, were the first to posit a strong notion of the individual self: the independent thinking and acting individual, the autonomous person that became the building block of the West's cultural tradition. Their society's highly developed individuality, Swiss historian Jacob Burckhardt had written earlier, was in total contrast to that of others which crushed it beneath the weight of group, caste and morality. Giving up their individuality, their 'infinite quantity of beautiful, lovely and pleasing individualities', Hegel said rather humorously, would have been 'a difficult thing for them'.

Free to be themselves, without the constraints, repression and renunciation from which, as Freud demonstrated, the modern 'free personality' is made, the Athenians, Pericles stated, lived exactly as they pleased. They would not get angry with their neighbours for doing what they liked; they would not even 'indulge in those injurious looks which cannot fail to be offensive' if someone did something they disapproved of.

Individuality was nevertheless inseparable from the whole, for the freedoms and the ends of the individual, the pursuit of happiness, socialised, integrated into this whole, were those of the polis. Stated most explicitly in Aristotle's Politics, this was the common property of all Greeks and what made them feel their society was superior to all others. Though feeling proud of their achievements, the unleashing of the power of the individual in the service of their community, they could not even imagine, as Carl Boggs wrote in his most stimulating *The End of Politics: Corporate Power and the Decline of the Public Sphere*, that the 'supreme virtue of (their) uniquely civic or popular life' would still be democracy's model two and a half millennia later. How can we go back to the Greek meaning of politics, Murray Bookchin, a major figure of the American Left, wondered, and restore and recover community structures? How can we empower our citizens to take control of their community at grassroots level and define our mutual obligations within it?

True, the Greeks made no attempt to portray in their arts a particular individual, George Washington, Pope Innocent X or Henry VIII. At least until the beginning of the fourth century BC, they strove, instead, for the perfect representation of the Athlete, the God or the Woman – 'Pheidias gave women dreams and dreams their looking-glass', exclaimed Yeats. Distinction was, of course, the individual's aim, and the flavour of one's personality, including a person's eccentricities, was the spice of city life. Neither of them could, however, be pursued outside the indivisible whole and certainly not at its expense.

The starting point was the community rather than the individual, the commuters, if I can put it this way, on that late night train from Portsmouth to London I happened to be on, rather than that man on his mobile phone who, to the irritation of everybody, insisted on his 'right' to talk sonorously to as many people as possible; or the customers in that pub I went to, rather than that woman who insisted on her 'right' to use the foul language she did while screaming at someone I presumed was her mother. The individual would not dream of claiming his 'right to...', if his claim ran against the rights of the community. Social and moral responsibility, involving in the latter case the community's right to protect the environment against verbal pollution, were essential components of the individual's freedoms.

It was these freedoms that Solon tried to protect when he admonished Thespis for the lies he was telling in his plays because, as he told him, 'such jokes in our theatre will soon creep into our contracts and our treaties'. The puritan ethos of the early age was evident in later times, too.

A man's right, unchallenged today, to spend his fortune on gambling, women, drugs, conspicuous consumption or extravagant parties as retail tycoon Philip Green did in 2005, when he reportedly spent £4m on a bar mitzvah party for his son, was nothing less for the Greeks than outrageously antisocial behaviour. Private wealth was a matter of public concern, for if it was spent for the gratification of the individual it could not buy a trireme or pay for festivals to honour the Gods. The loser would be the city. Social responsibility demanded that a wealthy Greek should, instead, defend his wealth by demonstrating the benefits the whole community accrued from it. The starting point was always the rights of the community, the whole, as opposed to those of the individual whose entitlements were expected not to antagonise the whole. The close connection that existed between politics and ethics led inevitably to a business ethical policy which, in spite of the socially responsible investment that is supposed to be gathering pace in our days, was miles ahead of our own notions of corporate citizenship.

In the same spirit, a sick person had, after receiving treatment, to return to normal life as soon as possible in order to minimise the time he was not useful to his community, and a man would refuse, as a matter of pride, payment for services rendered to his fellow citizens. Knowledge, for example, was not a commodity, and its spread was a pleasure as the Wikipedia contributors have discovered, even a duty to the community, rather than a service requiring remuneration as demanded by the Sophists. Ezra Pound, a Greek reader, if he had been an Athenian citizen, might have objected, like Mussolini, his idol, to Greece's culture of humanism and its democratic expression. But he would not complain about that 'tawdry cheapness', which, he expected, would outlast his own days. The Athenians, dismissed by the Corinthians for having been 'born into the world to take no rest themselves and to give none to others', were not buying life at a discount.

The skin of their inner being did not need moisturisers to ensure protection against the whole, because the whole was a part of their own inner being.

14. A High–Trust Society

The polis, H.D.F. Kitto, the British classicist, says in his delightful book *The Greeks*, enriched life to an extent that no social entity had done before or has done ever since. Its 'high-trust' society, a term used by author Francis Fukuyama, was founded on the expectation of regular, honest and cooperative behaviour, expressing commonly shared norms, and the city's unifying civic values, which, like the ritualised festivities, defined the community as a whole. This whole, rationalised, democratised and civilised, enhanced life and made possible the attainment of each citizen's wellbeing. The Romantics' mythical 'whole', which found expression in national socialism, was antipodal to the Greek classical whole.

The case for Athens, the city that God 'loved best' according to Hölderlin, 'the school of Hellas', was made superbly by Pericles in *Epitaphios*, his celebrated funeral oration. The Athenians, he stated without resort to any –isms, saw in wealth an opportunity for action, not a reason for boasting, considered idleness, not poverty, disgraceful, and regarded political discussion, not a hindrance to action, but its prerequisite. They were generous, not out of expediency, but from confidence, they knew the beauty of Justice, the dangers of ambition, the folly of violence. They ran their affairs relying not upon management or trickery, but upon their hearts and hands, loved the arts without lavish display, and things of the mind without becoming soft. Justice for all alike was secured by the law, but the claim of excellence was also recognised; citizens were chosen for public service, not as a matter of privilege, but as a reward for merit. 'Class considerations', he emphasised, 'are not allowed to interfere with merit'.

This speech, sections of which were being displayed on buses in England during World War I, will, incidentally, always be a source of embarrassment for me. We studied it as teenagers at school and the memory of it has me still in her arms for the wrong reasons. It never meant a thing either to me or to any other kid. All we could recall is the good laugh we had reciting his *Filokaloumen gar met' euteleias kai philosophoumen anev malakias* (we love beauty in simplicity and reflect without emolliating ourselves). The joke is in the word *malakia* which in modern Greek means masturbation – in ancient Greek it means softening up; not effemination, as some feminists claim.

Pericles' speech, the cultural epitome of a gentleman's approach to politics, would seem to give an idealised picture of the 'Republic of the Spirit'. Aware of it, Pericles himself said that a stranger, hearing 'anything above his station', would, indeed, suspect exaggeration. His speech did, however, describe an organic community that had at last come into its truth. The question, Raymond Williams, the English Marxist theoretician and novelist, once said, is not how we are governed, but how we govern ourselves. The Greeks had an answer to it since Solon's days: in the freedom to be responsible for ourselves and for our actions which is, nevertheless, the freedom which for a long time now we seem not to want.

Athens, even when her population had reached a quarter of a million people, had no hierarchies, no police force, no censors, no files on the undesirable, no politicians kissing babies to prove that they, too, have feelings, and no government to tell people what to think or say. There were no public prosecutors, for every citizen had the right to bring a prosecution, no professional judges, for justice was delivered by an elected jury, and people could not, since the early days of Solon, be imprisoned for debts. The rules by which the city was run were deliberately very few. Without anticipating Adam Smith's irritation at the unwillingness of the Greeks to make 'any attempt towards a particular enumeration of the rules of justice', Pericles explained: 'we trust less in system and policy than to the native spirit of our citizens'. Rules are important only when commitment to both principles and virtues is divorced from any substantial belief in the goodness of the human being. In any case, the Greeks had an aversion to rules and their ruthless application – they still do, which explains why they always seem to be given three times as many as they need.

Furthermore, the city did not exclude. Its community provided space for everything and everybody, including foreigners, the metics, who, despite postmodernist assertions, were free to settle and prosper. Some of them were even chosen over Athenians – people like

Apollodoros of Cyzicos, Phanosthenes of Andros and Heracleides of Clazomenai – to serve the polis as army Generals. Athens, a city so jealous of its citizenship, had no immigration controls, no central register for citizens, not even a land register. Taxation was based on self-assessment.

For a civilisation of honour a man's word was as good as, or even better than, any system of control. People, like Dicaeogenes, who tried to dodge the responsibility his wealth gave him, were publicly shamed. Their name appeared on a list in front of the statues of the cities heroes with a note: 'These are the men who promised the people they would make a voluntary contribution for the salvation of the city and paid nothing'. So-called ethical capitalism considered at some point doing the same by naming and shaming the banks which refuse to take measures to combat money-laundering. The Greeks obviously have something to teach.

Having invented both politics, whose root is in the word polis, and then the concept of democracy, the Greeks carried the whole process to its logical and also most radical conclusion. They ended up with what is called direct democracy, which, as it was practised particularly by the Athenians, had neither a precedent nor has it been seen anywhere else ever since. Direct democracy, giving all its citizens a 'steering capacity', denied altogether the division of the community into two groups, the rulers and the ruled. To accept rulers, or representatives of their collective will, the Greeks believed, would be tantamount to accepting the death of their community. The polis would no longer belong to its citizens. Their power would have been taken away.

The source of all authority was the community itself, the many thousands who came together at times of decisions, ready and willing to 'listen', as Protagoras said, 'to every man ... otherwise there would be no polis'. *Isegoria*, the full and complete equality of speech in Demos' ecclesia, the people's assembly which was the ultimate source of law and maker of policy, had been accorded an almost divine status. 'Fullers and cobblers' had as much right to make their views known as the great Pericles himself. They were all expected to express their views with *parrhesia*, the courage that goes hand in hand with political and moral responsibility. One has to assume, of course, that, whatever the high standards of the polis, demagogues ready to take advantage of any situation to advance their own interests, would always be there. As it happened, and miserably for Athens, they were there during the Peloponnesian war with catastrophic consequences for the city.

Full citizen participation in all government activities was possible in those days as the polis did not have the monstrous size of the modern State. An empire like the Persian, the Greeks thought, was suitable only for barbarians, for the true, the humanly-scaled State, Plato held, should have only about five thousand citizens. A state composed of too many, a city in which people did not know all the other people by sight, Aristotle, among others, also held, 'will not be a true polis'. Hence cities, even though they were neighbouring and had no physical barriers separating them, preferred to preserve their independence in order to protect the quality of their citizens' life.

Explaining the latter's importance for the benefit of our contemporaries, historian H.D.F. Kitto presented a record of an imaginary conversation between an ancient Greek and a member of the Athenaeum, modernity itself, who regretted the lack of political sense shown by the Greeks. The Greek asked the member how many clubs there are in London, to which he answered about five hundred. Well, well, what splendid premises they could build if they all combined, said the Greek. They could have a clubhouse as big as Hyde Park. But, said the member, that would no longer be a club. Precisely, answered the Greek, and a polis as big as yours is no longer a polis. Gigantism, as social philosopher André Gorz pointed out, is not a technical necessity, but a political choice.

But the decisions the Greeks had to make, and the dilemmas they faced, were not any simpler than those facing a modern State. Hence the differences between the Athenian and modern democracies were not just of a quantitative nature. The substantive differences were illustrated by Pericles himself when, for example, he declared that state policy regarding war could not be made by those who had no sons to lose. Such decisions had to be taken by those who would suffer their consequences, not by those who would salute the dead and their families for their bravery and sacrifice.

Though always battle-ready and reputed for being by temperament pugnacious enough to start fights on the spur of the moment, war was, incidentally, for the Greeks an evil, a monstrous transgression of civilised norms. The longing for peace and the horrors of war were mirror images of the human condition: 'in peace', as Herodotus said, 'sons bury their fathers, but in war fathers bury their sons'. Bloodshed, the 'folly of consuming one another', Empedocles held long before the blessings of 'surgical war', 'digital war' or 'zero-casualty war' were bestowed upon us, was the primal error. Plato, too, thought of the good life as a life in peace, probably with plenty of figs, which he loved. War was abhorred and de-glorified even in Homer's heroic era. To avoid being drafted, Odysseus, to whose warm humanity James Joyce, the great Irish writer, was so attracted, pretended he was mad. He began sowing salt instead of barley when he saw Palamides, the man who went to Ithaca to take him to Troy.

The Greek humanism, if humanism embodies, as Hegel said, 'the depths and heights of the human heart', or, as Cicero put it before him, ethicality, noble-mindedness, dignity and nobility of the human spirit, honour, grace, kindness and generosity, was evident even in victory. As opposed to the East, which as André Malraux observed, loved the cult of power and celebrated triumphs in terms of human suffering – a Rameses triumphant holding by their hair a batch of severed heads – the Greeks created Nike of Samothrace. This elegant female form whose timelessness and superb movement, that of a galleon in full sail, made it for many art's eternal symbol, was also the symbol of the Greeks' moral opposition to militarism. In this there is, of course, something ironic as even current Western notions of warfare have their ancestral home in fifth century Greece.

Citizens' responsibility for their city was the cornerstone of Athenian democracy. It necessitated the participation in the decision-making process of everyone, including, as Socrates disapprovingly said, 'fullers, cobblers, carpenters, blacksmiths, farmers, merchants, traders who think only of selling at a high price what they bought at a low one', i.e., all those 'who make up the Demos'.

The Athenian citizen, rather than just claim his sovereign right to tune in to BSkyB, was, thus, able to, and did, participate in all government activities, serving in turn as a soldier, an administrator, a judge and legislator. To serve as a magistrate a man had to satisfy the selecting body that, among other things, he treated his parents well. The bureaucratic nonrepresentative institutions which in our days are entrusted with the task of running the business of the State were not there. The Greeks had no civil service, no professional politicians or judges, no career officers, no police. The functionaries for nearly all public offices were chosen by lot and were rotated so as to ensure, not only that everybody had the chance to participate in the running of the city, but also that the city had a very large number of people acquainted with the day-to-day running of its affairs.

Rather than vertical, the distribution of power was horizontal, without 'responsible' ruling élites and hierarchies; and rather than one-dimensional as in modern democracies, Athenian politics were thoroughly entwined in the fabric of ordinary experience.

If democracy means, and it does, 'the power of the people', Greek democracy extended this power to the people over everything that was of common interest. Apolitical forms of power could not even be conceived, and neutrality in political disputes was not an option. Common affairs were the affairs of the polis. As such they were political by definition, i.e., the business of all citizens rather than that of professional politicians or experts, quangos, bureaucracies and committees whose meetings, in Russian poet Yevgeny Yevtushenko's verse, 'nourish neither heart nor mind'. The current de-politicisation and scientisation of politics, running contrary to the entire Greek political culture which rested on a shared civic consciousness and open discussion, would have been dismissed by the Greeks as the denial of democracy itself.

In such a world, and for the first time in history, all affairs were conducted openly, in public spaces rather than in smoke-filled rooms. Also for the first time, all public records were displayed in the Acropolis and the Agora, subject to public scrutiny and full accountability.

To function, the system required, of course, singularly well-informed citizens, able to participate in the decision-making process and run the affairs of the State. But the Greeks, as the nineteenth century English historian Thomas Macaulay remarked, had this singularly high level of education, possessed albeit because of their democratic system itself. The Athenian democracy, John Stuart Mill, the nineteenth century English philosopher and economist, said, had, indeed, 'raised the intellectual standard of an average Athenian citizen far beyond anything of which there is as yet an example in any other mass of men, ancient or modern'. For another English liberal, Edward Freeman, this crowd 'clothed with executive powers made one of the best governments which the world ever saw'.

'It is...Athens', Cornelius De Pauw, the Protestant polymath, said later, 'to which one looks for laws to build a new state just as one looks to Sweden for wood to build a ship'. In was in Athens, too, that Greek philosopher Cornelius Castoriades, an OECD economist and, perhaps, the most prominent Trotskyite of our era, looked for inspiration while looking for a society without bosses, managers, professional politicians, leading parties, priests, experts, therapists or gurus. The same Athenian political culture provided, however, 'the ideal type' and the 'classic model' for Karl Schmitt, the German nazi theoretician, on account of the existing identity between the state and its citizens which was Hitler's dream.

Run by amateurs, the polis was expected in turn not just to manage its business well but, in doing so, to stimulate the intellect and satisfy the spiritual aspirations of its citizens. Freedom, if it means absence of coercion, was not for the Greeks a value as it is for liberal democracy. Of value was, instead, the positive empowerment of man to fulfil his potential as a citizen and a human being, the development of all human capacities and the cultivation of social solidarity. That was politics on a human scale.

Startlingly, the community assumed responsibility even for the psychological welfare of its members. The delight the Athenians took in conducting the business of the polis, Pericles said, the games and sacrifices all year round and the elegance of life was a daily source of pleasure and helped 'to combat melancholy'. Rather than the free market's law and order preoccupations or socialism's class concerns, Athenian democracy, having elevated human happiness to the greatest goal worth pursuing, was reaching out to the daily, ordinary life of its citizens. The happiness of the individual, the highest human good as Aristotle confirmed later on, was not only the preoccupation of political theory but also the standard for political excellence. The result was a state with a human face the likes of which the world has never seen either before or after. Rilke, had he lived in Athens, might never have felt as alienated from his world as he did and might have never thought that it is 'our fate to be opposite and nothing else, and always opposite'.

Hence Greece remains a source of eternal inspiration. The Green root ideas, Robert E. Goodin wrote in the *Green Political Theory*, are founded on the conviction that people must feel part of their community, able to meet face to face with all its members, discuss all problems and options before them, and be confident that they can make some difference to the outcome. Similar resonances can be found in the writings of communitarian and also socialist writers. 'The link between socialism and popular democracy', John and Lizzie Eldridge stated in their 1994 book *Raymond Williams*, 'is literally the key to our future', which means that socialism 'has to go beyond the limited forms of representative political democracy, which has been historically the liberal modification of absolutist states', and move on to real sharing in all decisions that affect our lives.

A nonrepresentational form of democracy, i.e., a direct democracy, ensures the sought identity between law and popular will, but it does so only within a unified, homogeneous, 'organic' community; and it does accord the utmost respect to the will of the people, but it does not necessarily guarantee respect for higher values as the Athenians themselves had the opportunity to prove.

Yet the Greeks, Professor Ellen Meiksins Wood, the American socialist thinker, said in the '90s, still have a presence which 'can foster a democratic critique of capitalism', as they belong, Thomas Arnold, the nineteenth century English historian, held, to our present. They are 'virtually our own countrymen and contemporaries', the source, Bernard Knox, the American Yale university Professor of Classics, added, of our 'enduring enlightenment'. The Athenians, the nineteenth century American anthropologist Lewis H. Morgan stated, had, indeed, developed themselves into 'the most intellectual and most accomplished race of men the entire human family has yet produced'. Although much information about life in the hundreds of Greek cities, extending from the east coast of Spain to the eastern end of the Black Sea, from south Russia to Libya, all those scattered around the Mediterranean 'like frogs around a pond' in Plato's pictorial description, is missing, their most essential feature was this sense of community which generated a sense of belonging on which freedom was founded.

Shelley, the nineteenth century English radical poet, author of *On the Necessity of Atheism* which cost him his place at Oxford, exclaimed: 'Greece, the mother of the free'; and Joseph Campbell, the contemporary American cultural anthropologist, in lyrical tones, commented delightedly: The Greeks had learnt to live as rationally judging men, whose laws were voted on, not 'heard'; whose arts were in celebration of humanity, not divinity; in whose sciences truth and not fancy was, at last, actually beginning to appear. Society was not sanctified above the men within it. One can realise, after coming down through all these millennia of religion, what a marvel of new thought the wonderful, earthly humanity of the Greek *polis* represented in the world.

Socrates, an outspoken critic of it, objected to the democratic principle not so much on grounds of efficiency as on the grounds that it did not make sense. How come, he cried out, one would consult an expert in a trifle like the building of a wall, but in the infinitely more important matter of morals and conduct any ignorant could speak his uninstructed mind?

Yet those amateurs, to whom Socrates and Plato objected so vehemently, the 'masses' which even the great theoretical founders of modern socialism – Fourier, Saint Simon and Robert Owen – refused to trust, developed 'clearly the most civilised society that has yet existed'. Their achievements, which as German composer Richard Wagner, a former revolutionary socialist who manned the barricades in the Dresden uprising of 1849 only to succumb later to the mystical writings of Schopenhauer, said, have as yet to be explained. Unable to explain the Greek miracle himself, Wagner passed on to others the task of discovering 'what it is that has changed human beings so fundamentally, that we now produce merely the output of luxury industries' when 'the same human beings once made the works of Greek art'.

Marx, whose doctoral dissertation was on the difference between the Democritean and Epicurean philosophy, though a student of the culture of Greece, was, likewise, unable to explain the apparent contradiction between the ancient mode of production and the high civilisation built upon it. Like someone who had been told a joke he did not understand but did not want to show it, he remained puzzled to the end. The thesis he advanced in the *General Introduction to the Critique of Political Economy* according to which the 'eternal charm' of the Greeks is the product of 'the historical childhood of humanity, its most beautiful unfolding', inseparably connected with 'unripe social conditions', is, uncharacteristically, meaningless.

'The difficulty', Marx himself admitted whilst referring specifically to the Greek works of art, 'lies in understanding why they still afford us aesthetic enjoyment and in certain respects prevail as the standard and model beyond attainment'. If Marx's views make sense, Raymond Williams, the contemporary English Marxist, observed, it is only within the context of an ahistorical linear political development, 'a very crude and undiscriminated idea of progress'.

But as other Marxists, notably M. Lifshitz, an associate of George Lukács, argued, Greek society was inherently superior to the European class societies which succeeded it, and, therefore, its art retained certain essential human values which the later societies did not possess. For the free-marketeers, the answer must certainly be connected to the fact that the Greeks had to pay tax equalling just one hundredth of the price of the house they purchased.

The Athenian democracy fared well for nearly three hundred years. It failed during the Peloponnesian war to be denounced, as a result, by all the later centuries' monarchists, reactionaries and fascists as the rule of the mob. Yet, in spite of its failure at a critical time, which does not mean all that much as all systems have had their failures, this democracy has defined the meaning of democracy for ever. Obviously, it cannot be duplicated in our time. Water only goes downhill, the sun only moves west. Even so, it has provided the yardstick against which all democracies are measured.

As Goethe said, 'the brilliant passes, like the dew at morn; but the true endures, for ages not yet born'.

15. Freedom from Necessity

Emancipated from necessity, which means emancipated from consumption, the Greeks were not engaged in this unending drive to 'improve' their lifestyle. They had no need to work hard to earn money to buy lifestyle drugs, have a liposuction operation, take a holiday as far away from themselves as possible or see a psychotherapist, the alienated personality's spokesman, to recover from a life as bitter as the Siberian winter. The charms of the waste economy, which demands immediate consumption of everything produced or made if the world as we know it is not to come to an end, the era of avid consumerism had not arrived as yet. People did not need to learn simplicity, much as they did not have to make ecological protests by stabbing the tyres of parked cars in despair.

The predominant moral sentiment, Kenneth Dover, the English classicist, wrote, was hostile to any kind of consumption which gratified the consumer. Not slaves to needs, the Greeks did not want more at the cost of their souls' welfare – more space in a mansion ideally spreading over two time-zones, more than sixty minutes in the hour or a car for everyone. They did not behave, as Erich Fromm, the German-born social psychologist, would say, like 'overgrown babies' for whom the world was a big bottle or a big breast. They were not eternally expectant, hopeful, and disappointed.

Their lifestyle, 'a frugal meeting with the absolute', was extremely simple and materially undemanding – such simplicity, Schiller said, puts 'us to shame'. From Solon and Anaxagoras, who thought wealth an 'oddity', to Socrates, Plato and Aristotle, a noble, a dignified life, required only a minimum level of having. Socrates, the saint of the Stoics and a man who was never tempted by Ralph Lauren Purple Label Collection suits, held that acquisitiveness is 'the worst evil' in both society and the individual – D.H. Lawrence, a man who had grown up in poverty, described acquisitiveness a few millennia later as 'a kind of illness of the spirit'. Rather than sumptuous depravity and prestigious corruption, Henningsen lamps, Arne Jacobsen chairs, Eero Saarinen tulip tables, Le Corbusier lounge chairs and Eileen Gray side tables, the ideal, which in later times inspired the French Jacobins perhaps more than anybody else, was modest means. A man, according to Socrates, ought to be 'never in want and never in wealth'. Politicising his thinking later, Jean-Jacques Rousseau wrote: 'A citizen shall never be wealthy enough to buy another, and none poor enough to be forced to sell himself'.

He who was engaged in the further increase of his wealth rather than the attainment of *areté*, the man who would be drawn by lucrative contracts rather than deeds and words destined for immortality, being, thus, indifferent to his actualisation, was, indeed, despised. Only an idiot, someone who could drown in a cornfield, would, therefore, willingly sacrifice his freedom to become a slave, a slave of necessity.

Wealth, a 'cult' in our own days as Odysseus Elytis, the poet, said, did not move the Greeks. They were, indeed, proverbially blind to it. Thales of Miletus, the first of the giants of Greek philosophy, made the point early enough when he proved that philosophers and scientists could, 'if they wished, enrich themselves; but it is not in this that they are interested'. Rather than desirable, wealth was considered, instead, to be dangerous, for the very having of something could turn a man into its prisoner. As Thucydides and also Xenophon, the historian, argued, money creates an insatiable desire for more which is bad for both the individual concerned and his community. It can distort, Menander, the comic dramatist, believed, too, an otherwise virtuous character. For Euripides, the tragic dramatist, wealth offers a bad education for manliness defined by Spooner in Harold Pinter's *No Man's Land* as the essential quality that enables you 'to put your money where your mouth is'.

The contempt with which the Greeks dealt with possessions is almost as well documented as the World Cup final. Heraclitus, the philosopher, who would not have written anything if he had not faltered at the edge of silence, was living in mountains feeding on grass and plants – this is, at any rate, probably what his enemies who resented his superior tone said; and the Pythagoreans are presented by Aristophanes, the comic dramatist, in his *The Clouds* as half-starved ascetics. Empedocles and Anaxagoras, the philosophers, although rich, scorned wealth, and Democritus, a man as ascetic as all the other philosophers and as 'naive' as them in failing to grasp that whatever has no price has no value, associated wellbeing with moral wellbeing. Happiness, he said showing his contempt for financial rewards, does not reside in cattle or gold, but in the soul. It does not, he might have said, relate to the number of goals scored by Manchester United last Saturday, but, as he said, to 'just and lawful deeds'.

Socrates, a very simple man, completely indifferent to extreme hardship, was going around barefoot and ill-dressed – as it happened he was also, just like Marx, completely unable to support his family – and Diogenes the Cynic, 'a Socrates gone mad' according to Plato, the hippy of his time, had rejected as a matter of principle all, even the most elementary, comforts such as sleeping in a bed. Even Epicurus, the third century BC philosopher, vilified as a crude and unlettered sybarite, revelled in the pleasure of the body – on a diet, worse than prison's, of bread and water. Those, like the Colophonians in Asia Minor who deviated from the principle of simplicity, were denounced by their compatriot Xenophanes, the sixth century BC philosopher, for corruption by Lydian luxury to which the Greeks remained insurmountably shy.

Committed to a simple and frugal life, which later inspired, among others, St Just, Marat and other French revolutionaries, all concerned with the regeneration of ancient virtue, content, as Nicos Gatsos, the contemporary Greek poet, sang, with 'a bit of grain for the holidays, a little wine for remembrance, a little water for the dust', the wealthy Greeks never dreamt of retiring early to spend more time with their possessions. They preferred, instead, to live in a way that the poor of our days, those who have to live within their means even if they have to die for it because they cannot afford an operation in the private wing of the Royal Free, would contemptuously dismiss. 'Lessness', as Clint Eastwood, the American actor, neologising, said, was 'bestness'.

Even great statesmen like Themistocles and Miltiades, not needing a mansion where they could think with pleasure of their own importance, dwelled in humble houses, poorly furnished. They wore ordinary clothes and lived on the simplest food which hardly contained meat. Individual splendour, despised, was thought of as bad taste.

The diet of the Greeks, Archestratus informs us, was basic – cheese, olives, pulses, olive oil, honey, wine, fruits, vegetables pungent with fresh herbs and seeds, and more often than not barley for their staple. Incidentally, in *The Travels of Anacharsis*, a historical novel, Jacques Barthélemy wonders whether the Greeks were acquainted with melons. They also loved seafood, which is still regarded as an aphrodisiac throughout the Mediterranean, with the eel, which for the Egyptians was the greatest divinity, being the undisputed master of the fishmonger's stall.

Whether because of their diet or for other reasons, and though without smart toilets which perform instant computerised health checks, the Greeks managed to live a life which was twice as long as that of Europeans in the nineteenth century. Isocrates reached the age of 98, Gorgias 95, Sophocles 91, and Hippocrates, Pindar, Democritus and Phyrro, the founder of scepticism, 90. Diogenes lived to the age of 89, Plato to 81, Solon, Thales, Pythagoras and Epictetus to 80, Euripides to 78, Xenophon to 76, Plutarch to 75, Anaxagoras to 70 and Aristophanes to 68. Aeschylus was killed accidentally at the age of 71 and Protagoras perished at sea on his way to Sicily aged 70.

Agesilaus, the King of Sparta, when one would have thought he hardly had the time to reach his grave, was still leading his forces in the battlefield at the age of 80, and Xenophanes, with 95 years to his credit but still unbent by time, was still writing books – he was said to have lived to be over a hundred. Empedocles, if he had not jumped into the crater of a volcano just to prove that he was immortal, might have lived beyond the age of 150 some believed he had already reached – at the end, Bertolt Brecht, the German 'epic theatre' dramatist, philosophised, Empedocles 'died like anyone else'. None of them were subscribers to *Healthy Living* – 'nothing worse than fussiness about one's health', Plato held – and none spent their last years in residential homes, handing over their pensions and then selling their houses to pay for nursing care.

Life was, of course, simpler in those times and personal survival did not demand all the compromises we are forced into nowadays. But life was equally simple in the Alexandrian days and beyond, when the ethos of Presocratic Greece had been left behind and lifestyles were giving a foretaste of the world as we know it today. The Greek unyielding abandonment to beauty, their unappeasable pursuit of perfection, the purposeful turning of life into a work of art did not relate to circumstances. It related, instead, to an ideal, freedom from necessity, the kind of necessity which in our times forces us to take jobs we are not interested in to earn the money to pay for things we do not really need. Freedom from necessity gave them, if I can use the modern jargon, flexible working hours which ensured a 'work-life balance'. It ensured a minimum expenditure of physical and mental energy in a minimum of time, in other words, an order of abundance compatible with freedom that becomes possible only in a civilisation that has achieved its highest maturity. In the realm of freedom beyond the realm of necessity, they could, thus, freely pursue their desired 'lifestyle'.

The main features of the latter were becoming rather than being, creating rather than doing, and belonging rather than withdrawing into the garden of their private world. None of these, as notions, can, of course, be comprehended within the retail price index, in a world in which, as Seferis put it, 'we never sold or bought this kind of merchandise'. But, as a result, what Russian painter Wassily Kandinsky called the 'whole nightmare of the materialistic attitude, which has turned the life of the universe into an evil, useless game' never clouded the life of the Greeks.

The Greek passion for freedom, freedom from necessities, made no compromises over the nature of labour. Labour, though glorified in the last few centuries as the source of all values, praised, as by Thorstein Veblen, as the foundation of 'the good life', dehumanises the worker, denies him the fulfilment of his potential and stands in the way of greatness. The free Greek was not free if he had to work all his life to buy a pension, this expensive guarantee against uncertainty, engage in activities whose sole purpose is to ensure his merely being alive, concern himself with his biological survival. What is the point of being employed by someone, Eutherus told Socrates according to Xenophon, if, as a result, you give up your freedom, cannot move around and, perhaps even worse, you forego the right 'at least to answer back'.

Simone Weil, the twentieth century French philosopher and mystic, made the point in the diary of her daily experiences as a factory worker – its motto uses the line from Homer 'much against your own will, since necessity lies more mightily upon you'. Hence the Greeks' contempt for labour, equalled only by their intolerance of triviality, what we today call 'fun', bought in quantities large enough but never good enough, and also by their commitment to the time-consuming life of the citizen.

The challenge necessity poses stimulated the thinking of many influential thinkers of the modern era, from Wordsworth, Shelley and Wilhelm von Humboldt to William Morris, Tawney and Oscar Wilde. The right activity for man, Wilde held before he died in Paris in 1900 a broken man, is 'not doing, but being, and not being merely, but becoming' – a dream denied by necessity. The same dream of a society liberated from necessity and labour, as Hannah Arendt, the German-born American philosopher and political theorist, said, inspired by Pericles' Athens, galvanised generations of Marxist thinkers, too. Man, Sartre said, exists only to the extent that he fulfils himself.

The tone was set by Marx himself, who in his *Capital* wrote that 'the realm of freedom actually begins only where labour, which is determined by necessity and mundane considerations, ceases'. Freedom lies 'beyond the sphere of actual material production', in the individual's self-realisation, which for Marx himself was an absolute moral value. Theodor Adorno, the cultural theorist, Herbert Marcuse, the radical Frankfurt School philosopher, and André Gorz, the Austro-French humanist, too, built their views on the same basis.

The more we master necessity, they argued, the freer we become to realise our individuality through creative leisure, science, the arts, convivial activity and the like. The assumption that liberation from the drudgeries of life will lead automatically to other, 'higher activities' is, incidentally, anything but self-evident. Unfortunately, the skin of the dream is as tormented as the trunk of our reality, for, as Freud noted, the 'primordial struggle for existence' is 'eternal'. The pleasure principle and the reality principle remain consequently 'eternally' antagonistic.

Trying to move away from the problematic distinction between freedom and necessity, the ecocommunalists shifted the ground of the argument. True freedom or self-realisation, they argued, is not something that can be experienced only beyond 'bread labour'. It depends, instead, on how an individual's entire range of needs are integrated and satisfied. It is not 'freedom from', but 'freedom for'. The conquest of even such a restricted 'freedom for' rests, however, on the conquest of time, essential to contemplation and wisdom.

Yet the ideal which Greek society, particularly the Athenian, came as close to as no other is still present, teasing our realities, providing the inspiration for personal change outside the parameters set by the market and its culture. Placing no premium on ownership or social status, but, in what Ivan Illich, the Catholic thinker, called 'the nature of human satisfaction', and having a simple and materially undemanding lifestyle, the Greeks, Josiah Ober, the Princeton University Professor, wrote, have a good deal to tell the modern world about the nature and potential of democracy as a form of social and political organisation. His views were echoed by American professor Eli Sagan and others in what represents a millennium rise in the popularity of Greece.

The undemanding lifestyle of the Greeks gave them the time they wanted. So did the use of slaves which gave them some more. Slavery was not a means for the enrichment of the individual. To some extent it was considered necessary because of the disagreeable nature of all occupations that ensure the maintenance of life. But its prime function was freedom from, and the mastering of, the necessities of sheer life so that man could, as Plato said, 'practice excellence'. Maintenance was the least of the Greeks' concerns. Mere survival, it was thought, was identified with existence only by the animals.

Slavery was nevertheless not as important as Marxist thinkers, in particular, have under the influence of Engels suggested, or postmodernist thinkers, mostly women, have argued.

16. A Seditious Culture

Greece's spirit, 'armoured by Gods' as Hölderlin said, has since the Renaissance become the symbolic flag of humanity's battle for a world that makes sense. It has been the inspiration in the struggle of humanism against theocracy, of knowledge against ignorance, of democracy against tyranny, of republicanism against monarchy, and of Justice against social and political inequality. It is still so in our days in the struggle of Logos against modernist Reason, human values against fundamentalism, humanity against technology, beauty against utilitarianism, holism against fragmentation, civic ethics against profits and being against existing. As such, it has always been the flag of the Left – hence Thomas Hobbes' warning given in 1651, repeated later by the Marquis de Bouillé, the General who stood by Louis XVI against the French revolutionaries and was denounced as the accomplice of a 'bloody despot' in *La Marceillaise*, that there was nothing so provocative of sedition as the reading of classical texts.

Homer's 'divine race of heroes' was, of course, anything but perfect. It was often described by him as a murderous, deceitful and shameless lot – the dark and barbaric Eris, reaching back to an age of cruelty, Nietzsche said, could make her presence felt. A few centuries later, an angry Herodotus denounced the tyrant Periander because there was no crime against the Corinthians he would not commit – he even murdered his own wife, Melissa. Others such as the Athenian Cleisthenes bribed the Delphic priestess to deceive the Spartans; and Themistocles bribed his army commanders to get their agreement to fight the Persians in Salamis. Thucydides, the historian who, Plutarch said, made his narrative 'like a painting by giving a visual quality to the sufferings and the characters', noted in disgust that during the Peloponnesian war 'both sides had claimed to have the good of the community at heart, while both ... in their struggle for ascendancy indulged in the worst excesses'. He recorded excesses, bribes, blackmails, and betrayals of monumental proportions as, for example, in the case of Alcibiades, the fifth century playboy-statesman of Athens, and then, philosophising, he concluded 'the love of gain would reconcile the weaker to the dominion of the stronger'.

A century later, and admittedly in times less auspicious, Aristotle had no choice but to accept that it is 'the nature of the many to be ruled by fear rather than by shame, and to refrain from evil not because of the disgrace but because of the punishments'. As compromising was the inflated ego of the Greeks – Lucian, for example, records fierce arguments among philosophers relating to who sits where in symposiums held to examine the nature of virtue – or Aristophanes' story of a mature woman beaten up by her lover because someone was flirting with her. And the Greeks, as a postmodernist would argue, had neither societies for the protection of sacrificial animals nor public lavatories for the disabled.

But the numerous imperfections, which reflect the human condition, do not change the picture of a superb civilisation which Christianity attacked ferociously – even in 2006 the head of the community of Greek priests felt the need to denounce the 'degenerate' religion of the Greeks and its 'monstrous dark delusions'. Starting with Paul who promised to 'destroy the wisdom of the wise, and bring to nothing the cleverness of the clever', i.e., the wisdom of the Greeks as he said himself in his first letter to the Corinthians, the Christian culture consistently contrasted the thinking man with the simpleton who obeys unflinchingly the commands of God. Nearly two millennia since those days, the 'so-called intellectual' is still derided by our popular literature or the film industry on the assumption, which comforts the common man, that high intelligence is incompatible with the warmth of heart presumably possessed by the undistinguished. The myth was endorsed even by socialists, who failing to resist the post-Greek artificial split between intelligence and goodness, extolled and idealised the warm-hearted and morally superior Working Class.

The Greeks, incidentally, were not totally committed to the intellectualisation of virtue. 'I would rather have as a friend an ordinary man who is good', Euripides said, 'than a bad man who is more able'. But intelligence and virtue were indispensable elements of a well-structured man. Intelligence without virtue was dangerous, and so was virtue without intelligence. The dangers of the latter were highlighted by Euripides in Bacchae, his play which sounded the alarm over religious mass hysteria, or for that matter any mass hysteria.

Christian and also Gnostic hostility to Greek irreligiosity was succeeded, as Jennifer Tolbert Roberts, a New York Greek history professor, documented brilliantly in her book *Athens On Trial*, by a violent and ugly opposition to Greece's spirit. The parallel dogmatic and sterile appreciation of the classical tradition, which forced the disparaging comment by Voltaire that 'in England the governments of Greece and Rome are the subject of every conversation', and which motivated even Queen Elizabeth I to attempt to learn Greek, made no difference to it. Athens was, and still is, an ineluctable menace to any conservative establishment, whether authoritarian, religious or plutocratic, to modernism itself and its culture of profit. Modernism just cannot live with the wisdom of the Greeks. Even academia does its best, American academics Victor Davis Hanson and John Heath said, to denigrate the Greeks and kill, permanently if possible, knowledge of the classical tradition. 'Killing Homer', they said, academia is, however, also killing the understanding of our own selves. The botched-up twentieth century, hijacked by extremism, bears evidence of it.

The French monarchist historian Jean Bodin, whose work was most popular in Britain during the civil war, denounced, like Cicero, 'the dominion of the Athenian mob; the English monarchist Thomas Elyot portrayed Athens as a 'monster with many heads'; and Walter Raleigh, the English writer, disapproved of the democratic 'rascal multitude'. Robert Filmer, the English political philosopher who defended the divine right of kings, expressed his preference for the 1,200 year Assyrian stability over the unremitting evil of Greek democracy. God, Filmer explained, intended for Kings to rule, and to rule absolutely. For Thomas Hobbes, the Athenian democracy was at the mercy of 'wicked men and flatterers'; and for Jonathan Swift, the early eighteenth century Irish satirist who was also an Anglican cleric, it was 'a tyranny of the people'.

The violent attack on the 'wickedness of Greek democracy', and also on Greece's 'decadent' culture, which, as Jonathan Boucher, an English loyalist who opposed the American revolution, said in 1773, had created men who prefer the 'darkness and filth of Heathenism' to 'Christian verity and purity', continued well into the eighteenth century.

David Hume, fearful of Greek political radicalism, dismissed the Greek virtues as 'artificial', an obstacle to the expression of passions and desires in the service of self-interest, and disapproved of the 'Athenian mob'. Interestingly enough, though he himself considered 'negroes and in general all of the other species of men to be naturally inferior to the whites', he did not hesitate to denounce Periclean Athens for her policy on slavery. Edward Wortley Montagu, the English dilettante who, while in Egypt with a black paramour, adopted the Turkish dress and manners, warned his compatriots, likewise, that, if they did not mend their ways, they should only expect the Athenian 'universal idleness, effeminacy and corruption', complete decadence; and John Gilles, the Scottish historian, in 1786 wrote that Greece conveyed to the world only the evils of non-monarchic government. Democracy, he asserted, is 'a fierce and licentious form of government', with 'incurable defects' and a 'tyrannical spirit'.

That was, indeed, the view of all monarchists and reactionaries at the time monarchical absolutism was swept aside by the French revolution. The revolutionaries, on the other hand, were, as one might expect, appreciative of the Greeks' republicanism, which, as Robespierre, the leader of the Jacobins in the National Assembly, said, 'had raised them at times above humanity'. Republicanism, in its passion for equality and public virtue, attempted a partial restoration of the Greek tradition, but it failed because, to impose what was in effect an élite concept, it resorted to terror. Jean-Jacques Rousseau, although committed to egalitarianism, mounted a passionate attack on 'decadent' Athens which, he considered, had been corrupted by art. Rousseau's preference was for Sparta, 'that Republic of demi-Gods rather than of men' which he tried to understand better by trying to learn to read Greek except that, as he admitted, he failed.

The egalitarian Athenian democracy, and the notion of universal suffrage was further attacked by the conservative, indeed reactionary, founders of American democracy as a threat to the sanctity of property. Overwhelmed by fears that Greek democracy would, just like Marxism-Leninism, bring about the abolition of debts and the distribution of property, just as the distribution of sunlight, to all members of society, or, indeed, the tyranny of the poor over the rich, they – Benjamin Franklin, John Adams, James Madison and others – dismissed it, in Adams words, as 'the waves of the sea'. The chief objectives of civil society, Madison asserted, are 'the security of property and public safety'. Therefore, as Franklin advised his contemporaries, 'better to bring back from Italian travel a recipe for Parmesan cheese than copies of ancient historical inscriptions'. His pragmatism may not be inspiring, but, on the other hand, it enabled the United States to give the world the hamburger in whose name all the revolutions of the last quarter of the twentieth century were made.

Greek democracy was also dismissed in the twentieth century by Fascist and proletarian dictatorships – Athens, the land of the 'fierce democracy' and 'mother of the arts' according to the seventeenth century English radical, republican poet John Milton, had nothing much to offer them. Marxism-Leninism, focusing on historical processes, which, it was assumed, had decreed the discarding of capitalism into the 'dustbin of history', distorted antiquity before dismissing it as an extraneous occurrence; and capitalism, riding on the back of the Judaeo-Christian tradition, fearful of Greece, confined her to museums. The future, in blue jeans, rested, instead, with Coca-Cola. Similar was her treatment by a timid conservatism which, like Henrik Ibsen, the Norwegian playwright, disliked 'the doctrine that the common folk, the ignorant and incomplete element in the community, have the right to pronounce judgment, and to approve, to direct, to govern, as the isolated, intellectually superior personalities in it'. In our days the attack on Greek culture is carried on by postmodernist writers and university departments of political correctness. Rather than ask how we can emulate a superb civilisation, which politically, socially, culturally and ethically offers an alternative to the values of both capitalism and religious fundamentalism, they have denounced Greece on almost every account.

American professor of Classics Sarah Pomeroy decried the 'intolerable' exclusion of the Others, Margaret Wason denounced Thucydides' work as 'a record of trivialities unworthy of the dignity of history', Eva Keul, in her *The Reign of the Phallus*, the most vicious attack on Greek culture ever made, saw in classical Athens 'a kind of concave mirror in which we can see our own foibles and institutions magnified and distorted'. Miserably, even Bettany Hughes, the British broadcaster and writer, joined the belittling of the Athenian culture in her 2007 Channel 4 presentation of the

Athenian democracy. All she managed to see in it was slaves, the marginalisation of women, corruption and imperial designs. The most celebrated doctrine of postmodernism that no culture can be judged outside the specific limitations of its time and place went unceremoniously out of the window.

Others, including Martin Bernal, author of *Black Athena*, and then Cheikh Anta Diop and Yosef A.A. ben-Jochannon, denounced 'the Aryan model' in whose image the West has moulded the world. The core values of the West, they have argued, are rooted in Africa, instead – or in the Middle East according to Islamists. Islamic writer Ziauddin Sardar suggested likewise that the image of Athens through the centuries is 'mostly fiction' – to get the real picture, he said, 'think of Bush and Blair, Iraq and Afghanistan'. The Iranians, for their own part, and as soon as Hollywood's *300* was released, denounced Herodotus, the historian of the Graeco-Persian wars. Though Herodotus refers with respect to the Persians, he is, Amir Nasseri wrote in the *Persian Journal*, 'both the father of history and the father of lies'.

Postmodernist objections rest mainly on institutionalised slavery and the treatment of women. Either or both had been condemned to the barathrum by influential Greek thinkers such as Pythagoras, Plato, Diogenes, Epicurus, Epictetus, Callicles, Gorgias or Menander and many others, including Periander, the tyrant of Corinth, who attempted to abolish slavery. I would be tempted to include the Olympian Gods among those who did not support the institution of slavery. 'The Gods', the fourth century rhetor Alkidamas as quoted by Aristotle, said, 'made all men free, and nature had enslaved no one'. Indeed, unlike the Jewish God, who in Leviticus gives the Jews advice on where to get their slaves, i.e., from 'the nations round about you', or Paul, who in his letter to the Ephesians, commanded the slaves to 'obey your earthly masters with fear and trembling, single-mindedly, as serving Christ', the Olympian Gods had not given slavery the seal of their approval.

As far as Athens is concerned, agricultural slavery hardly

existed; and the Athenian economy depended much less than is often assumed on the labour of the slave population. Accounts of the Building Commission for the Erechtheion show, for example, that only twenty of its one hundred and seven workers were slaves receiving the same payment as the free citizens. The slaves, apart from those working in the mines, were, indeed, employed mostly for domestic purposes and had a function similar to that of housekeepers or, in our days, of the paid domestic help so many middle-class families can no longer do without. This did not free the Greeks from the need to work. Indeed, the entire Greek literature portrays the Greeks as working citizens of the Republic rather than idlers working on their tan.

Moreover, as Aristotle acknowledged approvingly, the slaves were, and had always been, part of the family often treated with great affection. Relations were sometimes so close that, as Plato rather disapprovingly mentions, Euthyphro, the son of a wealthy family, prosecuted his own father for the murder of a family dependent, a slave. Slaves were often protected by law in other ways, too – raping a slave, for example, was an offence – and Athenian citizens were known to have been sentenced to death because of criminal acts they had committed against their slaves.

Often, as in the comedies of Aristophanes and Menander, the slaves outwitted and patronised their masters. Sometimes, more vocal than the citizens, they would not, as fifth century arch-conservative pseudo-Xenophon complained, 'step aside to let him pass in the street'. Dressed the same as the free citizens and thereby visually indistinguishable from them, they were also in Demosthenes' time able to attend the theatre, participate in mystery rites, and even join the demos. 'You can find plenty of slaves here at Athens', Demosthenes said, 'who have more freedom to speak their minds than citizens have in some other states'. Several of them, like the famous Pasion, the best-known slave banker, ended up as a man of substantial means.

The respect with which they were often treated is evident in

Aeschylus whose Cassandra, the princess taken forcefully by Agamemnon to Greece, proves herself superior to him on all accounts – as a slave to her conqueror, as a foreigner to a Greek, and as a woman to a man. A slave who is good, Euripides in *Ion* had no difficulty admitting, was in no way inferior to a free man; and Creusa, in the same play, was more than happy to help her old slave to walk up the steps. Hence the slaves were able to feel part of the whole, their polis. Thucydides, making the point, mentions that when the Thebans attacked the Plataeans, the defending men charged the attackers while the Plataean slaves and women pelted them with stones and tiles.

Women in Greece, though far from having elevated themselves to the position of honorary men, were not exactly extolled for their feminine helplessness, either. The Goddesses, as the archetype, were anything but helpless objects of desire, and priestesses, from the most famous to basket bearers and handmaidens, were prominent and indispensable executives in the civic sphere. Christianity, professor Joan Breton Connelly said after extensively studying ancient inscriptions and vase paintings, needed 2,000 years before it could offer women a comparable status. Aristocratic women, likewise, held considerable power. As Bettany Hughes says in her book *Helen of Troy*, 'women like Helen were more than just golden, sitting ducks, waiting to be hunted down ... If wealth was the honey-pot which attracted suitors like Menelaus, women like Helen appear to have owned and enjoyed the honey'. Helen was the perfect example of a Greek archetype, but for the Christianised West this was a difficult concept to deal with.

The mortal women's rights as human beings could not easily be dismissed, either. Charisios, in a Menander comedy, did just that when he treated his wife harshly after she bore him an illegitimate son. Recalling, however, soon after that he himself had begotten one, he reproached himself as a 'merciless barbarian'. The Greek males were, of course, not known for their passionate love affairs with their wives. But despite heavy penalties against adulterers

– and also against rapists – wives, on the other hand, were not as submissive as postmodernism would expect us to believe. Herodotus, for example, mentions the 'rumoured' illicit relationship between the wife of Isagoras, Cleisthenes' opponent, and Cleomenes, the king of Sparta.

Incidentally, he also mentions that the son of Sesostris, the Egyptian king, who was blinded, was told that he would recover his sight if he washed his eyes with the urine of a woman who had never slept with any man except her husband. He had to try really very hard.

Women, who could remarry after the death of their husbands as Perictione, Plato's mother, did following the death of her husband Ariston, often had to work to earn their living. Euripides' mother, for example, used to sell parsley from her garden – others traded in other commodities such as flowers and perfumes, dresses and make-up. Interestingly enough, women's aesthetic needs, their concern about their looks that is more pronounced now than before the feminist revolution, could even then support a section of the manufacturing industry.

Several women had also distinguished themselves as thinkers – Diotima of Mantinea, Aspasia the Milesian, Theano, Perictione, Asclepigenia of Athens, Hypatia of Alexandria; others, including Clytaemnestra, Antigone, Medea, Electra, or Deianeira had often been portrayed as forceful and assertive characters; and others like Olympias, the mother of Alexander, or Artemisia of Halicarnassus possessed considerable political power. Sappho's 'I would rather watch the delightful way she walks and see the sparkle that lights her face than gaze at Lydian chariots or warriors in glittering armour' is a damning condemnation of the male culture of her time; and Lysistrata's 'honey, how'd you do something so stupid', directed to her man, was a clear demonstration of women's political views, forcefully expressed. Women did not, of course, participate actively in the affairs of the polis. But they did not spend their time watching *Footballers' Wives*, either: when Lycidas suggested the capitulation of Athens to the Persians it was women who lynched him.

The Spartan women were, perhaps, even more powerful than those American women who only a few decades ago were happy to let their husbands decide on the rights and wrongs of the Vietnam war while confining themselves to the trivial tasks of life, things like buying a house or choosing their children's education. The Spartan women, Plutarch says, 'were bold and masculine, overbearing to their husbands ... and speaking openly even on the most important subjects'. As Will Durant said in *The Story of Civilisation*, they lived in liberty at home while the men bore the brunt of frequent wars. The exact position of Greek women, whose education was neither encouraged nor forbidden, is still disputed among scholars. There is no consensus regarding the criteria by which judgment can be made.

Whatever the exact position of slaves or women, the dismissal of Greece on these postmodernist grounds is as good as dismissing Christianity for no reason other than that all the twelve disciples of Christ were men or denouncing the great European civilisation as the product of white and heterosexual males. It is, indeed, as good as dismissing the past altogether in favour, presumably, of an idyllic present guaranteed culturally by Hollywood, commercially by the WTO, financially by the IMF and militarily by Anglo-American Tomahawk land attack and AGM-86 air-launched cruise missiles.

To mention the failures of the Greeks is necessary. To place the emphasis on these failures, which occurred two and half thousand years ago, and trivialise or dismiss the Greek culture on their account is as good as criticising the Greeks for their inability to maintain computerised records of their public debates, produce books with beautiful photographs, which, as Günter Grass, the German socialist poet and novelist, said, show 'clearly what napalm can do', or inform the public what to do in case of a nuclear Apocalypse. Suspending intellectual judgment to indulge in political correctness, the kind which offers US college students the same consumer choice enjoyed by a Tesco customer, has nothing much to recommend itself for.

The Greeks simply cannot be seen as failed contemporaries. Postmodernist persistence in doing so reveals only, if I can borrow a line from Rilke, an intellectual 'incoherence that's ours, but which we can't appropriate'.

The Greek failures were and are, in the last analysis, the failures of mankind. Slavery is one of them – only in the 'illustrious' centuries of Europe over sixty million Africans, perhaps the first ever global commodity, were 'in the name of the most Holy Trinity' shipped over to the 'new world' where they perished; and slavery, though officially abolished in the West only as late as the nineteenth century, is still with us.

It is still practised in India, Pakistan and Nepal where hereditary 'debt bondage slavery' holds hostage to its practice ten million people whose debts pass from one generation to the next, in Buddhist Burma, in line, its dictatorship claims with the Buddhist cultural tradition, in some Arab countries and also in Western Europe. The latter harbours many thousands of either black household slaves or women from Eastern Europe who, prostituted, are the slaves of criminal gangs who have turned human trafficking into the third largest moneymaker, after drugs and weapons. Slavery can be found in the trade of babies, too, when parents from tribal villages sell their children for a pittance to baby traffickers who resell them to wealthy Westerners for exorbitant sums. As Kevin Bales has argued in his book *Disposable People: New Slavery in the Global Economy*, there are still, at a conservative estimate, perhaps as many as twenty-seven million slaves in the world today. They also include Mexican slaves in the US, Haitian slaves harvesting sugar in the Dominican Republic, child prostitutes in Brazil servicing the workforce of the mines, young women in Thailand, who, sold by their parents, are the property of brothel owners, cocoa farm workers in the Ivory Coast or women from Eastern Europe, Africa and Asia sold as prostitutes in Europe.

The role of slavery in the global economy is striking, and even expanding as the end of the cold war eliminated barriers between states. Slavery, a lucrative industry, is still an issue, and hence it is on the UN agenda as one of those our contemporary society has failed to eliminate.

Women, on the other hand, have been discriminated against through the millennia. Thomas Aquinas propounded the doctrine, which remained influential with the Church through the centuries, that women, inferior to men, were only ever conceived under adverse circumstances; and modernism gave them the vote but only in the 1920s. The position of women did not really begin to change until the last quarter of the twentieth century.

Greek society has also been attacked by cultural theory for its phallocratic values. Although, as James Davidson, author of the engaging *Courtesans and Fishcakes*, says, the Greeks never rebuked anyone with a 'fuck you' and never described a loser as 'screwed' or 'buggered', Kenneth Dover in his *Greek Homosexuality* sees anal penetration in particular as placing the penetrated in a subordinate social position. Society is, thus, split between 'us', the penetrators, the adult male citizens, and 'them', the penetratees, women, slaves and male prostitutes in the role of the Others. Of particular interest in this context is what Davidson called the 'Platonic mirage' which forced upon Foucault the belief that Greek males were more interested in boys than in women.

Sexual relationships between male adults and boys certainly had the blessing of the Gods. After all, Zeus himself abducted Ganymedes, the most beautiful youth alive, and turned him into his bedfellow. Orpheus, likewise, although a married man who once went to great lengths to bring Eurydice, his wife, back to life, seemed, as Roman poet Ovid indiscreetly mentioned, also to have a preference for boys. The Greek myths, Robert Graves writes in *The Greek Myths*, were fully exploited by Greeks and Romans alike to justify a grown man's love of a boy. But such a preference was distinct only in the Dorian parts of Greece, in Sparta, Thessaly or Boetia. Though the rules for the élite were different, public opinion in Ionian Greece and Athens was decisively against it. Considering, however, that the cultural legacy of Greece is that of the Athenian élite, conservatives have consistently mistranslated the Platonic texts to prove that homosexual conduct was regarded as intrinsically shameful, immoral and, indeed, depraved or depriving. Sex between males, professor of Classics at California's state university Bruce S. Thornton wrote, was viewed as a sexual outrage with the male who had allowed himself to be penetrated viewed with disgust. Male sexual passivity meant, indeed, inferiority, submission to domination and acceptance of servitude, which is what led several postmodernists to denounce Greek culture as phallocratic.

But again this is correct only in terms of popular feeling which the élite was only too happy to dismiss; such feelings, Pausanias made clear in the *Symposium*, are immature, incomplete and inferior. The masses' heterosexuality, the *Pandemos eros*, had something basic about it that a noble and idealistic man of culture could never contemplate. The path to heaven was offered to him, instead, only by *Ouranios eros*, the spiritual and intellectual love affair between men, what is known as Platonic love. This is the nineteenth century scholar Benjamin Jowett's initial interpretation of Platonic love which, however, wrongly denied its physical consummation as the very sexual relations between Socrates and Alcibiades, Pausanias and Agathon or Patroclus and Achilles were well-known in their time. Even Heracles, the hero of the Greeks, according to the story fell in love with young prince Hylas – the two were together 'morning, noon and night' until Hylas fell in love with the nymphs and disappeared, leaving behind his heartbroken partner.

Prior to the Christian tradition, Chicago University professor Martha Nussbaum argued, there is no evidence that natural law theories regarded same-sex erotic attachments as immoral, 'unnatural' or improper. Hence, she said, the natural law theory which rebuffs homosexuality is 'inherently theological'. Plato himself, who apparently never knew love between the sexes, denounced sodomy as against nature, calling the Ganymedes' myth a 'wicked Cretan invention'. But he also used the myth to legitimise his own affections towards his pupils.

The gap in perceptions between the populace and the élite however, had implications, as in the celebrated case of Timarchus, a male prostitute who urged the Athenians to oppose Philip the Macedon. Discussing it, Foucault linked politics and sexuality. 'What was hard for the Athenians to accept', he wrote, 'was not that they might be governed by someone who loved boys, or who as a youth was loved by a man, but that they might come under the authority of a leader who once identified with the role of pleasure object for others'. Several other postmodernist scholars, including Jack Winkler and David Halperin, have since interpreted Greek history through this sexual-ethical 'activity'/ 'passivity' angle. Some went as far as the very end of their vocabulary to denounce the 'tyranny of Greece'.

I do not think Greece's spirited eyes of pride blinked.

Part II: Faith and Profits

1. As Elusive as the Holy Grail

The buoyancy of the youthful, diligent, optimistic, universalist Greek world was undermined by the war between democratic Athens and oligarchical Sparta. The war, also involving the two cities' respective allies, began in 431 BC and ended 27 years later with the defeat of Athens and the horrors of the thirty tyrants' regime led by Critias, a former pupil of Socrates. Boundaries had nevertheless begun to crumble right from the start of the war. Outwards, and in spite of disasters including an horrific plague that obliterated one third of the population of Athens including the great Pericles himself in 429, everything looked amazingly the same as before. The city was still able to indulge in grand designs, power still rested in the hands of demos, the people's assembly, philosophy and the arts were flourishing. But doubt, underpinned by democracy's serious failures of judgment, the resulting calamities of the war and unnecessary acts of cruelty, had begun to creep in destroying the puritan commitments of the previous generations.

The situation became much worse at the end of the war which saw a new and much resented Spartan 'New Order', a very short-lived Spartan-sponsored tyrannical regime in Athens the end of which left a legacy of hatred, fear and suspicion, and the reoccupation of Ionia by the Persians. These most disastrous developments marked the end of Greece's *akme*, the 'pink of perfection' reached at the time of Pericles, and the beginning of *parakme*, the decline that gradually, over the centuries, dissolved Greece's proud features in the rain of the ages.

The new era, reflecting profound social and psychological changes, was as outstanding as the one that had just ended. Its creativity and imagination had, however, taken a different direction. Unhappy people, robbed of their bliss, as John Dryden, the seventeenth century English poet and dramatist, might have said, began to lose faith in their institutions, to distrust the world they were living in, to distance themselves from politics and to look elsewhere, rather than in their fellow human beings, for support. The cosmocentrism of the earlier Greek thinkers became anthropocentric, 'subject-centered'. The inward search introduced by Socrates, with his emphasis on ethics, and the flight towards otherworldliness, articulated by Plato, was carried on with the impatience of a storm. 'Farewell, O wings and fragrances, ideas, dreams, farewell, O multicoloured precious filigrees of air', Nicos Kazantzakis would have said.

The rot appeared with the first postmodernists of our world, the ancestors of our disillusionment, the Sophists, practitioners of the art of dissuasion and persuasion. Excelling in the unscrupulous exploitation of logic, banking on their wit which they turned into a profession, and almost as good as Richard Branson, the English Virgin entrepreneur, in grabbing the headlines, they denied truth, objectivity and virtue. Protagoras, a major intellectual force and the best known among them, argued against objective truth, which means that there is no such thing as good or evil. His views, which laid the foundations of contemporary subjectivism, relativism and postmodernism rested on the belief that each man has his own truth which can be better than the truth of another man but nevertheless not truer. Moral considerations were accorded the respect the dog has for the lamppost; rhetoric, a persuasion technique practised in our days by politicians, PR consultants and advertising executives was morally as good or bad as rain.

Rather than the objective truth about physical reality, the philosophers' views, Protagoras further argued, reflected only their subjective understandings. For appearances and reality are two different properties – 'the stick in the water appears bent, the hallucinations of the insane, the faces in the clouds, they are all appearances that are clearly at variance with reality'. Had he lived in our days, he would have also said that something does not even exist unless it is on television, as Italy's former prime minister Silvio Berlusconi asserted after he turned Italian life into the world's longest running reality TV show. Taking these views as their starting point, twentieth century phenomenology, founded by Edmund Husserl, held that phenomena deserve to be studied in their own right – for in the psychology of perception, significant is the form of the object as perceived by the individual and not the object itself or its material description. People's ideas about reality, expressing views without visible means of support, are, therefore, good insofar as they offer a rich mine of psychological understandings.

All the Sophists were concerned about had to do with the intellectual merits of the arguments they advanced, the creation of the right impressions, vital particularly if misleading. A pioneer in the study of language and semantics like Parmenides before him, Protagoras claimed to be able 'to make the weaker argument the stronger' – hence he was also able to earn more money than ten statue-makers together. Language, losing its genuinely communicative use to attain common goals, which is the inherent telos of human speech, became, in Habermas' terminology, a strategic or success-oriented speech, parasitic on the former. The meaning of words, Thucydides recorded, no longer had the same relation to things. It was changed by the Sophists as they thought fit. Just like 'enhanced interrogation techniques' by which the CIA means torture of political detainees, 'reckless doing', Thucydides said, 'was held to be loyal courage; prudent delay was the excuse of a coward; moderation was the disguise of unmanly weakness; to know everything was to do nothing'. Freedom remained the supreme good, but reinterpreted by Gorgias, the rhetorician, it became one's freedom to have things done his way in everything. Sophocles had warned 'time is the umpire in all human business'.

Protagoras is best remembered, however, for his 'man is the measure of all things', which introduced the concept of utilitarianism which looks upon everything as a means to an end – upon every tree as potential wood or, as Aristotle said, upon a deer or a wild goat as the evening's meal. This subjectivism led German classicist Werner Jaeger to the belief that Protagoras and the other Sophists were the 'first humanists' on account of which he embraced the Greek culture for its truly humanistic education. But subjectivism, as Heidegger, Hans-Georg Gadamer and others pointed out, has nothing to do with humanism, whose substance had been equated from the middle of the nineteenth century onwards with secularism, personal liberation, enlightenment and later on democracy.

Protagoras' inherent anthropocentrism, which devalued the world and nature, everything there is, and which ran against the grain of Greek thought which despised the sheer vulgarity of consistent utilitarianism, was violently opposed by both Plato and Aristotle. Aristotle objected to the 'absurd' opinion of those 'absolutely ignorant' people that man is the highest being and everything else is subject to the exigencies of human life. Plato, too, thought the Sophists were wicked, and Aristophanes, the comic playwright, equally annoyed at them, said that trying to be too clever, selling two-

153

for-the price-of-one, has its inherent complications and limitations. But the tide of public opinion had already begun to turn against the spirit of classical Greece. The young Athenians had already begun to fall in love with the richest widows south of Delphi.

Truth and morality, elusive as the Holy Grail, were turned in the name of a new, 'deconstructive' realism into relative values – it all depends on what you mean by 'virtue'. Thrasymachus, the Sophist, held that there is no such a thing as Justice because the powerful of this world always make sure that the law works to their advantage. Though never as vulgar as he would have liked, he did, nevertheless, make clear that he did not disapprove of it on the grounds that nature supports the survival of the fittest. Giving philosophical respectability to all the justice money can buy, he further argued against conventional morality, which, he said, brings injustice since it deprives the strong of their natural right to exploit the weak. Antiphon, another Sophist, considered that traditional morality conflicts with self-interest, Callicles preached that the law of the stronger is the law of nature, and Xeniades of Corinth said that nothing at all is true. Words in Greece were never in search of an idea.

The disillusionment with public life in the shattered world of the Greeks was brilliantly articulated by Socrates, a very ugly man according to Xenophon, 'uglier than all the Silenuses in the Satyric drama'. His teachings, a gallant effort to retain and develop the humanity of the earlier times, marked the shifting of Greece's loyalties from the objective to the subjective, from the community to the individual, and from the search for eternal moral laws to an inward search for self-knowledge and truth. Although he never bothered to put his thoughts within the safety of a book, Socrates placed his emphasis on the virtue of the individual rather than the nature of the world or the life of the city; as he said in his *Apologia*, the philosopher's mission was to search into, and understand, himself and other men. In line with the Delphic wisdom *Gnothi safton*, Know Yourself, his axioms turned into the very foundation of existentialism and modern psychology.

Man with him became, as Karl Jaspers, the German existential theologian, said, conscious of his being as a whole, of himself and of his limitations. Self-questioning became the method, and self-knowledge the goal of philosophy. The change which was accelerated during the Hellenistic times, dramatic and epochal, was, according to Joseph Campbell, the main feature of 'the Greek – the European – miracle', which Europe, larger than Athens's cemetery but much quieter at the time, was to view later in awe. For Nietzsche, on the contrary, Socrates was the symbol of decay and the atrophying, size zero life-instincts on which Reason, as understood by modernism, later built its empire.

Socrates' main drift was to establish virtue on a rational foundation, which, he believed, was lacking from traditional morality, and to define precisely ethically significant concepts. Virtue, he said in his sinewy style, is knowledge, which he constantly claimed he did not possess – 'I only know that I know nothing' was his dictum. His philosophy was matched by his high regard for traditional Greek values – moderation, simplicity, temperance and Justice – and by his emphasis on constant self-improvement. To get through life, he held, you do not need to disable others; just improve yourselves. His view that it is never good to do wrong, was founded on the belief that the benefit one might gain by doing the wrong thing could not compensate for the evil done to one's own self. He believed in life after death, and his indifference to his own death in 399 BC, which he faced fearlessly and nobly, was a triumph of his spirit. In his life he associated politically with the anti-democratic camp and men harmful to his city. He himself adhered, however, strictly to the principles of legality and Justice.

The great old man, whose 'wonderful consistency' enabled him, as Kierkegaard, the 'father of existentialism', said, 'to remain true to himself', had a tremendous influence over all subsequent thinkers. Incidentally, the encomium of Kierkegaard, a man who as H.J. Paton said, 'hardly ever thinks of anyone but himself', seemed, however, rather inconsistent with Kierkegaard's own dismissal of rationality and what he himself called the 'teleological suspension of ethics'.

Socrates can only be compared to Christ. Unlike Christ, he based his arguments on Reason rather than faith, but, like him, he called for a revolution in consciousness leading to spiritual transformation. In doing so, Christ offered tailor-made solutions, while Socrates, the thinker, wanted his followers to think for themselves. Comparing the two men, professor Oliver Taplin also drew attention to the dissimilar way they faced their death. Socrates, he said, remained calm and poised, for his philosophy had saved him from pain and passion. Christ, on the contrary, died after hours of torment and doubt. Socrates impertubably took the cup of hemlock; Christ in the Garden of Gethsemane cried out, 'Take this cup from me'.

Each one of Socrates' students was, as a result, himself a master. Many founded schools of their own. Aristippus, one of them, called on the citizens to abandon politics to win their freedom, and declared, like the Cyrenaics later, that the supreme good is sensual pleasure; he soon discovered that hedonism in circumstances decidedly impoverished, with 'neither a date nor a dollar' as poet Nicos Pappas might say once again, is not a practical proposition. Others became great generals, statesmen, heroes of all kinds, not heroes in martyrdom, strong in suffering, but in action and in life. Socrates, Hegel wrote, had 'no mould into which he wished to pour his characters and no rule according to which he might have desired to even out their differences'.

Most unfortunately for Europe and the world, it was nevertheless Christ rather than Socrates who was to become the founder of the new religion, with Jewish theocracy rather than the free, rational and humanistic spirit of the Greeks as its foundation. The world, apparently, cannot do without gurus.

The aristocratic views of Socrates, developed in the years Athenian democracy was being tested, combined with his humanism and moderation, made him a mild conservative of the one-nation party. Socrates was not, however, one but two: Socrates himself and Plato's Socrates who was gradually merged with Plato and his doctrines which endeared the reactionary Right. Plato, Socrates' pupil, his Judas, according to Karl Popper, the Austrian-born British philosopher, exerted an immense influence in the thinking of mankind. He dominated Christian philosophy in the first millennium AD, influenced western philosophy and even Islamic thinking, and remains inspirational even in modern times. A.N. Whitehead, the British mathematician-philosopher, saw all later philosophies as just a footnote to his, and Nietzsche regarded him in the same spirit. Yet Plato, although a genius of the very first order, led the movement towards the bankruptcy of the human spirit. His views, Castoriades held, were the total negation of Greek thought and, indeed, of political thought.

His time was even more dispiriting than Socrates'. The internal disasters continued unabated with another major war, the Corinthian, from 395 to 387, and then the Theban from 371 to 362 which ended with the defeat of mighty Sparta. Athens had slightly recovered in the meantime, but the age of melancholy was making no allowances for optimism and hope. The Greek states relapsed into separatism and chaos, and people began to look after themselves because, the feeling was, if they did not, nobody else would. Materialism, in full contradiction to the spirit of the previous generations, started to raise its head, and so did corruption. Aristophanes, who mocked the ethos of his days by extolling the pleasures of food, drink, sex and sleep, denounced the *nouveau riches* – 'no one', he said, 'gets rich quickly by being honest'. And Aristotle warned: 'Mankind does not acquire or preserve virtue by the help of external goods, but external goods by the help of virtue and happiness'. Three hundred years of stable political development and social articulation was approaching its end amid nostalgia for the passing ancestral virtue still thought to be recoverable.

Like Socrates, Plato was actively interested in politics. Unlike him, however, he strove to define, not the good individual, but the good community. He, too, believed, though only in a legalistic sense, in Justice, and was convinced that there is 'Good' whose nature can be ascertained. But at the same time he moved the argument into an entirely different sphere, a far-reaching intellectualisation of all there is, in Heidegger's terms 'the forgetfulness of Being'. Combining Parmenides' notion about the indestructibility of the 'substance' that makes change illusory, and Pythagoras' otherworldliness, he arrived at a new synthesis described by St Augustine as 'the most pure and bright in all philosophy'. His transcendental Form of Good, an eternal world dazzling like the sun, provided Christian absolutism with all it needed to proclaim the end of thinking.

Plato's theory of Forms, developed at a time that Greece craved some stable and unchanging reality beyond the flux and chaos of appearances, ridiculed empirical science and set the basis of idealism for all succeeding generations. The real, timeless, unchangeable and 'good', Plato held, is beyond the grasp of ordinary experience – the naked evidence of Being was erased and replaced by the ontological precedence of the 'idea'. The scene for the philosophical controversy lasting to our day about the essence of the true Being against the constantly changing multiplicity of appearances had been set. The senses, for Plato, perceive only something like the mirror-image of the 'real' which is beyond what we can see, smell, taste, hear or touch, beyond us, in the mind of the universe. The 'real', in a ring of invisibility, is the absolute, eternal deity of the universal religions, the mystical God to be apprehended only by the intellect. 'The soul cannot have true knowledge while in company with the body'. Despite all its splendour and bright beauty, the world we live in is, thus, a world of illusion silently witnessed by the immutable.

His theory of Forms, embalmed by Christianity, split the human being into two opposing parts, the immortal soul and the perishable body – Augustine was grateful to Plato, for, as he acknowledged, Plato had convinced him that reality had two fundamentally different sides, spirit and matter. Rejecting fully the Oneness of the Presocratic universe, Plato, thus, introduced the dualism of soul and body, mind and matter, object and subject, reality and thought, humans and nature, and ultimately society and the individual that have since become inherent in the highly fragmented world of the West. The soul, subject to metempsychosis, reincarnation, was further divided into three parts roughly corresponding to Reason, emotion and desire; their harmonious coexistence according to his sense of 'Justice' constituted what he called 'good life'. 'Justice' for Plato was the perfect Justice which exists in another world, is known to the immortal soul, and comes to us at birth in some imperfect form, as *a priori* knowledge.

Politically, Plato, a crusader against the 'permissive' society of his time, was the advocate of modern day totalitarianism. His fear of 'democratic extremism', rather entertaining in our days, envisaged a world in which sons have no respect for their fathers; citizens are indistinguishable from foreigners; the teachers fear and pander to their pupils; the elderly ape the young; the slaves have the same liberty as their owners; there is complete equality and liberty in the relations between the sexes; the least restraint is resented as intolerable; and people, in their determination to have no master, disregard all laws. In his *Politeia*, identifying his views with the will of God, the polis is run by a 'golden' class, a ruling élite of experts who stand above the rule of law or the people. His ideal, Aldous Huxley's terrifying *Brave New World*, is set against, not only the fundamentally democratic culture of the Greeks, but also their understanding of the whole man.

A rigid censorship ensures the public receives no 'harmful' influences. Homer and Hesiod, the creators of Greece's romantic myth, are banned as are all the dramatists and the relaxing Ionian and Lydian music. Brainwashing techniques ensure all stories, even those told in private, extol the virtues of faultless male heroes of good birth, and all children, taken away from their parents, are trained by the State to be fearless and 'free'. His ideal state is entitled to resort to 'noble lies' in the 'public interest', which people, like the Americans, though they know that the Iraq war was entirely a grab for oil, were happy to accept. It also decides what is 'good' for its citizens, what kind of specialised work the individual should be doing, even what kind of marriages can take place and what kind of children are allowed to live.

Plato hated wealth, and his Utopia makes no allowance for the rich and powerful. Neither wealth nor poverty exist – the ruling class live in Spartan conditions, friends share everything including women, and women have equality with men in all respects. Unity, for him, to which Aristotle objected as it would 'reduce harmony to unison or rhythm to a single beat', was 'the greatest blessing for the state'. Although he established an Academy, Europe's first university, to advance his ideas, Plato's impact in Greece herself was, however, minimal until the arrival of Christianity. But his politics and metaphysics provided inspiration to the dark ages and forces, including the Nazis and the American neoconservatives.

Aristotle, Plato's pupil, was and still is regarded as the supreme philosopher, 'the master of those who know', according to Dante, a 'Florentine by birth, not by character'. It took two thousand years, Bertrand Russell said, before the world produced any philosopher who could be regarded as approximately his equal. Aristotle exerted a decisive influence on the thinking of Thomas Aquinas and through him on the thinking of the Christian Church after the 12th century, and was a major influence on Hegel and also Marx. The latter, a left-wing Aristotelian, had frequently acknowledged his debt to Aristotle, this 'great thinker who was the first to analyse so many forms, whether of thought, society or nature, and among them also the form of value'. On account of his empirical biological studies, he was a thinker who hugely impressed Darwin, too – Darwin acknowledged him actually as the father of biology.

'How fortunate the man was', René Descartes, the seventeenth century Frenchman often thought of as the father of modern philosophy, confided almost enviously: 'whatever he wrote, whether he gave it much thought or not, is regarded by most people today as having oracular authority'. Aristotelianism was attacked for both its physical theories and its metaphysics. Yet Aristotle's work, interpreted and reinterpreted, exerts a powerful influence to our day.

Aristotle was basically a great systematiser of knowledge. Guided by a rational thinking which, he believed, unites the world, as opposed to the irrational that divides it, he subjected all knowledge to a sort of clinical criticism whilst at the same time non-dogmatically advancing new assumptions of his own. Basically, he affirmed that the physical world, being not a mere illusion as Plato had held, was subject to change just as Heraclitus believed. But the other world, what Plato had called the 'real', eternal and immutable, was stable and permanent – the Parmenidian 'nothing ever changes' because 'being is'. This distinction, which from the twelfth century onwards became the basic doctrine of medieval philosophy and cosmology, brought a cosmic reassurance to Christianity's frightened world. Aristotle's own reasoning dictated that the soul, being the form of the body, perishes with it – a view that troubled medieval theologians. Man, he believed on the other hand, partakes in the divine which is immortal – he partakes more if the divine in his nature increases in terms of virtue.

Rejecting explicitly Plato's Utopia, he endorsed democracy as the best system among bad ones and ridiculed tyranny in the same manner that Machiavelli, the Italian sixteenth century political philosopher, did after him. He 'advised' tyrants, in this sense, to execute or assassinate their opponents, build a police state and a network of informers, divide, impoverish, corrupt and censor their subjects, engage them in great public works which would keep them busy, and, failing all this, send them to war provided, of course, that, unlike Iraq's war, travel expenses could be covered. Embarrassingly for him, and although he freed his own slaves on his deathbed, he endorsed slavery as the natural state of affairs.

In spite, or perhaps because, of his intimate knowledge of Alexander whose tutor he had been for several years, Aristotle remained fully committed, like all the Greeks until his day, to the small-sized city-state. Bigness was an enemy to be fought against.

In doing so, he reasserted the classical political doctrine according to which the State exists, not to regulate financial transactions and prevent crime, which is what the free market is about, but to provide good life to the whole. The Greeks were convinced that the large state, because of its size, would never be able to do so, for it would not be run by its citizens but by a bureaucracy. The whole for him was not an aggregate of individuals but of families – hence his view that discussion of politics should begin with the family, even with one's own self. He stood for equality, but his 'equality according to proportion' left something to be desired: proportion was seen in terms of virtue which is, of course, immensurable. He also adhered to the holistic concept of *areté* as it had been understood until then by the Greeks.

In Aristotle's ethics, which is seen as a branch of politics, good is what would satisfy the two parts of the soul, the moral and the intellectual. This is what he called virtuous activity on which *eudaemonia*, happiness rests. Virtues are a means to an end, namely happiness, which according to his famous doctrine of the golden mean, is the fruit of a life in accordance with Reason. Every virtue is a mean between two extremes because each extreme is a vice. In what constitutes a studious protest against consumerism, Aristotle stressed that virtue and happiness are more likely to be found among those who, though they possess only a moderate share of external goods, are highly cultivated in their mind and character than among those who possess useless external goods and are deficient in higher qualities. Perhaps this explains why many people in the most developed countries of this day find that the size of their happiness does not depend on the size of their mansions – as Demetrios Antoniou, the seaman who, like Joseph Conrad, wrote many of his poems on cigarette boxes and scraps of paper aboard ship, said, 'the precious things in life take little room'.

Aristotle was the last of the Greek philosophers to treat the world in a positive spirit. He was also the last to believe in the destiny of Greece. The country's northern races, he said, are spirited, and the southern, intelligent. The Greeks alone are both spirited and intelligent, and, if united, they could rule the world. But the European Union of the time was never really an option. The Greeks valued the independence of their city-states too much to consider an alternative.

After Aristotle, the last representative of a society to which no other eye-witnesses existed, there was only defeatism and retreat. Ordinary citizens, gazing at the world with useless eyes, 'readier', as Aristotle had already established, 'to submit to compulsion and punishment than to argument and fine ideals', were more concerned with their private affairs than those of their cities. The latter, unable even to raise an army, had to outsource their national security and rely increasingly on mercenaries. 'What astonishes me, men of Athens', Demosthenes, admonishing his fellow citizens, thundered in 349, is that rather than do something to help your city, 'you just sit there!'

Material possessions began to be seen as compensation for the lack of meaning in life, and glamorality won respectability even when corruption and fraud, widespread, were involved. The elegant simplicity of the classical era had gone amid the silent screams of the new times. Meidias, Demosthenes thundered again, built a house in Eleusis big enough to overshadow his neighbours, drove his wife to the Mysteries with a pair of white Sicyonian horses, and swaggered about the agora with three or four attendants. Still, the new spirit of ritual consumption was pretty measured. 'Only three or four servants?' James Davidson, the contemporary British historian, asked for the fun of it; 'Only one house? Not in Athens, but in Eleusis? With neighbours?' And without jeroboams of Crystal Roedener White?

Individuals, celebrities unhampered by achievement and known for nothing else but their celebrity status, useless men in times of no meaning, made a footnote in history's books because of the size of their graves, monuments to their vanity and riches. Triviality replaced the aspirations of the bygone era – an entertaining example of the latter was given by the legal action an Athenian took against a fellow Athenian to whom he had hired his donkey, but not the donkey's shadow which he, albeit unsuccessfully, claimed for himself on a hot summer day.

Comedy reflected accurately the tensions of the lost weight, the days which looked like pieces of a puzzle that did not fit together. Though recalling with sadness the good old days, its inspiration was being drawn, as in the work of Menander, not from the life of the city, but from the domestic life of its citizens with jokes about the price of eggs, incompetent doctors and fat housewives causing tremors on the bathroom scales. The new trend was reflected also in the arts, which were becoming introspective, portraying men rather than Man, and in literature that had begun to look for romance and thrilling escapes rather than the fight of man for survival and justice. The new, 'romantic' element valued sensibility more than Reason and the individual more than the community – concerns of the previous era were as authentic as, Greek-born American surrealist poet Nicholas Calas would have said, 'leather furniture of genuine linoleum'. The 'literature of masterpieces', in which, Virginia Woolf pointed out, 'there are no schools, no forerunners, no heirs', had reached its end.

Life had lost the previous centuries' authentic concern for immortality without at the same time capturing the future's metaphysical concern with eternity. Dinner parties with exquisite dishes and craters of wine, flute-girls, harp-pluckers and acrobats, which came at times to be so extravagant that people kept writing about them for half a century after the tables had been cleared, had taken their place. 'Let the dinner start! Slaves, the flutes, the torches', Kavafis, the philosopher poet the Greeks themselves respect more than any other twentieth century Greek, poet or otherwise, mockingly commanded. Bono, the Irish singer, would have loved to be there to promote a basket of must-have consumer products and services – including American Express credit cards, Gap T-shirts and Emporio Armani sunglasses – aimed at raising funds to fight plagues in Africa. A few men, like Praxagoras, did, on the other hand, call for the complete socialisation of all wealth.

Jay Robert Nash, the crime writer, described Al Capone, the notorious American gangster, as 'a near illiterate who acquired millions and knew not where to spend a dime of it'. The sophisticated Greeks of *parakme* would never have been found guilty of such an ignobility.

2. Maundering in Time

Considering himself an apostle of Hellenism, in 334 BC Alexander launched the military campaign which made him known worldwide, from Dallas to Minneapolis and from San Diego to New York, as President George W. Bush would have testified before the Iraq war. As fortune favours the bold, the campaign ended ten years later with the conquest of territories stretching from the Adriatic to the Indus, and from the Caspian to Upper Egypt. Europe, the backward outpost during the Golden Age of Asia, had nothing to attract a conqueror. The Hellenistic era which lasted for just over three hundred years until 31 BC, when Cleopatra was defeated by Augustus, the first Roman Emperor, had begun. The world got its first taste of globalisation.

Hellenism, as a cultural force supported by the establishment of numerous Greek cities all over this vast empire and the politically motivated intermarriage between Greek males and non-Greek females, spread in Asia and Africa. It inspired new religious and aesthetic forms in India, China and even, ultimately, Japan. Babylonia was profoundly affected and Alexandria turned, in the years that followed, into a Greek city that outshone those of mainland Greece. The Middle East, which was completely hellenised, adopted the Greek language. Stubborn resistance to its hellenisation was maintained only by the Jerusalem Jews, who in 170 BC, and then again in 164 BC, revolted against Antioch, recaptured the city and established what was essentially a theocratic state. The victory, as decisive for the Jews as the battle of Marathon was for the Greeks, is still celebrated at the annual festival of Hannukah.

But all these epochal developments affected Greece, too. The old Greek city-states, although still maintaining the old civic spirit, had lost their independence, freedom, financial muscle and their social and cultural formations. They became powerless, demoralised and apathetic. The new ones Alexander had established were in an even worse shape. Being a mosaic of different ethnic, religious and cultural groups run by Greek adventurers, they were unable to form a cohesive political unit. To bring back the old community spirit, the Greeks introduced their own cultural forms which had grown organically in the old world. But, like today's media, the more they moved away from their distinct communities, the more disjointed they were from their reference group. 'Modernised', they lost their seminal meaning and turned into a show. Alexander's multiethnic, multilingual and multicultural global village, which was split after his premature death in Babylon in 323 BC into the European, the Asian and the African territories, was making no sense.

The clues of chaos were evident in everything as the global village, forcibly appropriated by feuding and unprincipled warlords operating with the support of mercenary armies, just maundered in time with no purpose, no principles, no moral justification for anything it was doing, not even a ruler strong enough to keep it under control. Rupert Murdoch would have been delighted to be there to lend a helping hand; so would Disney, ready to supply the global village's mouse.

Greek in terms of culture, the empire had little of the Greekness of the earlier times. Run by Alexander and his successors in the Greek democratic spirit of acceptance of all cultures and respect for the individual, the *oekoumene*, the inhabited world, was anything but an oppressed entity. But democracy, with which Alexander had replaced tyranny, had only ensured the monopolisation of power by the wealthy. The balance of power had shifted decisively in favour of the rich. As in today's world, 'democracy' had won. As in our days, all rulers were 'democrats'.

No longer masters of their fate, people, men and women 'neither of yesterday nor tomorrow but of never', as Antonio Machado, the poet, might say again, completely lost interest in public affairs. The globalisation of markets, their 'liberalisation' and the import of cheap labour from the east had brought unemployment, wage reductions and insecurity. The new world, though commercially attractive, had only contributed to the spread of disillusionment with the political system. Life had become full of things destined to be forgotten. Impotence had killed the political will. As Hannah Arendt said, what makes mass society so difficult to bear is not the number of people involved, or at least not primarily, but the fact that the world between them has lost its power to gather them together, to relate and to separate them. Social and cultural formations, dislocated, were deactualised, togetherness could be found only in alienation, discontent was on the ascendent.

In a climate of disarray, the dwindling cadence of a great era amid fears springing from an unknown address and the provocative display of a decadent lifestyle imported from the East, there were no ideals worth living for, let alone dying for, nothing worth looking forward to, no institution commanding respect, and no man capable of driving the rats and mice out of Hamelin with his pipe. Judgment, worth and merit became a matter for the 'free' individual to decide. Truthfulness, honesty, commitment, thrift and cooperation left the streets of the Hellenistic global village, like leaves deserting the trees in autumn. As British essayist Erich Heller might have said, 'we can no longer be sure that we love the lovable and abhor the detestable. Good does no good and evil no harm'.

Authors and poets like Theocritus, detaching themselves from their realities, turned for inspiration to the exotic or the pastoral; and scholars, like Apollonius, preoccupied themselves with the precise meaning of dried words, forgotten in the streets of inconsequentiality. Greece had obviously lost the plot; or, as Canadian novelist Margaret Atwood might have said, she had got tired of saying Onward.

As an ugly mood was sweeping across the country, everyone 'beg'd relief, which none would grant'. An escape route was likely to be offered either by retreat – into one's own self or into imported Eastern mysticism – or the unscrupulous pursuit of material self-interest. The age of vulgar materialism was in full swing – even the temples, the habitations of the Gods rather than houses of worship, had turned into banks, lending money at interest rates which would have forced the CBI to man the barricades. Phryne, probably the most glamorous über-slut of all ages, the woman who, when sauntering down the street made everything in pants turn his head towards her like a sunflower following the sun, as Costas Taktsis, the novelist, would say, had acquired such enormous wealth that she offered to pay herself for the rebuilding of the walls of Thebes. Her condition: an inscription on them acknowledging that 'Alexander destroyed them, but Phryne, the haetera, rebuilt them'. Yet as the monkey told Mephistopheles in *Faust*, life wasn't healthy, 'but, given gold, I'll be consoled'.

The new world had brought together Greece, India, Persia, Egypt and the Jews outside Jerusalem, i.e., many races, tribes, civilisations and religions. This offered very fertile ground for the cross-fertilisation and also multiplication of the mystic cults – gnostic and hermetic. Mergers, religious rather than corporate, became the order of the era. The twelve Olympian Gods inspired new religious approaches in the East, but at the same time, new oriental beliefs, facilitated by the time's easy promiscuity of sympathies, entered the Greek-speaking world and were mixed with Orphism and the Mysteries. A lethargic Eastern fatalism and Babylonian magic, finding favourable soil in the vicissitudes of the time, fell, as Professor Murray wrote, 'upon the Hellenistic mind as a new disease'.

So did astrology, the study of cosmic timing, celestial alignments and radiations from various stars and planets. Although a booming business in Wall Street, the Greeks until then had little regard for astrology. The contention that the future is predictable, and man is, therefore, the hostage of fate had been repulsive to them.

The magicians used formulae from all known religions, with Kabbalah, the Hebrew occult belief-system which accepted reincarnation, the recycling of souls, and undermined the rational study of the Torah, being the most influential. The influence of Kabbalah is still evident in the Tarot cards and in interviews given by Hollywood actors. Astrology and divination came from Babylonia, scrying from Persia, chiromancy from India or China. Numerology, on the other hand, is credited to Pythagoras, the sixth century BC philosopher. The world, with a good range of unamusing expressions, the face of 'drowned fears', had as a result become, according to Madame Blavatsky, the Russian Godmother of the New Age of our times, 'more spiritually advanced than we are'. Hebetudinosity, home grown or imported, was given divine status and the hours lost control over their minutes. The dawn of the age of the common man had come. Pythia no longer prophesied in verse.

At a time, as Umberto Eco, the Italian novelist and semiotician, said, dazzled by ecstasies and peopled with theophanies, emanations, demons and angelic hosts, mysticism and philosophy blended into many new forms; and, as in our times, everything was as good or as bad as anything else. All modes of worship, Edward Gibbon, the eighteenth century English historian, wrote, were considered 'by the people as equally true; by the philosopher, as equally false; and by the magistrate, as equally useful'. Mythology, which in pre-Christian times gave man self-confidence, was searching now, in Yannis Ritsos' verse, 'for some deeper correlation, some distant, general allegory to soothe the narrowness of the personal void'.

The *kosmopolis*, a term coined at the time to describe the Alexandrian global village, had brought people together – people sharing the same exquisite taste in cars, clothes, aftershave and wives. This laid the historical foundations on which Coca-Cola later built its empire, and created a huge demand for mirrors in front of which people needed to stand to confirm themselves. 'The transitory, the fugitive, the contingent', the phrase Charles Baudelaire, the nineteenth century French poet and critic, used later to describe his own era, dominated the experiences of the time, expressed its blasé attitude.

Reflecting the social, political and philosophical disintegration, the retreat from the world around us into the prison of the self because there is 'nothing' one can do out there, the era inevitably produced a new line of thinking. Moral theorising, as Marx, followed by Nietzsche and Foucault, explained, are only secondary phenomena relating to the form of power and the modes of social practice.

Yet, against all odds, the new thinkers, keeping watch at posts long lost, did not lose their humanity. Passing over in succession as before, like an endless row of cranes flying off towards the horizon, they kept their countenance. They did not succumb either to the serene calls of Eastern mysticism or to the theological populism of their time, and never abandoned the premises of human-centred Reason. Even in its decay, Hegel said, the free and liberal spirit of the Greeks remained majestic; amiable and cheerful, 'it accompanied their rational morality to its grave'. Making the best out of their dispirited, and yet still civilised, era, the new thinkers argued that its arrival made no difference to the life of the 'wise' individual. Wise men, they held, could always, as citizens of the world, fraternise with other wise men. The eyes of the Greeks had not yet lost their mobility.

The era produced four major schools of thought – the Cynics, the Sceptics, the Epicureans and the Stoics. They were all intellectual children of their disfigured age, but still superb representatives of Greece's splendour, present even in failure. The thinking of all of them, still able to start fires, exerted a major intellectual influence in Europe from the sixteenth century to modern day. Even Jean-François Lyotard, the philosopher of postmodernism in the 1980s, managed to associate, though rather incomprehensibly, his own vision with the 'nonhegemonic Greek philosophy'. What appealed to him was 'the guerilla warfare of the marginals, the foreigners, the non-Greeks, against the massive repressive Order of Aristotle and his successors'.

Diogenes, the founder of the Cynics and a man who, like Margaret Atwood's Zenia, did not just enjoy contradictions – he created them – was a sort of a professional anarchist. His entry in the *Who's Who* would have read, 'a citizen of the world'. Diogenes declared no allegiance to the established religion, the State, or the family, and like his later counterpart Jean-Jacques Rousseau, he preached a return to nature and a life devoid of any luxury, pride or malice. Unlike the Sophists, and in spite of his contemptuous rejection of all 'civilised values' as reflected in the way people dress, house themselves, eat, behave to each other and interact either socially, intellectually or politically, he was still, however, a moralist.

He stood against the class system and its stinking aura, condemned slavery and proclaimed his brotherhood with the whole world, the *oekoumene*, which included animals. His vigorous philosophy was a cry against powerful evil, a healthy emotional reaction to the politics of domination and manipulation. But it was also the attitude of a man who had nothing to look forward to. His search in the streets of Athens in broad daylight with a lantern for a 'just' man was not so much an eccentric gesture as a political statement damning the world he lived in. The Cynics' views, later fashionable in Alexandria and hellenised Palestine, have retained their sparkle to our day.

The Sceptics, whose influence on Descartes, Hume and many others has been paramount, refused dogmatically to commit themselves to any belief. The old road full of certainties had fallen into disuse. Pyrrho of Elis, the fourth to third century BC philosopher who established their tradition, a shadowy figure himself, held that arguments held in favour of an opinion are never better than the arguments against it – his principle was *ou mallon*, 'no more this than that'. Timon, his disciple, intellectualised the concept further by denying even the possibility of establishing general principles, which the Greeks, following a deductive way of thinking, had until then taken for granted.

As Descartes would later, the sceptic argued that any proposition must be judged in accordance with a criterion which, in order to select, needed another criterion based on another criterion, *ad infinitum*. Those who believed they had some sort of an answer to fundamental issues, people like Democritus, Aristotle, Epicurus or Zeno, were for the Sceptics 'dogmatists'. The real Sceptic, Sextus Empiricus explained, does not vote for any thesis, not even that 'nothing can be known'. Lucian, the second century AD Greek writer of prose satires, unable to stand the Sceptics' dogmatic uncertainty, just ridiculed it. In his imaginary slave market for philosophers, Pyrrho kept an open mind as to whether he had been sold as a slave while he was being carried off by his master after he had been sold as a slave. The sceptic kept an open mind and everything fell out.

Relativism and suspension of judgment, appealing to a world socially disintegrating and morally lax, found a few more powerful exponents such as Aristocles, who argued that each individual thing 'no more is than is not, or it both is and is not, or neither is nor is not', or the Cretan Aenesidemus, who, not surprisingly, denied the possibility of knowing whether God exists. But then he added: admitting that God exists is an impiety, for if he does exist, he controls everything and is therefore the author of evil things; and if he controls some things or nothing, he is impotent. In spite of their dogmatic doubt about everything, two Sceptics, Carneades and Clitomachus, nevertheless watered down the original Pyrrhonian version and also set themselves firmly against the incursion of oriental magic into Greece.

The Epicurean school, disillusioned with a world that no longer made sense, focused, instead, on the needs and pleasures of the individual. The individualism it embraced did not, however, have the antisocial overtones of the capitalist era. To begin with, Epicureanism denied the culture of unlimited needs and desires. 'What is insatiable', Epicurus, the founder of 'hedonism', held, 'is not the stomach, as people say, but the false opinion (that it needs) unlimited filling'. His view was that we spent a life trying to get what is, in fact, unnecessary and even undesirable, things, probably, like watches 'that adjust the date automatically for the next 100 years'. Neither did his individualism embrace the cynicism or the selfishness of the 'me' society. As he said, it is really 'not possible to live pleasurably without living sensibly and nobly and justly'.

For the founder of 'hedonism', the beginning and the end of *eudaemonia*, the blessed life, is *ataraxia*, freedom from trouble, anxiety or pain. Happiness could be found in the dailiness of life – certainly when taking off those tight shoes at night – and pleasure had to be pursued with prudence. Unlike the Indian *nirvana*, *ataraxia* was the choice of the rational mind which did not deny the existence of the world – the Epicureans were thoroughbred materialists. Epicurus' views were echoed later by Bentham, whose doctrine was a maximum of pleasure and a minimum of pain, and also by the contemporary Californians, who, as Isabel Allende said, leave nothing unchecked in order to avoid the anguish of living. For John Stuart Mill freedom dwells in the pursuit of happiness by every individual as he sees fit rather than in a substantive and unique vision of the common good.

Having no interests whatsoever outside individual happiness, Epicurus advised, thus, withdrawal from public affairs – 'free yourself from the prison of politics'. He also rejected luxuries and fame, and stood for the liberation of the individual from fear – fear of death and of the afterlife. To overcome the latter fear, he denied the existence of supernatural powers and the notion of the immortality of the soul. He was consequently denounced by the Christians later on as the embodiment of the Antichrist – Dante said he found Epicureans in the fifth circle of hell, where no coffee is served.

Though committed to sensual pleasures, Epicurus' own lifestyle was, however, very austere. He valued the pleasures of love and friendship, believed in the free will of the individual, and accepted as equals in his communities both women and slaves. His religious beliefs were typical of Greek religiosity. He believed in the existence of the Gods, whom, however, he considered as neither the creators of the universe nor its guardians – Spinoza's 'God exists, but only philosophically' was already in the air.

The Stoics, for their part, opted for the resigned acceptance of life as it was without even the consolation prize of happiness in the afterlife. You will die, Marcus Aurelius said, and 'you will be no one and nowhere, even as Hadrian and August are no more'. Epictetus, one of the main representatives of Stoicism, though a Greek, was after all in his early age a slave of Epaphroditos, a wealthy freedman of Nero who had sadistically tortured and crippled him. Still, the Stoics, whose teachings had something heroic, made, perhaps, the most enduring contribution to humanity's thinking. Their influence can be traced through the Christian faith, Rousseau, Adam Smith and Kant, who saw himself as the representative of the Stoics in the modern age, even in the Austro-Marxist thinkers as Otto Bauer acknowledged.

The humanism of the Stoics carried on in the proud Greek tradition. They defended fiercely their belief in free will – 'the fates guide him who will, him who won't they drag', said Seneca – and they advocated the primacy of moral choice. Virtue for them, personal virtue disengaged from civic virtue, was an end in itself, its own end, its own reward and its own motive to be sought for its own sake. 'Virtue', Diogenes Laertius asserted, 'is a rational disposition to be desired in and for itself and not for the sake of any hope, fear or ulterior motive'; and success, which the Professor in James Joyce's *Ulysses* thought might bring about 'the death of the intellect and of the imagination', had to be measured only in terms of doing what needs to be done regardless of results. The Greek tradition which had linked virtue to happiness, to the fulfilment of desire had been broken. Kant proceeded on the same lines later on. Virtue, however, did not debar the individuals from the pleasures of life as long as these pleasures were virtuously enjoyed.

The Stoics objected, furthermore, to distinctions based on gender, ethnic origins, rank or property, and declared allegiance, not to the laws of the city, but to those of the *oekoumene*, which, they held, were carved on the human soul. The laws of the *oekoumene* were for them in harmony with the laws of nature. Nature's order, implying a natural equality between humans in conditions of political equality, was, thus, both a political and a moral law, the law which lay the foundations of the *jus naturale* doctrine of a later age's struggle against medieval despotism.

Zeno of Citium, the founder of the Stoic School, firmly on the side of a corporealist view of the world, refused to subscribe to the Platonic otherworldliness and the immortality of the soul. For his school, God was not separate from the world. It was, instead, its soul, which, described as an 'intelligent fiery breath', later displeased philosophically-minded Christians. 'You yourself', he said, 'are a fragment from God; you have a portion of Him within yourself'. Zeno's leading disciple Posidonius, a man of tremendous encyclopaedic knowledge, elaborated the approach further by concluding that physics and theology are two aspects of one knowledge. Science, he said, deals with the material body of which God is the living spirit. God was intelligence, knowledge and right Reason.

Like the PreSocratics, the Stoics viewed all things as part of the One. Right action had to conform to the law embodied in nature itself, the cosmic order. Emperor Marcus Aurelius, the last of the Stoics of antiquity, argued that the universe is one living being, having one substance and one soul; 'Frequently consider', he advised himself, 'the connection of all things in the universe'.

In spite of the introspectiveness of their time and the now familiar Oriental philosophical brooding on the alternating influences of the yang and yin in the cosmic harmony of heaven, earth and man, in spite also of the social, moral and political disintegration of the Hellenistic times, the Greeks never abandoned the scientific premises of their thinking. None of the difficulties affected the further and most impressive development of science and technology whose advances Europe could not absorb fully until the nineteenth century.

Two millennia before the heliocentric system was introduced by Copernicus, Aristarchus of Samos was, thus, able to explain 'that the heaven is at rest, but that the earth revolves in an oblique orbit, while it also rotates about its own axis' – Copernicus was familiar with the Aristarchus theory through Ioannis Argyropoulos, Theodoros Gazis, Ianos, Constantinos Laskaris, Marcos Mousouris and other Byzantine thinkers whose lectures he had attended while in Italy.

The era produced, likewise, great mathematicians and geometers like Euclid, Eudoxus and Theaetetus, and great astronomers and geographers like Eratosthenes, who figured out the existence of America, Posidonius, and later Ptolemy of Alexandria. Their views, communicated by Plethon Gemistos to the Italian mathematician and astronomer Paolo Toscanelli and sent by the latter to Christopher Columbus in Lisbon, provided the ultimate foundation of the great navigator's confidence.

Great engineers like Eupalinos, great physicists like Archimedes and Apollonius and great physicians like Herophilus and Erasistratus, and later, in the second century AD, the greatest of all, Galen of Pergamus, made more breathtaking discoveries. Included among the latter was the 'world's first computer', an astronomical calculator discovered off the island of Antikythera more than 100 years ago but unlocked only in 2006. Regarding Archimedes himself, very recent findings have established that he was even ahead of Newton, who guessed at numbers and volumes whereas Archimedes himself was able to calculate them precisely. Great linguists, too, like Diogenes of Babylon created the first semantic theories. The last of the great scientist-philosophers of antiquity was the Alexandrian John Philoponus of the sixth century AD.

Rome, in the meantime, was gradually building its vast empire, which, just like the Alexandrian, made no attempt to impose uniformity on its subjects. As long as the latter were prepared to conform to its wishes and finance Rome's wars, the cities, in the hands of the well-to-do who became Rome's allies, were left 'free' to carry on with their business. So were the individuals, who, without many obligations or expectations, could freely pursue their own interests – video games, reality TV shows and internet porn. Several of them, those favoured by circumstances, became citizens of the empire without abandoning their local identity. But in the 'most artificial and empty culture' of the Latins, which André Gide compared to the 'thoroughly natural civilisation' of Greece, the feeling of alienation from the world, the sense of going but to nowhere, had benumbed large sections of the population. The kettle was boiling once again, but still there was 'no corner of comfort, no tea and no newspapers', as Vladimir Mayakovsky, the Soviet futurist poet and dramatist, might have said.

After the sacking of Syracuse, the old Greece's bastion in the West, in 212 BC, Rome was hellenised. 'Conquered Greece conquered its fierce conqueror', Horace, the first century B.C. Roman poet, acknowledged. Caesar's famous 'et tu, Brute', uttered when he was stabbed to death by the son of his former lover in 44 BC, was gasped out in informal Greek 'kai su ei ekeinon, o pai' (you are one of them, child). The Romans looked up to the Greeks with admiration, for the latter were better at everything except road building, plumbing, legal codes and military capabilities. Later on, they were also comfortable with the world-loving approach of Hellenism as opposed to the world-improving ethos of the Christian era.

But Rome, like Greece earlier, fell under the influence of oriental beliefs and practices. Even Marcus Aurelius was persuaded by a magician to throw two lions in the Danube as a means of achieving victory over the Germans. Half-comprehended religious practices from the East, together with Babylonian, Persian and Egyptian superstitions, magic and belief in karma crept further into the empire in the third century, this age of despair caused by unprecedented violence and destitution. Civilisation, as it was known until then, finally ended when Diocletian transferred the empire's capital to Nicomedia, in Asia Minor, and the Roman empire turned into a veritable oriental state. The preceding long

Roman peace, like the Hellenistic period before, had opened the gates to the notion of a universal culture, which the Romans, with diminished confidence, had eventually delivered straight into the arms of Eastern otherworldliness.

As deaf to Reason as the ass to the lyre of Apollo, and able to feel only their impotence, men and women placed all their hopes in God, whatever their understanding of deity was. In the absence of anything else to believe in, without any certainties, hope or reassurance, without even a clear identity, a divine company had, indeed, become necessary if human existence was not to be annihilated altogether. It was at this point that Christ arrived on the scene. 'What is astonishing', C.H. Sisson, the English poet and a deeply devout man, exclaimed, 'is that he came here at all where no one ever came voluntarily before'. Christ presented himself as the light, only acknowledged as such nearly four centuries later, for people refused obstinately to be convinced by his truth. The light, after all, as Kavafis said, could 'perhaps be a new tyranny'. But what Hegel called 'the objectification of the deity' had begun. It went hand in hand with the corruption and slavery of man.

The Greek awesome, breathtaking, magnificent joint venture of intellect and intuition, thinking and feeling, rationality and morality was ruthlessly destroyed by crude and monolithic mental structures, the barbarism of the centuries that followed. The Olympian system was defeated by Christianity, the empire of the Soul, which, though philosophically in debt to Plato and the Neoplatonists, adopted the dogmatism and the morals of the Jewish fundamentalists. God was there only to be killed with reverence. The mind was contemptuously dismissed in favour of the soul, and morality, confined into the bedroom of our existence where it has remained ever since, was separated from Justice. In the process, Logos was exorcised as if it were an evil spirit, and holism, which as a word is rooted in the Greek *holon*, which means whole, was replaced with a monism, which, in the name of the One, set as life's purpose the identification with the divine. Life and its pleasures were decried.

The benefits of life in the grave were, obviously, available only to those who loathed life and, particularly, their body.

3. A Theology of the Heart

The esoteric tradition of the West goes back way before Henry Ford, the car manufacturer, decreed that the only history worth a tinker's damn is the history we make today. Its origins lay in the Orphic movement whose profound mysticism exerted, through Pythagoras, an influence on the thinking of several philosophers and played a part in shaping both the Christian and Gnostic theology.

As a spiritual cult, a parareligion, Orphism appeared late on the scene, in the sixth century BC, when an upsurge of religious feeling swept through Greece. This is likely to have originated, Joseph Campbell said, in the archaic Bronze Age order, which in its last phases underwent a negative transformation. He termed the latter the 'Great Reversal'. At that time, following centuries of invasion, murder and pillage, a literature of lament arose from Egypt to Mesopotamia, and the focus moved from this world to the next. Expressing it in Greece, the Orphics renounced the pain and weariness of this world in favour of the true life in the stars, and claimed access to a mystic universe through union with God. The teachings of Orpheus himself, if he existed, are not known. Legend has it that he was the greatest musician who had ever lived and that he was reborn after his death, wiser.

Orphism developed from the 'divine madness' of Dionysos, the raving God of fertility and wine, whose cult represented the opposition to the culture of rational Greece. Its love for the primitive, a more instinctive and passionate way of life, was in constant search for *ekstasis*, a means of enabling the soul, 'out of the body', to show its true nature. *Ekstasis*, achieved by intoxication, partly physical through alcohol and hallucinogenic laurel leaves, and partly mystical, expressed itself, however, with murderous ferocity. The frenzied dances of the laurel-chewing Maenads, the female followers of Dionysos, on the bare hills for whole nights – orgiastic, savage and barbaric – included tearing wild animals to pieces and eating them raw. 'They stripped the flesh off their bodies faster than you could wink your royal eyes', the herdsman, a witness, told Pentheus, the king of Thebes, who later was to suffer the same fate at the Maenads' hands.

Orpheus, after he lost his wife Eurydice and swore never to have sex again, was himself their victim. In a frenzy of sexually crazed bloodlust that followed the murder of their husbands, the Maenads tore him limb from limb and threw his head to the river Hebrus. Reborn, and wishing that women for their amusement would instead try on each other's shoes, Orpheus condemned human sacrifice and the Maenads' promiscuity. Heraclitus, not standing for barbarity and the 'unholy manner' of those practices, exclaimed: 'They purify themselves vainly by defiling themselves with blood, as if a man who had stepped into mud were to wash with mud'. Equally disturbed, Euripides denounced the Bacchic cult of mass-emotion, the mass-surrender to the supernatural resulting in cruelty which inspired nothing but horror.

Orphism took from the Dionysian cult the ecstatic element but it spiritualised it, substituting mental for physical intoxication. The 'juice that streams from the vine-clusters to give us joy and oblivion' became a sacramental symbol taken over, together with the symbolic swallowing of the slain god and other basic elements of Orphism, by Christianity. Orphism, although it influenced Plato's *Phaedo*, never, however, gained the upper hand in Greece as similar religions did in the East. It clashed head-on with science, which checked its development and ensured its subordination to Reason. Greece, Bertrand Russell says, was saved by its scientific schools. If not for science, Greece and, as a result, Europe might well have taken the same road the Chinese, the Indian or the pre-Columbian cultures did. She might have been lost 'in some blind lobby... or corridor of Time... in the dark' with 'no thread', as Penn Warren, author of *All the King's Men*, might have put it. But, again, as someone would argue, if the sea boiled, we would have boiled fish.

From another point of view, the Orphic mysteries, a flight from the irksome demands, burdens and restrictions of civilised life, were an escape into primordial experiences through visions associated with sex, death and rebirth. This was the kind of vision the rational life of the polis could not, and would not, entertain. The price of civilisation, as Freud said, is repression and a heightened sense of guilt, and man is, as a result, not the rational, but the repressed animal. Repressed impulses reflecting the archetypal human being, though disappearing from consciousness, are nevertheless present in the unconscious, in 'the psychopathology of everyday life'. The latter, yearning for the original freedom, denies rationality. Repression and socialisation, the same reality viewed from within and without, are, thus, inevitably in an epic conflict with each other.

Interpreting the Orphics along Freudian lines, Marcuse, following Nietzsche, Schiller and Rilke, saw their cult as the 'Great Refusal' to accept the sequesteredness from the libidinous object or subject, a revolt against the realm of Reason and its culture, one based on toil, domination and renunciation. The image of Dionysos and Orpheus, and also of Narcissus, he said, is that of a world that is not to be mastered and controlled but liberated. In this joyous and fulfilling world, responding, according to Nietzsche, to 'the wonderfully alluring call of the Dionysian bird', the voice does not command but sings, the gesture offers and receives, the deed, which is peace, ends the labour of conquest. 'Being is experienced as gratification, which unites man and nature so that the fulfilment of man is at the same time the fulfilment, without violence, of nature'.

Pythagoras tried subsequently to reconcile the Orphic mystical intuition, which presupposes and demands the abdication of Reason, with rational science. His intellectual mysticism, which was dismissed by Heraclitus as 'artful knavery', intellectualised religion and spiritualised Reason. It turned religious fervour into an intellectual fervour, the religious and emotional *ekstasis* into an intellectual *ekstasis*. *Theoria*, an Orphic word meaning contemplation – in the case of Pythagoras of the orderliness of *kosmos* – was, he believed, the road to *katharsis*, the purification of the soul, and *gnosis*, 'the knowledge of things that are'.

The reputation of Pythagoras in antiquity was so great that, as Isocrates said, people who claimed to be his students received for their silence more admiration than those with the greatest oratory skills. His influence on the ideas, and thereby on the destiny, of the human race, Arthur Koestler, the former communist turned mystic, says, was 'probably greater than that of any single man before or after him'. Though perplexing, his thinking influenced profoundly, among others, Plato, St Augustine, Thomas Aquinas, Descartes, Spinoza, Leibniz, even Wittgenstein and his analytic philosophy which metamorphosed all philosophical speculation into mathematical calculation – 'Come, let us calculate'. But for Pythagoras, Bertrand Russell says, Christians would not have thought of Christ as the Word; but for him, theologians would not have sought logical proofs of God and immortality.

Religion and science came together as two inseparable aspects of a single way of life, and mathematical relations turned into the key to philosophical wisdom in its contemplation of the One. The essence and power of Pythagoras' vision lies in its all-embracing, unifying character which gave a new meaning to the philosophical holism of the Greeks. It is, however, arguable whether Pythagorianism was fundamentally a monistic philosophy, as Cornford, the English philosopher, believes, or dualistic, as Aristotle holds. The argument focuses on the exegesis of the Pythagorean belief that life consists of pairs of contraries, say good and evil, as two separate forces or as two parts of the same unity; if taken as One, the next question is whether we have a single One or a 'plurality of ones'.

Believing in metempsychosis, Pythagoras claimed to remember his own four previous incarnations. Considering also that the human soul could be reincarnated in the form of other living things, he regarded all living things as akin. A militant vegetarian, he advised his followers never to approach butchers and hunters, and he accepted women as equals in his Orphic Brotherhood. Following his death, his school did, however, split, like Hegelianism or Freudianism did later, into two sects, the Right and the Left, the mystics, ancestors of the Gnostics, who tended to be otherwordly, and the 'mathematicians', the scientists.

Though despised by rational, civilised, Greece, Orphism was officially celebrated in many cities, including Athens, in state-sponsored rituals. Likewise, its God, Dionysos, coexisting with the Olympian Gods, was properly honoured, notably in the famous Eleusinian mysteries which were both protected and administered by the Athenian polis. Exclusiveness was alien to the spirit of the Greeks. The same spirit, evident both in Hellenistic and Roman times, made possible the coexistence of all religions in a way which also enabled them to discover what they had in common. But the ground in latter times had shifted dramatically, for life had lost its authority. Reality, the material world, evil and repulsive, was not reality but a mask of it, a mere appearance behind which the real reality, celestial or divine, was hidden. This reality, God himself, would reveal itself if the soul were open. To such a soul, the Greek-Egyptian body of the Gnostics affirmed, 'nothing is invisible, not even an incorporeal thing. Mind is seen in its liking, and God in his working'.

The Gnostics, whose theology preceded that of Christianity, anxious to eliminate anything people enjoyed with or without their clothes on, led the field. Gnosticism was the religion of *Gnosis*, knowledge, the knowledge, however, of pure spirit. Man could escape to its realm by spiritual purgation usually through initiation into certain 'mysteries', in an undecodable ecstatic union with a divinity impervious to human feelings. 'Abandon the search for God, and creation', one Gnostic teacher said; 'ask who it is within you ... learn the sources of love, joy, hate and desire ... and you will find God in yourself'. The 'root of evil', too, was hidden within the self itself rather than the Satan of the Christians. *Nous*, as in Pythagoras and Plato, was superior to the soul; and the opposites, 'light and dark, life and death, good and evil', were in reality, as a Valentinian writer explained, pairs of interdependent things, each implying the other.

Their teachings leaned on the Presocratic and the Stoic philosophical tradition which was, however, robbed of its earthliness and humanism. The Gnostic Oneness was a mystic One, Oneness with God in ourselves. The Greek Holism, the Oneness in life as it manifested itself in everything, seemed as if it belonged to the age of the apes. So did the Greek concept of beauty which both Gnostics and Christians associated with the virtues of spiritual life – beauty became Seraphic and Cherubic.

In the second century, Christian Gnostic Marcion, 'the most dangerous foe Christianity has ever known', rejected the God of the Jews as a hopelessly inferior being, the product of some pre-cosmic fall and the creator of evil. The whole material universe was for him an evil place, a prison and a trap. Having been appointed for the purpose by a higher God, of which he knew nothing, he then crusaded to eradicate the Judaizing influences on Christianity. The Jewish Bible was vehemently opposed because, he held, of the perversity of its 'an eye for an eye and a tooth for a tooth' doctrine. Based upon the Old Testament, Blavatsky wrote later, the Christians extended their laws 'of conquest, annexation, and tyranny over races which they call *inferior*'.

Plotinus, the third century philosopher, founder of Neoplatonism, rejected Christianity because it personalised religion and saw salvation through faith. His own God was a supreme principle, light, or the absolute Good, something like the source of a river, separated from its lower reaches by all the intervening waterfalls. The ultimate Being, the One which was 'beyond being' as it transcended, and also was the source of everything, projects itself into lower forms, firstly through the *Nous* and then through the

Psykhe (soul) which is a projection of the *Nous*; the weaker forms, for their part, seek to return to the source, achieve mystical union with the One and experience unity with the universal principle of life and the rational order of the universe. For Plotinus, reality had a higher level not perceived by the senses, and was accessible only by intellectual intuition. 'Poor mind', the senses had asked the intellect rhetorically many centuries earlier according to Democritus: 'do you take your evidence from us and then try to overthrow us? Our overthrow is your fall'.

Neoplatonism, the fusion of Greek philosophy and Christian doctrines with Orphism and oriental beliefs, articulating philosophically the existing mystical beliefs, subsequently exerted a profound influence on medieval and Renaissance philosophy and theology. Porphyry, Plotinus' pupil and biographer, vehemently opposed Christianity because it had put Christ in the place of the One – his books were burnt in public at the end of the fifth century to the dismay of his publisher; and then Iamblichus, Porphyry's pupil, associated the Neoplatonic dogma with magic and superstition. Proclus, the fifth century A.D. philosopher, and the Gnostics of his Athens School, which in the early Christian centuries commanded the heights of philosophy, developed Neoplatonism further in a pagan, anti-Christian direction that threatened what became latter-day Christianity. Philo, 'a sort of Jewish Plato', for his part, combined it with Judaism, and so did Spinoza who combined it with the pantheistic elements of kabbalism creating a metaphysics without any supernatural deity.

Plotinus' Neoplatonism, on the other hand, as modified by Origen, who introduced an adequate Christian philosophy, and then modified again by Greek Church fathers, notably the Cappadocians, and by Latins, including St Augustine, the Pythagorean Boethius, who was executed for treason before he could work out whether squareness existed, and St Thomas Aquinas gave Christianity the foundation of its theological beliefs. Similarly important in this respect was the work of Pseudo-Dionysius the Areopagite, revered as Saint Paul's first Athenian convert – he was in all probability the bishop of Antioch Petros Grafeas, a follower of Proclus, brought to the West by Johannes Scotus Erigena, a Neoplatonist, in the ninth century.

The pre-Christian Gods, never really completely demystified, nourished the Gnostics, and enabled Gnosticism to thrive on diversity. Without feeling threatened by a multiplicity of cults, Gnosticism was, in a sense, nothing but a universal religion which attracted, as it still does, many thinkers as a means to the spiritual union of humanity. As such, it opposed, and was bitterly opposed by Christianity's monolithic consensus. 'Drive out the wicked from among you', Paul had urged the catechumens.

In the centuries that followed, the Gnostics, vague shadows in the land of a dreary obscurity, rejected all things irrelevant to God such as the authority of the Church, its hierarchies and its rituals, and opted for the concept of *ecclesia spiritualis* involving meditation and chanting. Likewise, they all called for spiritual awakening to discover the divine within and aimed at a state of *apatheia*, a nirvana, in which they could have divine visions, make eye to eye contact with Christ, John the Baptist or the Virgin, and see the future. Meanwhile, a most primitive paganism had staged a comeback with Apuleius, who recommended the worship of Isis, Apollonius, who vaunted the virtues of the Neo-Pythagoreans, or Heliodorus, who introduced the cult of Sun-worship.

Gnosticism, as a theological belief system, disappeared in the fifth century. But its mystical beliefs, and its anti-conformist spirit, survived in most of the major Christian heresies. The period did, however, end with the triumph of Christianity, a religion which, though certain of its philosophical beliefs derived from Plato and the Stoics, and certain of its theories from the Orphics and kindred cults of the Near East, was hatched in the theocratic Jewish world and its monolithic consensus. The *Torah*, the will of God as revealed in Mosaic law, lies at the very heart of the New Testament. The triumph of Christianity, 'the triumph of religion and barbarism' as Gibbon wrote, remains, however, an enigma. Christianity was a latecomer in the field, Christ was long regarded as an obscure figure, and his teachings, often confused by outsiders with Judaism, were seen as unlikely to found a religion of universal appeal. If a new religion was to replace the Olympian Gods, Gnosticism was the most likely candidate.

Christ appeared on the scene soon after the long and terrible Jewish civil wars to which the Sadducees and the Pharisees had been driven by religious madness and which had turned the 'Promised Land' of 'the people of God' into absolute hell. For the Essenes, one of the three leading Jewish sects, Armageddon seemed to be in full swing – the end of the world looked as if it was only a few prayers away.

Identifying humanity with the Jewish people, the Jewish mystics, members, as they considered themselves, of the final generation, set themselves the task of preparing, in the desert of the Dead Sea, for the ultimate battle: the planned forty-year war which would enable them, with the Messiah's help, to conquer the world. The Lord had after all promised Abraham that, in return for their exclusive loyalty, he would lead the Jews to glory. Christ, as it happened, was not their Messiah, the 'Teacher of Righteousness' they expected. His coming did, however, spring from the myths and expectations, and also from the authoritarianism, of their Dead Sea communities. Some, including the English deists, actually considered the Essenes to be the predecessors of the Christians, and, though the evidence is very confusing, others still claim that Joseph and Mary, Christ, John the Baptist, John the Evangelist and others were Essenes themselves.

The new religion instantly split the universe into two: the Christian and the non-Christian parts of it. 'There is no such thing as Jew and Greek, slave and freeman, male and female', Paul stressed in his letters to both the Galatians and the Corinthians, 'for you are all one person in Jesus Christ'. That would have been nice if Paul, formerly an anti-Christian Jewish fanatic, had not with his usual unlicensed indelicacy instructed, as a Christian, his followers 'not even to eat' with non-Christians. Christian teaching was not about reconciliation but war. 'I have not come'', Christ said, 'to bring peace, but the knife' – *machaira* in the original Greek text means knife, not sword. 'I have come to set a man against his father, a daughter against her mother, a son's wife against her mother-in-law; and a man will find his enemies under his own roof'.

Calling the faithful to love their enemies but hate their loved ones must have certainly baffled a few of the early adherents. But the early Christians did not mind challenging the family, setting its members against each other if and when this was necessary for the spreading of their religion. As Greek author Dimitris Kyrtatas pointed out, the family became 'holy' only after the fourth century, when Christianity's enemies had been defeated. Its break up has ever since become an act directed against the Christian religion itself.

Denouncing wealth as incompatible with Christian goals, Christianity looked, at first, as if it had a radical social edge: the rich seemed to be excluded by definition from the pleasures of eternal life. 'It is easier', Mark warned, 'for a camel to pass through the eye of a needle than for a rich man to enter the kingdom of God'. Luke, for his part, cautioned good Christians: 'You cannot serve both God and Mammon'. Man had to make his choice in the knowledge of both the benefits and the costs in afterlife.

But Christianity, just like Tony Blair's New Labour, had no desire to alienate the rich and powerful of the world. Hence Peter, in his First Letter, called the faithful to 'submit to every human institution ... Accept', he emphasised, 'the authority of your masters with all due submission'. Clement of Alexandria, the influential Athenian theologian of the second and third centuries AD and a saint until the seventeenth century, when Pope Clement VIII deprived him of his sainthood because of 'a certain elitism in his thought', fought passionately for the rights of the rich within the Christian communities; and John Chrysostom, a leading light of the Church, in the fourth century subsequently turned the concept of submission into a paraplegic dogma. Submitting to their masters, the Christians, he argued, were, indeed, submitting to the will of God, tasting thereby on earth the feeling of 'real freedom'. When St Anselm explained man's relationship to God, he, likewise, did so in terms of the relationship of disobedient tenants to a feudal lord. The parallelism ensured no criticism would ever be voiced against feudal masters.

The most enlightened of the Church Fathers, the Cappadocians – Basil of Caesarea and the two Gregories, all somehow appreciative of classical culture – raised social issues in the fourth century. But the new religion had not come to challenge the existing social order and its institutions, including that of slavery. The underpinning of the latter was, instead, a duty to the Lord – hence the Church of England became the owner of one of the largest slave-using plantations in Barbados.

Christianity separated God from the world, grouped its faithful, identified itself with the state and deprived religion of its essence. In their denial of Orthodox dualism, the mystics, on the other hand, saw God as a living God, who is not apart, but within all and beyond all definition. He is born, Eckhart, the German Christian mystic preached in the fourteenth century, in the soul as he is in eternity. The soul is one with God – not united; 'the Kingdom of God is within us'.

Eckhart was, of course, given something to write home about – he was excommunicated by the Pope.

4. The End of Wisdom

Christianity triumphed in the first half of the fourth century, when Emperor Constantine the Great transferred the capital of the empire to Constantinople and then proclaimed and defined for all mankind the will and nature of God. For some unknown reason, he then killed both his son Crispus and his wife Fausta. Though much later than advertised, Christianity had at last been accorded equal status with all other religions. Half a century later, in 380, Theodosius the Great declared it the only religion of the State whose refusal to accept constituted a criminal offence. The first ever Christian state, a decadent falling away from the primordiality of the Greek experience, was ironically born on the soil of Olympian Greece. Theodosius' imperial decree marked the beginning of the Dark Ages, the barbarised era that really had nothing wrong that Deukalion's Flood could not fix. Darkness leaped back with a culminating crash. The Olympians became the memory of spring – 'kind Gods', Hölderlin, the great German lyric poet, lamented, 'we are poor without you'.

With the West crumbling under the blows of the barbarian invasions, 'in outer darkness' until well beyond the times of Charlemagne, Byzantium, 'the brightest jewel of a disturbed age', as R.R. Bolgar of Cambridge University called it, enabled Christianity to win its crucial battles. The Byzantine empire, whose splendours overshadowed those of Rome and whose influence extended from Kiev and Turkestan to Syria, north Africa and Italy, had no ideology. The homogeneity of the early Greek times together with the commitment to the cultural values of the polis were not there to hold it together. Christianity was, thus, able to force the state to identify with it. Constantinople, on the other hand, looking for a unifying force, was only too pleased to use Christianity for its own imperial purposes.

Having embraced the Jewish doctrine that all Gods but one are false and evil, Christianity became a branch of imperial politics. One God and one oecumenical Emperor were destined to control the *orbis terrarum*. When in 669/70 the armies of the Empire crowned the two brothers of Constantine the IV as his co-emperors, they did so again in the name of God: 'In the Holy Trinity we believe, three Kings we crown'. God was officially objectified, the cities, 'cities of silence', were depopulated of ideas, the garden of the old world was abandoned by the birds. 'Even the chattering water dried up', an anonymous poet wrote in the fourth century. Classical morality became the prototype of evil, sagacity was whisked away by the hissing winds of bigotry, moral indignation, in our own days the prerogative of impotence, became a technique used, as Marshall McLuhan, the philosopher of the mass media, pointedly said, 'to endow the idiot with dignity'. Virtues, which for the Greeks were principles expressing dispositions, distinct from rules and law, became rules and law.

The destruction of what was left of old Greece by the Christians, those 'ignorant or unintelligent or uninstructed or foolish persons' as the second century Greek writer Celsus called them, began earnestly with a horrendous violence. Eros, 'the handsomest among all immortals', able, as Hesiod says in his *Theogony*, 'to overpower the intelligence in the breast of the human beings and all their shrewd planning', was one of the first victims of the manic Greek Christians of the third century. They turned his bronze statue in Alexandria into a frying pan. Perhaps there was some logic in it as they can both burn you, Palladas, the fourth century AD Alexandrian epigrammatist and a man trapped in poverty and a sense of futility, wittily commented. The launch of the Christian era at a time unconscious of the calamity befalling the innocent was, indeed, funny, very funny, except that it could not prove it even to itself. 'They say', Palladas again scornfully observed, that 'we, non-Christians are dead, and only seem alive. I say, we're alive but life, instead, may be not'. His epigram looked nevertheless more like a valedictory note to a disappearing age.

Hypatia, the eminent Alexandrian Neoplatonic philosopher, had no better luck at the hands of God's *Sturmabteilung*. She was lynched by Christian devotees of the new culture of love, who, in all their modesty, chose to remain anonymous. 'She was torn from her chariot', Edward Gibbon tells us, 'stripped naked, dragged to the church, and inhumanly butchered: her flesh was scraped from her bones with sharp oyster-shells and her quivering limbs were delivered to the flames' of burning books. It is the kind of story that makes one miss a night at Bates Motel. Patriarch Cyril, who orchestrated this horrendous violence, beatified by the Church, is known among good Christians as St Cyril.

'In almost every province of the Roman world', Gibbon carried on, 'an army of fanatics, without authority and without discipline, invaded the peaceful inhabitants; and the ruin of the fairest structures of antiquity still displays the ravages of *those* barbarians who alone had time and inclination to execute such laborious destruction'. The famous library of Alexandria, the jewel of the ancient world containing about 400,000 books – Greek, Egyptian, Babylonian, Jewish, Zoroastrian and Buddhist – was possibly another target of the emerging viciousness. It was destroyed, Gibbon says, by a Christian mob at the very end of the fourth century. The charge is not, however, self-evident as the famous library is likely to have also been heavily damaged by the fighting between Caesar and Ptolemy XIII in 48BC while another section of it was lost later, in the third century, when Emperor Aurelian suppressed a revolt by Queen Zenobia of Palmyra. It is also possible that part of its contents were taken to Constantinople later in the fourth century.

Books were, in any case, of no use to the fiery Christians. As contemporary fundamentalists, all those 'incapable of surmounting their ferocious goodwill' as poet Charles Causley might have said, still demonstrate, reading of anything but the scriptures is a denial of God. Knowledge, 'vain inquisitiveness', in Augustine's words, 'dignified with the title of knowledge and science', 'knowing for knowing's sake', is a sin. The only knowledge to be desired is knowledge of God. Silence notices, put up in towns, were looked upon with amazement, by, to use Byron's verse, 'the ghost of vanish'd pleasures once in vogue'. Ennobling ignorance became a precondition for Christian self-realisation. The mind, considered to be infested with demonic powers which distort and confuse our thinking, was dismissed; and grammar was made illegal but for the theological élite.

Appropriately, Palladas observed that it is not only nouns, but also poor grammarians that decline. Not surprisingly, with the possible exception of *The Divine Comedy* of Dante Alighieri, the fourteenth century poet, the thousand-year long Christian culture produced no literary work equal, even by approximation, to that of an Aeschylus or a Shakespeare.

Christian faith had achieved the objective of God, who, as Paul, in his first letter to the Corinthians, said, had promised to 'destroy the wisdom of the wise, and bring to nothing the cleverness of the clever'. Greeks, 'we no longer concern ourselves with your tenets', a delighted Tatian, the second century Christian author, acknowledged: 'we follow the word of God'. Socrates had already answered him when he said that it is only among fools that the wise are judged to be destitute of wisdom. In the new world, silent as a stone, God had, indeed, 'made the wisdom of this world look foolish'.

'Where we pass, nothing ever grows again', the prospector who represented the violent forces of capitalism cried elated in Jean Giraudoux's play *The Madwoman of Chaillot*. The Christians had certainly surpassed him. They 'mutilated', as Friedrich Nietzsche, the man who saw himself as the last inheritor of the aristocratic Greek spirit, said, 'the human spirit and its freedom'.

Assuming that nature is corrupt and the Christian Church incorruptible, free from any restraining sense of the absurd, the Christian misanthropes and their fellow-travellers denied the self's human nature. They freed it from 'the tyranny of the body'. The monks, most of whom did not work, abstained from pleasure, and did not even wash, for lice, called 'pearls of God', were a mark of saintliness. The hermits, the most extreme manifestation of early Christian rejection of life on earth, had condemned themselves to an exchange of silences and perpetual self-inflicted pain. The Platonic duality of soul-body had narcissistically turned into a theology of schizophrenic dimensions.

In the new jargon for the masses, the earth was 'the filth and mire of the world, the worst, lowest, most lifeless part of the universe, the bottom storey of the house'. Life on it was a life lived in the waiting room with no dancing girls to bring some relief to the Flagellants and make them feel human again. In a climate of flowering hysteria and profound nihilism, life on earth, this vile lowland, was seen only as a preparation for the life to come, in heaven, in the ethereal highland, divided between God at the top and the lowliest forms of existence at the bottom. Pseudo-Dionysius, who adapted Proclus' philosophy to Christianity, articulated the divine order, class structured, to perfection. This medieval universe ensured nothing could move from its preordained rank and place. Rigid, static, hierarchic, petrified, it placed its dispirited world into a deepfreeze to protect it from the subterranean winds of change and the power of Reason. What had to be defeated was the devil, omnipresent and responsible for all the ills of the world.

'The one moment abandoned the other', Odysseus Elytis, the poet, said when lamenting the death of a friend in the war, 'and the eternal sun ... suddenly left the world'. He could have said the same about the triumph of the religion of the cross. The face of Christianity is, of course, more agreeable today, but this is so only thanks to the influences to which it was subjected by secular, non-Christian and even anti-Christian forces in the last two centuries. Its transformation, anything but complete, came, however, too late. The church lights are on, but the congregation fails to show up.

Trapped, like rivers in their cemented banks, in wars, famine and epidemics, oppressed by feudal rulers and the Church, obsessed with sin, fearful of evil spirits, ignorant, superstitious and wretched, the populations of Europe had no choice but to look only to heaven for salvation. Interestingly enough, the tears which Pseudo-Dionysius' angelic orders could not even wipe off their faces, rather than lessen, increased the intensity of religious feeling; and the Church, which in the thirteenth century pronounced that 'it is a necessity of salvation for every human creature to be subject to the Roman pontiff', exploited this feeling to the full.

Preoccupied with market share, profits and power, and devoted to the pursuit of a healthy spiritual connection with its bank balance, the Church was, thus, unable to energise religious feeling. 'Truth' was in any case the least of its concerns, and virtue just an investment to cash in upon arrival in heaven. As Paul had promised the Ephesians, 'whatever good each man may do, he will be repaid by the Lord'. Antigone's sacrifice, without expectation of reward, made no sense in the context of what Kierkegaard, a very religious Christian, still called the absurdity of Christian faith.

In the spiritual vacuum created by the managers of Christianity's spiritual affairs and given the identification of Christianity with all worldly evils, the field was, thus, left open to the mystics and their 'theology of the heart', unhierarchical and close to the message rather than the messenger. For the Christian Church they were 'heresies' to be brutally suppressed. The Manichean heresy, launched by the Persian prophet Mani in the third century, combined Zoroastrian with Buddhist and Christian-Gnostic ideas. With the cheerfulness of a willow tree, it asserted that the world is corrupt because it had been created by an evil God, the Prince of Darkness, but it held that redemption was possible through personal virtue. Evil was embodied in matter, and good in spirit, the soul, which, reincarnated several times, could reach the ultimate release through illumination. St Augustine was a Manichean before he became a Catholic.

Vegan and against sex, the Cathari, a resurgent variant of the Manicheans in the twelfth century, regarded matter as essentially evil and believed that the wicked would transmigrate into the bodies of animals. Further West, Johannes Scotus Erigena, the Neoplatonist Irishman whose extensive Greek education enabled him to translate Pseudo-Dionysius into Latin at the request of Byzantine Emperor Michael III, denied God as the creator. The account given in Genesis, he said, was allegorical. His view of God as the end and purpose of all things led him to the rejection of Christian orthodoxy and to the embrace of some sort of pantheism.

The Gnostics' influence was also evident in the Paulicians, a Christian heresy of obscure origins which developed in the eastern provinces of the Byzantine empire. The Paulicians, and their *ecclesia spiritualis* which involved only gatherings for the purposes of praying, rejected the church and its hierarchy, the worshipping of the cross and the icons. The Bogomils, who were a fusion of Manicheans and Paulicians, in the Byzantine world again, rejected the cross, the icons, the sacred mysteries and the hierarchy, scorned the rich, hated the Emperor, and refused to obey any authority. Churchmen like the Patriarch Cosmas, well aware of the social origins of several of these heresies, tried to turn the Church into a responsive institution. He was, however, accused of Bogomilism himself and was driven out of his seat in 1147. The Messalians, another heretic movement, believed that in every man lives the devil in person who can, however, be expelled by continuous praying in places offering monastic life.

All those deviations from the Christian doctrines affected, in one form or another, most of Europe and, through Byzantium, reached as far as China. They all retained a pantheistic view while maintaining the esoteric tradition of their early days, the time when at nightfall one could hear only the crying of the bats.

Meanwhile, the old religious beliefs had not been demythologised. Driven underground, they had become, instead, an anti-cosmos of demons whose presence was traced everywhere, in caves and wells, animals, black Ethiopians or lascivious women sporting Prada bags and top-class lingerie. For the Christians, all bad things were the work of the devil. Even a man like Digenis Akritas, the greatest hero of the Greek Byzantine world, disclaimed responsibility for the rape of a young woman he could not resist, for it was, he said, the work of the devil. Confidence in God was shaken and individuals had no difficulty praying to the devil, 'the master of the world'. 'Eyes wide and fat with fear' were witnesses to satanic rituals inspired by opposition to the ghastly Christian love of God.

In an era armed with the sense of humour of a bat, depressed and dispirited, even laughing was thought to be unbecoming to all good and God-fearing men of Christendom. Hierocles, the

Neoplatonist philosopher who in the fifth century AD spent a life compiling the first ever collection of jokes, failed to muster more than twenty-eight. Humour, incomprehensible in the void created by intellectual vacuity, had died of incomprehension.

Mysticism flourished despite the splendid terror of the Pope's religious armies, and swayed even major thinkers like Roger Bacon, the thirteenth century English philosopher and scientist, who had placed his faith in magic and prophecies. Superstition was not the prerogative of the uneducated masses, those who thrived in their well-earned obscurity. The ruling class, too, accepted that there was in all these things 'a grain of truth'. The rulers of Pergamus, a city threatened by Arabs in 717, were, thus, happy to sacrifice an embryo and then rinse their hands in its juice in order to become invulnerable before counterattacking. The sacrifice, if anyone wonders, did not help as the Arabs took the city. Even a Byzantine Emperor, Nikiphoros the First, ordered the slaughter of a bull in a ceremony involving magic against one of his opponents, and another one, Alexander, tried to overcome his sexual impotence with the help of magicians. After he failed, he was pleased to discover that the rich, as Plato had said, when old, have many other consolations.

Black magic, associated with Ahriman, the Persian power of evil, and his followers in the world of spirits, was often mixed by the mystics with alchemy, the science of the Middle Ages. Astrology, viewed as a branch of science or even 'the Queen of all Sciences', was as widespread and used by the War Departments of all major religions. Luck was also considered to be a force ruling the world, and miracles became a frequent phenomenon from the sixth century onwards.

In the meantime, Mohammed appeared in the seventh century as another prophet empowered, this time by Archangel Gabriel, to improve the world's state of religiosity. Things, apparently, were not bad enough already. Mohammed contended that Christianity, particularly in relation to its Trinity preachings, seemed to detract from pure monotheism as preached by Abraham, the Father of the

Semitic religion, and he, 'the last prophet' after Abraham, Moses and Christ, was to put things right once and for all. A 'rightwing' purist, Mohammed demanded from his adherents adherence to a most strict code of worship, and Islam, the most proselytizing of all faiths, embarked upon a policy of conversion of the world's population to its doctrines. In its course, in 700 AD Omayyad caliph Abd' El Malik banned the Greek language from all government departments – this was the end, Fernand Braudel, the French cultural historian, said, of the *modus vivendi* by which Christians and Muslims had lived in mutual tolerance. Islam could have, indeed, confined Christianity to oblivion if Charles Martel, the Frankish ruler, had not turned back its armies at Poitiers in 732. Had he failed to, Oswald Spengler, the twentieth century German historian and philosopher, pointed out, we would have ended up with the Great Frankistan!

But at the same time, Arab philosophers introduced Neoplatonic ideas into the Muslim world, and some of the Gnostic doctrines were actually adopted by Sufi sects. The Sufis, the mystics of Islam, whose theology was formed by Plato's *Phaedo*, the Christian Monophysite and Nestorian sects and also by Buddhism and Hinduism, seek the union of man with God through the power of love. Suffering is a necessary condition.

At that stage, the Gnostics' belief that the material world had been created by an evil God as a prison for the divine in man did not seem too far fetched. Determined right from the beginning 'to overthrow the existing order', and thus silence the 'Jews (who) call for miracles' and 'the Greeks (who) look for wisdom', God had, indeed, as Paul, in his first letter to the Corinthians, said, 'chosen things low and contemptible, mere nothings'. Yet, so much wretchedness could only be the work, not of a decent God, but of a pervert. Hence Christianity, whose spiritual bottom demanded far more comfort that its head could justify, neither won nor lost the affection of the population. It bought submission by the promise of salvation or extorted it by terror.

Waves of moral disgust at the greed, simony, cruelty, lust for, and abuse of power, the wickedness of the clergy, turned the heresies into radical movements, conservative in terms of their nostalgia for a return to earlier times but also revolutionary in terms of their opposition to the existing social order. In a few instances they did, indeed, turn into political movements. But overall, into the cult of poverty, they went for personal holiness which is what made them, as allies, unattractive to the political forces hostile to the Pope. Much more interesting is, however, another feature of the mystics, the fact that, uninterested in either power or wealth, they united rather than divided the peoples of the world which the orthodox religions in the name of God did their best to split apart.

All of them were, of course, barbarically suppressed by internal Christian crusades and spontaneous massacres by mobs convinced, as Byron said, that 'all the Apostles would have done as they did'. The Inquisition, that Procrustean bed initially for Jews and Muslims and then 'heretics' and Protestants, founded by Pope Gregory IX in 1233, articulated the process to perfection: it burnt its victims. The job was carried out mainly by Franciscan and Dominican monks, 'brainsick fools' according to Desiderius Erasmus, the sixteenth century Dutch humanist and scholar. Generations of people in the West and its colonies, from Brazil to Angola and the Philippines – Byzantium was by comparison a tolerant force – were 'christened' with blood, exterminated by all those good Christians who were looking for spiritual exercise, job satisfaction and good money, the latter albeit to be paid later in heaven. The earth was stained with 'irrational streams of blood'. 'If the blood of the martyrs', Henry Charles Lea, the American medieval historian, suggested, 'were really the seed of the Church, Manicheanism would now be the dominant religion in Europe'.

But for Alice Bailey, the twentieth century mystic, and her Tibetan gurus, Christianity, although it is 'being superseded by a new formulation of truth not yet revealed', has, however, 'served humanity well'. It has 'done its divine work'.

Divine work, like a woman's work, is nevertheless never done.

If proof of it was needed, Jesus W. Christ offered it in his statement 'God wants me to be president'.

5. The Old Giant

Despite the sub-zero temperatures during the one thousand year long European winter, the spirit of Greece was anything but dead. The cultural tradition inherited from the pre-Christian past had not been interrupted, and de-Christianisation was a regular occurrence. Byzantine philosopher-Emperor Julian the Apostate, a Neoplatonist, in the fourth century even tried to revive the pre-Christian religion of the Greeks. He did not succeed, but the classical tradition, though 'distant in memory like those breasts' as Seferis might say, continued to exert a powerful appeal. Classical studies found fertile ground in the Academy of Athens in the fourth and fifth centuries, the philosophical academy of Alexandria and the Academy at Trebizond which became a renowned centre for scientific studies. The university of Constantinople which, founded in 425 by Theodosius II and recognised as such in 849, was likewise involved with secular subjects only to the exclusion of theology.

The beginning of the humanist period can be traced back in the ninth century when patriarch Photios, an avowed Aristotelian self-conscious of his Greekness, made a determined effort to reconnect with the ancient world of the Greeks. His *Bibliotheca*, a collection of extracts from 280 volumes of classical authors, was an invaluable contribution to the emergence of the new consciousness. Great eleventh and twelfth century thinkers such as Michael Psellos, the philosopher and mathematician considered to be the forerunner of the Italian Renaissance, Ioannis Italos, his student, the mystic Euvagrios, a disciple of Origen, Eustathius of Thessalonica or Michael Choniates, a humanist scholar, archbishop of Athens and political writer, had a definite preference for the values of the Hellenistic era. Indeed, Psellos, led the eleventh century mini-Renaissance, which, in the following era of the Comneni created the first age of Greek medieval humanism. As Ioannis Tzetzes, a philologist who admired the ancient culture wrote mockingly, everybody in his day produced poems: women, toddlers, artisans, and even the wives of barbarians. Old pagan cults, the worship of Pan, meanwhile kept springing up long after Christianity had won the day.

In the thirteenth century, Thomas Aquinas, the Italian theologian, discovered Aristotle, 'that buffoon who has misled the church', as Luther said later, and the first rays of sunshine broke through to the forlorn streets of the Middle Ages. Aquinas had been won over by Aristotle who, as opposed to Plato who held that true knowledge could only be obtained intuitively by the eye of the soul, stressed the importance of experience – *empeiria*. His attempt to establish the truth of the Christian religion by rational arguments did not, however, take him far. He was prevented by his dogmatic commitments which, though they left the letter of Aristotelianism intact, transformed its meaning. But the reintroduction of Reason was a break from the thousand year long Christian anti-rational tradition and the very timid beginning of a new era in which looking for the truth was not considered to be deviant behaviour.

Meanwhile the Byzantine humanism was reaching its zenith with what British historian Steven Runciman called 'the last Byzantine Renaissance'. Georgios Pachymeris, the thirteen century philosopher whose influence was evident in the work of René Descartes, Spinoza and Gottfried Leibniz, Maximus Planudes, the thirteenth to fourteenth century grammarian and theologian, Manuel Moschopoulos, the commentator and grammarian considered to be an early founder of social theory, Demetrius Triclinius, who edited the works of the Greek poets, or Nikephoros, the humanist scholar who wrote a 37-volume history of Byzantium, were among its most prominent members. They were all very familiar with the classical tradition. Meanwhile, as the urbanisation process had already began and trade was flourishing, Dionysian carnivals marginalised the circus spectacles, and anti-clericalism was on the ascendant. In an unique urban revolt in 1342, the Zealots, a secular, anti-aristocratic movement, seized power in Thessalonica and held it for eight years in the course of which they established a civic self-government, confiscated the aristocrats' wealth and ran their society along egalitarian lines.

The eyes of intelligence were opening once again, but the era was only the prelude to the intemperance of the centuries that followed. A century later, the rise of national monarchies in France and England, the emergence in Italy of a rich commercial class, the increase of knowledge in the laity and the papacy's loss of moral power created the conditions for emancipation from the authority of the Church.

The explosion, the liberation from the tyranny of the Church, the long-delayed spring-clean came in the fifteenth century with the Renaissance which reconnected, first, Italian culture with the life-enhancing Greek world, and then the learned people of the time with the brilliance of Greek art and science. 'The old giant had risen up again with renewed vigour', Max Weber noted. Europe had grown tired of sitting in one frame of mind for so long. Or, as Hölderlin put it, "Godly fire (could) not bear captivity'. Humanism, the term employed at the time, meant both reconnection with the classics and interest in man's relation to society rather than God.

The change was dramatic, phenomenal, epochal. The fire of the indomitable, inquisitive Greek spirit, as vigorous as in the times of its *acme*, reappearing in all its glory, dazzled the Europeans. Greek manuscripts, downloaded from their dusty shelves and translated by superb Greek scholars like Marsilio Ficino, Pico della Mirandola, Agostino Nifo and Zabarella, altered the philosophical discourse of the time and restored faith in human greatness. Fascinated by the ancients, whose work came to the West initially through the Arabic fringes of Europe and also the Graecophone Sicily, the humanists, as Philippe Monier, a historian, said, 'copied them, imitated them, repeated them, adopted their models, their examples, their gods, their spirit and their language'. The West became all of a sudden obsessed with the Greeks. 'There is contempt for the faith', complained the Greek theologian Gennadios who in 1454 became the Patriarch of Constantinople; people turn to Hellenism and there is 'strong infidelity everywhere'. One of the Hellenists was the 'impious and arrogant' Iouvenalios, one of the most devout disciples of Plethon Gemistos, who was accused of polytheism and also among other things of speaking against virginity and celibacy. Just before 1450 he was dismembered and, while still alive, thrown into the sea where he drowned for 'God's pleasure', as Gennadios informed us. It was one of the worst atrocities of the Greek Orthodox Church.

Ironically, at the same time classical Greece entered a second youth the Greeks themselves came face to face with a catastrophe, worse than anything they have experienced either before or ever since. On Tuesday, May the 29th 1453, a date no Greek can forget, Constantinople fell into the hands of the Ottoman Turks – Tuesdays have since been considered ill-omened days by the Greeks. 'The fount of the Muses is dried up for evermore', Pope Pius II bewailed immediately after the event, and Byron lamented many years later: 'turbans now pollute Sophia's shrine'. Greece, the West's leading light for millennia, was no more. The Turks, Henry Miller said, 'converted her into a desert and a graveyard'. The subsequent four centuries of unbroken Ottoman darkness made sure that the Greeks, when freed again and, as Seferis would say, put to sea but 'with broken oars', never really caught up with time. In the same year, 1453, but BC not AD, Moses is believed to have led the Jews to their 'promised land'.

But, as it happened, the Ottoman horror forced thousands of Greeks 'endowed with learning' to escape to Italy. They settled principally in Venice, Florence, Bologna and Rome. Venice, cardinal Bessarion observed, became 'almost another Byzantium'. The Greeks were familiar with the classical tradition – education in the Byzantine empire had not been dishonoured just as science had not been disowned – and the educated Greek of the middle ages knew the works of the ancient poets, historians, philosophers, dramatists and scientists. Their arrival in Italy helped the restoration of Greek culture in the West enormously and underpinned the Renaissance.

The heroic age of Western humanism started in 1397, when Manuel Chrysoloras, a Greek diplomat, began his Greek lectures in Florence. He was followed later by Bessarion, Argyropoulos, Theodore Gaza of Thessalonica, Chalcocondyles of Athens, George of Trebizond, Isidore of Kiev, Constantinos Laskaris, Demetrius Cydones and others, all of whom, intoxicated with the spirit of Greece, translated ancient texts and taught throughout Italy. Gemistos Plethon, the most prominent but also the last Byzantine philosopher, was the most distinguished, and also the most controversial, among them all.

A Greek nationalist passionately devoted to Greece, Plethon outraged the Christian establishment of his day by championing the abandonment of the Judaeo-Christian religion in favour of a *religion naturelle* as perceived by the Greeks. Christianity, he held, a religious neoterism that grew on falsity, had caused the destruction of Greece whose rebirth could not be achieved without the destruction of Christianity itself. His call to the Greek *ethnos* to strive for the creation of a Greek state embracing all Greeks, with its own Greek army and a social and political structure modelled on classical Athenian culture, was the first ever nationalist call made centuries before modernisation destroyed traditional societies and nationalism became a force. Plethon's last work, *Code of Laws*, was burnt by Patriarch Gennadios II and lost to mankind. The Church, Machiavelli observed one generation later, 'made us irreligious and evil... The religion of classical antiquity exalts greatness of soul'.

The new, Dionysian, spirit of the Renaissance, its exaltation of humanity, culminated in an intellectual and artistic renaissance, an orgy of art, poetry and creativity, the dance of the spirit. Greek and Roman art, the 'Pheidian forms cut out of marble Attic', inspired artists such as Leonardo da Vinci, Michelangelo, Raphael and Titian, great writers such as Boccaccio and Petrarch, whose efforts to learn Greek were not successful, and architects such as Brunelleschi and Alberti. It connected Europe to its roots, the culture of joy, its sensuality, carnal pleasures and playfulness that contrasted so vividly with the preceding madness of the religious fundamentalists. To recall Byron, 'the glasses jingled and the plates tingled' once again. 'Hard and painful virtue' is 'the extreme of madness', Thomas More decreed in 1516 in his Epicurean *Utopia* which was inspired by Plethon's treatises submitted to the Byzantine Emperor Manuel II Palaiologos that were translated and probably given to him by Erasmus. St Augustine's 'we here below are travellers longing for death' was forgotten as Christians were able to enjoy life once again free from guilt or fear. Christianity was fast losing its old yellow teeth.

Together with the classics, the West discovered the Greek scientists, too. Dioscorides' botanical work, with its exquisite illustrations, was copied and re-copied, Ptolemy's Geography with its mathematical cartography changed the picture of geography, and Galen's impressive anatomical work, transformed by the divinely gifted hand of Leonardo da Vinci into the first correct anatomical drawings, elevated him almost to the status of a God. In the pantheon of science's heroes a most prominent seat was also occupied by 'the superhuman Archimedes, whose name', Galileo said, 'I never mention without a feeling of awe'. Others included the mathematician Diophantus, the philosopher and botanist Theophrastus, the zoologist Pliny, the astronomers Philolaus, Aristarchus and many more, including of course Aristotle whose work on physics and mathematics no sixteenth century student could ignore.

The work of many of them often arrived in the West through the Arab world, which, since the translation of these texts into Arabic in the eighth century, had made striking progress in science, medicine, mathematics and philosophy. The West had nothing to compare with the great Arab thinkers of the earlier age.

Erasmus, the Dutch humanist, whose published collection of

moral sayings from the ancient world had an extraordinary appeal, influencing, among others, Rabelais, Gascoigne and Ben Jonson, declared triumphantly that the 'golden age' had come back, together with its humanism. Erasmus, whose translation of the Greek New Testament outshined the Vulgate, Thomas Hobbes, translator of Thucydides' *History of the Peloponnesian War*, Charles Blount, editor of Philostratus' *Life of Apollonius*, and Thomas Paine, the English political writer, all bitterly opposed the doctrinal and metaphysical dogmas of the church and its theocratic powers.

Great Spinoza, the Jewish atheist philosopher, in turn, returned to the roots, the Presocratic philosophy, and reasserted the Oneness of the universe, which, undivided and infinite as Parmenides had held, had one substance, 'God or Nature', uniting body and mind which Plato and Descartes had split. Spinoza differed from the mystics because of his emphasis on the power of Reason, which he thought capable of producing a rational and enlightened morality, and on the indissoluble mind-body unity. His difference from the Reason of industrialism laid in his acknowledgement of love, 'the intellectual love of God', which led him to the rejection of industry's drive towards the domination of everything.

Shakespeare, at the same time, unwilling to seek comfort in faith, and dismissive of the immortality of the soul – 'our little life is rounded with a sleep' he says in *The Tempest* – celebrated in a most unChristian manner the beauty of the world and, as in *Timon of Athens*, classical, non-Christian love. In this moment of 'joyful liberation', which relished the many pleasures of life, and allowed Greece to triumph over the Judaeo-Christian set-up, the modern world was born.

But the old order was not giving up. Revolting against both the corrupt papal authority and the intellectual and moral freedom of the Renaissance, early in the sixteenth century Martin Luther, the German theologian, launched the Protestant Reformation which eradicated the Greek philosophical thought absorbed over the centuries by Christianity. Clement of Alexandria, Origen, Athanasius,

Chrysostom, Thomas Aquinas, Augustine, the Cappadocians, Boethius, pseudo-Dionysius the Areopagite, Philoponus and others had apparently contributed only to the corruption of Christian thinking. Going back to the roots meant that the Christian religion had to return to the aphilosophical, raw moral code of the Old Testament best represented in our days by the US evangelists. As Greek novelist Emannuel Roides said scornfully in his *Pope Johanna*, a historical novel, Christianity became something like garlic sauce without the garlic. Incidentally, too, as scholar Demetrios Dedes reminded me, Christ became Jesus. *Christós* in Greek means the 'anointed one' but later on was identified with Logos, albeit the *christós* Logos. Jesus is a word which, though Hellenised, derives from the Hebrew *Yehoshua*.

Further, in his drive towards 'modernisation' Luther and, what Hegel called, his 'Christian police institutions' objected to Reason, 'the Devil's Whore', which had to be rejected by anyone who wanted to enter the kingdom of heaven. Like Calvin, the French Protestant theologian who was forced to flee to Switzerland, Luther also considered Copernicus a 'fool' – his truth was, obviously, fatal to the truth of the Bible. Aristotle, this 'blind heathen teacher', was in his black books, too, for, as everybody knew, he had been sent by God 'as a plague upon us on account of our sins'. Speaking on the subject of 'Christian Nobility', Luther urged the faithful to ignore Aristotle's *Ethics* as 'no book is more directly contrary to God's will and the Christian virtues' than his. Still, although preoccupied with theology, Luther's century, by accepting the principle of individual conscience over ecclesiastical authority, prepared, against Luther's own will, the ground for modernity's inwardness and individualism.

Hostility to the bright spirit of Greece emanated from another quarter, too, for the age had retained the preceding centuries' superstitious beliefs, even witnessing a revival of the swirling occult of the Hellenistic times. Ficino translated most of the Renaissance's occult texts into Latin, including what was believed at the time to be the work of Hermes Trismegistus, an Egyptian seer of very old times. Like Mirandola, who believed that nothing gives 'more certainty of Christ's divinity than magic and kabbala', Ficino, a Neoplatonist, did not consider occultism incompatible with Christianity. The return to supernaturalism, which discredited the classical tradition, was noticeable mainly in Prague where, at the end of the sixteenth century, Emperor Rudolf II established what one author called an 'academy of the occult'. Alchemists who flocked to it 'like gnats to sweet wine' turned alchemy into 'the greatest passion of the age'.

Following in the steps of Roger Bacon, the thirteenth century English polymath, they combined chemistry, or iatrochemistry in the case of Paracelsus, with the search for spiritual rebirth. Its first principle was the existence of a certain Universal Solvent, *menstruum universale*, which possesses the power of removing all the seeds of disease from the human body, of renewing youth, and prolonging life.

The alchemists, whose ranks included outrageous fakers and phonies like Edward Kelley, and also people like Johannes Kepler, the German astronomer, who believed he held the key to the structure of the universe exactly as it was in God's mind at the Creation, and Giordano Bruno, the philosopher who was attracted to the magical tradition of Hermes Trismegistus and was sent to the stake by the Inquisition in 1600, presented their findings in the language of mystical Christian symbolism. All of them were violently opposed to the Greeks. For Francis Bacon, who had adopted a spiritualistic view of the world, the study of Aristotle was a great waste of time. Paracelsus, the sixteenth century Swiss physician, more enthusiastic in his denunciations, used to start his lectures by burning books of the Greeks.

The Middle Ages finally ended with the arrival of the age of Enlightenment, and repressed sexuality could express itself again with something more substantial than a small 'Oh', as in 'Oh dear'. By 1700 the mental outlook of educated men, urged later by Goethe to 'reach towards the highest form of existence', was completely modern. Reason, reborn, was, however, murdered in its youth; and man and nature were marginalised once again. The Enlightenment passed a Clean Air Act only to necessitate the passing of a second one which is nonetheless still waiting to be drafted. From the one extreme we succeeded in effortlessly reaching the other.

But, as Virginia Woolf's Mr Pepper might say, there is nothing to regret in life except our fundamental defects which no wise man regrets.

6. The Age of 'Reason'

The Enlightenment, displacing the prejudice and superstition, bigotry and brutality, the crudity of the age of unreason, promised that the horrors of the Dark Ages were a thing of the past. Light, as Kant said, had triumphed over the powers of darkness. Reason, which following the decline of hell, took the place of faith, would not allow a rerun of the medieval show. Christianity, Voltaire, Diderot and Holbach held, represented a barbarian, oriental, superstitious world, maintained in power by force. Its absurdities, Montesquieu, Condorcet and Rousseau, too, asserted, could no longer be tolerated. The new man, the autonomous individual, Denis Diderot, the eighteenth century French philosopher, proclaimed, is an investigator who 'trampling underfoot prejudice, tradition, venerability, universal assent, authority – in a word everything that overawes the crowd – dares to think for himself, to ascend to clearest general principles, to examine them, to discuss them, to admit nothing save of the testimony of his own reason and experience'.

Sapere aude! – Dare to know! Kant, likewise, urged the emerging new world. Think, use your own Reason against any kind of imposed or external authority, spread light into the dark corners of the human mind. Greece was back with a vengeance.

From then on, knowledge, whether about nature, society, morality, politics or history, taken away from the clergy, was to be scientific. Nothing would be accepted any longer without verification. Proceeding at a breathtaking pace, science did, indeed, transform, the face of the planet. But so did the political principles which the Enlightenment espoused: popular sovereignty, equality before the law, individual liberty and the brotherhood of men united by Reason in the pursuit of knowledge, democracy and progress. Progress, the *philosophes* of the Enlightenment believed, was possible because humans were basically good, not fundamentally evil as Christianity had taught. The French Revolution, with a huge debt to the Enlightenment, made sure that these ideals did not remain the property of an intellectual élite.

The Enlightenment, long dismissed in England as 'shallow and pretentious intellectualism', was optimistic and positive, a call for freedom, democracy and equality, for the freest possible development and expression of one's own personality. Diderot saw Reason and *sensibilité* walking hand in hand, and Kant, likewise, combined the power of the intellect with the heart's commands. Athens, 'a sort of heavenly city', in professor Richard Jenkyns words, 'a shimmering fantasy on the far horizon', was once again the model, particularly in Germany where the 'New Humanism' was initiated. The greatest German minds from the mid-eighteenth century onwards – Winckelmann, Schiller, Hegel, Goethe, Hölderlin, Nietzsche and Marx – were taken by the 'eternal charm' of Greece to such an extent that a book published later in the twentieth century chose as its subject *The Tyranny of Greece over Germany.*

As soon, however, as the principles of the dawn were grounded, modernity, on the blue horse of its insanity, betrayed itself and the human spirit. It turned into the vandal to shame all vandals. Thought inspired by the inquisitive culture of the Greeks, it replaced Christianity's dogmas with its own absolute truths. Instead of priests we now had scientists. Geometry, Johannes Kepler said, preceded the creation of the world and gave God a model for its decoration;

'God', Paracelsus triumphantly boasted, 'can make an ass with three tails, but not a triangle with four sides'.

Descartes' *Cogito ergo sum!* – 'I think, therefore I exist', which provided the intellectual justification of the individual's search for knowledge, became ever since the neutral, value-free, objective image of pure science as the sole force capable of leading the world to its truth. Science itself, instead of searching disinterestedly for the truth, turned into a tool of big business and the military, and through the development of means for mass destruction it has prepared the suicide of mankind. 'The drama of progress', Theodor Adorno, the influential German sociologist and political thinker, said, has only taken us 'from the slingshot to the megaton bomb'. Progress, science or objective knowledge gave us cars, digital television or means of arresting the ageing process. But fatally it ended up by eating its own tail. 'You are my creator, but I am your master; obey', the monster tells Baron Frankenstein. Logos, just like chivalry or town-criers in our days, was a thing of the past.

The two independent realms of Descartes, that of mind, *res cogitans*, and that of matter, *res extensa*, brought nearly to completion the dualism which had begun with Plato. For Western man, whose intellect had been sedated by the Church, existence was now completely identified with the mind. As a result, Europe went straight from the religious extremism of the Middle Ages into the extremism of a Reason that denied the spirit, the soul and the body, and also nature.

Reason, called by Heidegger 'the most stiff-necked adversary of thought' and denounced by Marcuse as the repression and renunciation of the instinctual, aesthetic and expressive aspects of our being, subjugated everything to its own narrow aims. 'As the absolute model of knowledge and the measurement of all truth, science became the tool to master the universe, 'to make ourselves', as René Descartes proclaimed, 'masters and possessors of nature'. Descartes, though he claimed he was a Catholic, never escaped the Vatican's wrath for having set the stage for the destruction of the medieval Christian worldview and the 'death of God'. To make matters official, in 1994 Pope John Paul actually denounced Descartes' evil influence to the satisfaction of a crowd clamouring for Christian clarity. The edge of anger, 'the spring of all life's horrors' as Euripides put it, is in some instances never blunted.

True, good and right were identified with what was, and still is, true, good and right for capitalism itself. Economic growth, which Aristotle had already warned could not be an end but only a means to an end, became the new God to worship. Enmeshed in a net of means, Reason became exclusively instrumental, and destroyed the humanity it first made possible. The Enlightenment, in the form of instrumental rationality, Jürgen Habermas, the German philosopher and a leading contemporary representative of the Frankfurt School held, instead of a means of liberation turned out into a new source of enslavement. While proclaiming the universal values of Reason and freedom, Michel Foucault, the French philosopher, also stated, it was supported by their very opposite, a tightly knit system of domination and repression. It led, as T.S. Eliot, an influential voice of his disillusioned generation said, to 'the deformation of humanity'.

With a view uninterrupted by humans, rationality became the condition of efficiency and profitability, the means to control nature, society and the individual, culture, art and science. This is what robbed man of his spirit and pulverised his earlier aspirations, imprisoned him in the illusions created by the forces of the market, and disempowered him.

Europe, the world were taken by storm. The emerging capitalist eternity brutally colonised and dominated all 'underdeveloped' peoples in the name of Reason, enlightenment and progress. Its intellectual arrogance and universal truths forced mankind to conform with European preconceptions; its controlling drive made democracy the servant of big money; and its greed exploited and repressed the working class at home.

The 'almost miraculous improvement in the tools of production',

Karl Polanyi, the economist-philosopher, said, was matched by 'a catastrophic dislocation of the common people'. E.P. Thompson, the eminent British social historian, made the case brilliantly in his classic *The Making of the English Working Class*. The experience of the industrial revolution's immiseration, he said, came upon those who served it in a hundred different ways: for the field labourer, the loss of his common rights and the vestiges of village democracy; for the weaver, the loss of livelihood and of independence; for the child, the loss of work and play at home; for many groups of workers whose real earnings improved, the loss of security, leisure and the deterioration of the urban environment. This violence was done to human nature. In this sense, we may still read it, like Marx, as the violence of the capitalist class.

From another standpoint, it may, however, be seen as a violent split between the traditional community and patriarchal ties, the technological differentiation between work and life. For, E.P. Thompson wrote, what casts the blackest shadow over the years of the industrial revolution, which arrived with the smile of a tornado, is the general pressure of long hours of unsatisfying, immoderate labour under severe discipline for alien purposes. That was the source of the pain which inspired much of Charles Dickens' fiction, and of the 'ugliness' which, as D.H. Lawrence wrote, 'betrayed the spirit of man'. Dickens himself had to work from the age of twelve in a blacking warehouse, and Lawrence, one of five children of a miner, had to give up his education at the age of 15.

Sharing the modernist beliefs, the social scientists, too, attempted to understand human nature in terms of general laws on the model of physics. Reason was supported in this by an empiricism associated with John Stuart Mill and Herbert Spencer, that 'mediocre thinker' whose influence, Hobsbawm, the British Marxist historian, said, was then greater than any other's anywhere in the world. Empiricism discouraged 'useless speculation' about consciousness and human nature, values, feelings and spirituality. Unconcerned with human ends, it valued only the skill of the process, a form of madness, as

Bertrand Russell said. Progress, indeed, though married to science and technology, sleeps habitually with madness.

Human relations, objectified, turned into mere commodities, and facts were separated from values, which, not being a measurable quantity, were dismissed. In the new world of the industrial Middle Ages, there was no room for ethics or purpose other than economic growth and the financial benefits associated with it, no space for the holistic understanding of the Greeks whose sunshine had been robbed of its sun. Its 'V' sign was not for victory but vultures, though the latter, in spite of the bad publicity they have received, never attack even the smallest living creature. 'Love, where is thy church?' George Seferis, the Greek poet who won the Nobel Prize for Literature in 1963, wondered in despair.

The most influential thinkers of the nineteenth century, Comte, Darwin and Marx, all believed in the absolute truths of science. Auguste Comte, the French philosopher and social theorist, coined the term 'positivism' to describe the 'scientific' status of historical laws and to comprehend social realities. His theory rejected everything that could not, in principle, be empirically verified, and asserted arrogantly that human behaviour, institutions and political organisation could be interpreted, even controlled, as if they were machines or substances. That was Comte's principle of the unity of the sciences which was used to dehumanise humans, even treat them as a herd whose social consent, as H.J. Eysenck, the disagreeable behavioural scientist, said, could be 'engineered'.

Happiness, an immeasurable quality impossible to verify statistically, was left for dreamers and poets. Values were dismissed as nonsense. A new religion, the cult of the fact, swept Europe; it is still enthusiastically subscribed to in our own days even by the fact-free tabloids.

Charles Darwin, who developed what the evangelists call the 'satanic doctrine' of evolution, and Karl Marx found truth in the material laws governing society. 'Just as Darwin discovered the law of development of organic nature', Engels wrote in the climate of intellectual euphoria that had crept in, 'so Marx discovered the laws of development of human history'. Like Hegel who had placed unbounded confidence in progress, demonstrable if only we turned a 'rational eye' to look for it, the Marxists subsequently never questioned its merits. Marxism, Maurice Thorez, the celebrated French Communist party leader, said at a time when one could make such statements without fear of ridicule, is a 'proven, scientific theory'.

Historical materialism became economism, man *homo economicus*, and human interactions relationships between commodities, a process which Lukács called reification. Marxism, Soviet Marxism in particular, never understood that human beings have their place in the world as distinct and unique individuals – that they are subjects, not objects. The Marxists, the elder generation of them, were, thus, able to claim, together with the Liberals, all the honour of the Enlightenment's crude rationalist tradition which generated the worship of progress on which the current materialistic utopianism rests.

Utilitarianism, the dominant ideology of the industrial revolution and beyond to our time, dictated an understanding which legitimises what maximises our benefits. It became one with eudaemonism. Good and right make sense only when the pleasures outweigh the pain. It is, as Jeremy Bentham, the English philosopher and jurist, said, the sum of pleasures minus the pains.

Its early and predominantly English philosophical contingent, Bentham, Mill and, at the end of the nineteenth century, Henry Sidgwick, defined moral virtue in terms of the pleasure the individual derives from his choices. Economist Gary Becker, the 1992 Nobel laureate, took the concept a step further, when he argued that our personal behaviour is defined by the market. Even marriage, he held, is to be judged in the 'marriage market' in terms of profit and loss – parties, he said, would only sign up to marriage if they thought it might be profitable to do so. The anaemic assumption behind his thesis, rooted in a mathematical theory called game theory according to which people are concerned only with maximising their utility, questioned by behavioural economics, a hybrid of economics and psychology, is nevertheless in the foundations of modern politics which treat people like calculating machines. One can only expect that people will act accordingly.

Morality, having nothing good in itself, is determined, as in a pizza festival or a Harrod's sale, by the happiness or the cash benefits it delivers. The notion, backed up by Methodism, this 'desolate inner landscape of utilitarianism', as E.P. Thompson described it, did not work to the benefit of the greater number. It only maximised capitalist profits. Methodism, E.P. Thompson said, just 'forged the last links of the utilitarian chains riveted upon the proletariat'.

Pragmatism, that quintessentially American approach hostile to theory, and utilitarian in its beliefs, was rooted, likewise, in ideas which, as William James, the nineteenth century American pragmatist philosopher, said, we can 'assimilate, validate, corroborate and verify'. These are, of course, the ideas which have a practical usefulness, i.e. pay off. Reason, Charles Peirce, another American pragmatist, elaborated, is only what we choose to believe; and what we choose to believe is as good as its practical results, i.e. success. Meaning and truth were relegated to the second division, torn apart – Kierkegaard's subjectivism, his 'I', taken from its metaphysical heights to the streets of New York, had to become inevitably streetwise to survive.

Taking the same dogma to politics, John Dewey, the last major American pragmatist, gave it a populist twist. His aim was to reconnect philosophy with the human values of the early Greek times. In doing so, he directed it, however, towards an instrumentalism which was totally alien to the Greeks. Men, Alexis de Tocqueville, the French political thinker, said nearly one and a half centuries ago, contracted the ways of thinking of the manufacturing and trading classes, and forced their imagination to fly to the level of the earth.

Modernism, the Empire of the Mind, had reinstated Reason to its ranks but only in order to kill its spirit at leisure. Reason, taken out of its moral context, and thereby desacrilised, turned into the means to master the world – to conquer, dominate, exploit and destroy. The world, high on the scent of money, was no longer, in Hölderlin's verse, 'touched by the spirit of the sun'. Freedom and Justice, on which morality ought to rest, became words which, signifying nothing, were only used as bricks to build walls behind which we can hide. The whole, objectified, was split between its constituent parts, which have all been, in turn, commodified. Nothing in our fragmented, digitally confused universe has an intrinsic value and nothing is valued except as a means to an end which is itself as confused as a fish caught in the net.

What we have today, in our languid, unrecommended times, is neither God nor Reason, but the desiccated footsie logic of the stock exchange; 'heaped papers, trifling cares, small wretched sorrows' as Costas Cariotakis, the Greek poet, wrote just before he 'died of disgust' in the first half of the last century aged 32. 'Destruction shines with such beauty', Margaret Atwood, that great novelist once described by *Time* magazine as 'the mistress of controlled hysteria', melancholically reflected.

It is not, of course, that 'mankind' did not gain from 'civilisation'. Making the case for it half way through the nineteenth century, John Stuart Mill referred to the physical comforts, the advancement and diffusion of knowledge, the retreat from superstition, the softening of manners or the progressive limitation of the tyranny of the strong. But, on the other hand, he said, the price paid for these gains was high – the loss of proud and self-reliant independence, the slavery to artificial wants, the effeminate shrinking from even the shadow of pain, the dull, unexciting monotony of life, a life with no blame and no praise, and the passionless insipidity, and absence of any marked individuality, in people's character. It looks as if we cannot escape our destiny. The principles of progress, Nestroy, a Viennese playwright, remarked, have failed to abolish destiny. The tale is still being told, if I may borrow a line from Dante's *Divine Comedy*, 'in words of flowing tears'.

Despite the tremendous advancements in all fields of knowledge, the rationality that enabled Europe to emancipate itself from the tyranny of the altar and the crown brought mankind back into the arms of a new absolutism as controlling as the one it had deposed. In the smoke of all those burnt out expectations, the powerful of this world succeeded in turning enlightened Reason, which had sought the truth, into an instrumental rationality which, reduced to technical talk about means and divorced from ethics, served only their own goals, purposes and interests. Whatever did not, and still does not, fit in with the crude materialism which our world calls rational thinking has become irrational. Irrationality, modernism's madness, has become Reason. We may not know where we are riding to, but we are making progress. 'Don't ask me', Freud says Itzig answered when asked to state his destination; 'ask the horse'.

Yet the Enlightenment, what Jürgen Habermas called the 'unfinished project', which is eagerly held in humanity's toil-embrowned hands after the long and unlamented winter of the Middle Ages, cannot be discarded. It cannot be dismissed because modernism distorted its values, and it cannot be replaced by either postmodernist cynicism or a New Age mysticism which evokes living memories of sinister political and intellectual currents in European history. The Enlightenment's dialectical continuation is vital but, as Professor Terry Eagleton, the British critical theorist, remarked, it demands the affirmation of its essence with the rejection of its distortions. In a world which is no longer as monolithic as it used to be, it also necessitates a new interpretation of its basic tenets. Contemporary philosophy, Habermas emphasised, needs to be post-metaphysical, and yet not post-rational.

For Nietzsche, a new future, post-postmodernist so to speak, would have to reappropriate the Greek values the Enlightenment endorsed and betrayed. But these are, of course, 'generalities', and 'generalities' in a society of 'fret-sawyers and stamp collectors', as Aldous Huxley, the English novelist commented before he left for

California where he plunged into Eastern mysticism, are 'evils', albeit 'intellectually necessary'.

But as an Indian inscription reminds us, 'there are so many daybreaks that have not yet dawned'.

7. A Life-destroying Culture

The opposition to the soul-destroying elaborate errors of the industrial revolution and its twin Gods, speed and noise, and also to the Enlightenment's conviction that Reason alone could unlock the mysteries of the universe began with the eighteenth century anti-rationalistic, anti-Enlightenment philosophers – Vico, Georg Hamann and Johann Gottfried Herder. Reactionary theologians were at the forefront of the counter-attack. Vico, the Italian philosopher of history, turned his attention to mythology and to symbolic forms of expression used by primitive societies, and Hamann, a theologian with an extremely conservative background, saw the philosophical issues of his day in theological terms. So did Herder, another theologian. They all opposed the Enlightenment's conviction that knowledge could be attained through Reason alone, rejected rationality because, as Hamann said, 'the heart beats before the head thinks', and denied the existence of a common, universal human nature. The Greek inheritance was anathema to them.

David Hume's scepticism, and its inherent conservatism as manifested in his docile acceptance of the *status quo*, was a weapon in their struggle against Kantian rationalism. Hume, though irreligious, doubted the power of Reason to define the individual, morality and the world or to access the truth. This did not prevent him, however, from endorsing the passions of his century's propertied classes, including that for female chastity, a means of passing property safely to a man's legitimate heirs.

Like Pyrrho of Elis – who held that arguments in favour of a belief are never better than those against it, and man, therefore, should not bother all that much about anything and live by appearances – Hume was ready, as he wrote, to 'look upon no opinion as more probable or likely than another'. Hence his advice was to follow our nature and, perhaps, enjoy like him, the company of good friends and a game or two of backgammon. Hume's scepticism was moderated only by his belief that 'nature breaks the force of all sceptical arguments in time'. 'Philosophy', he explained, 'would render us entirely Pyrrhonian were not nature too strong for it'. His naturalism brought him close to Rousseau except that when the latter visited him in England the two could not stand each other.

These anti-Enlightenment views were taken up by the Romantics, who, in spite of their debt to Rousseau, who profoundly influenced romanticism in literature and philosophy in the early nineteenth century, were at first mainly German. Concerned with the 'soul', they rejected the orthodox cognitive understanding of values, the universal standards to which all human activity had to conform, the objective criteria by which art or morals had to be judged, and industrialism, greed and the exploitation of nature. Breakfasting on feelings and poems, trying to charm the moonlight, and unconcerned about what the contemporary Greek poet Manolis Anagnostakis called 'the epic of the everyday', they favoured, instead, histrionic sincerity and melodramatic passion.

Science was denounced by Jean-Jacques Rousseau, the first Romantic, for the ruin and corruption it had brought on the human race. All ills, he said, derived from civilisation – culture denies nature. Fashionable, instead, became the distinctly human, 'subjective', evaluative reality of the individual, and human subjectivity with all its inner invisibilities, itself dissociated completely from 'inhuman' objectivity. In the new emotionally coloured culture, in which the Diana syndrome is enveloped, passion, feelings and intuition became much more important than Reason, calculation and intellect. The rules of the new game, inherently relativistic, entitled everybody to a personal and arbitrary opinion, with no need to explain it by reasoning.

Driving a coach and six horses, the Romantics embarked on a journey away from their time, to a lost home or haven. Theirs was the search of the pearl for its oyster. To reverse the march towards 'progress', many of them, full of nostalgia for *temps perdu*, embraced the simplicity of the Middle Ages, the time when, as Robert Bloomfield, a working class English poet, versed, 'the chatt'ring dairy-maid immerses in steam, singing and scrubbing midst her milk and cream'. John Clare, another English working class poet who spent the last twenty years of his life in a madhouse, longed, too, for the days the shepherd 'from labour free, dances his children on his knee'. J.R.R. Tolkien, creator of *The Lord of Rings*, condemned the world of street-lighting and cars, and so did Ludwig Klages, who, in his notion of cosmic love, wanted a return to pre-industrial stability, the 'divinely willed' natural rhythms of the Middle Ages.

Likewise, they extolled the simple, 'organic' community of the Middle Ages. 'Organic' development, as opposed to 'mechanical', something in the context of which things 'grow' rather than 'are made', was hailed as a welcome alternative to individualism, social instability and cultural discontinuity. The word 'holistic', of more recent origin, was not used, but the community, in opposition to capitalist individualism, was linked to a holistic way of life, albeit medieval in its outlook and repressive, as the whole was superordinate to its parts. The Romantics' contempt for commerce, finance, and the 'unnatural' life of the big cities was undisguised, as was their opposition to classicism, socialism, democracy and the universalism of the Enlightenment. Essentially anti-materialists, some of them did embrace what Marcuse called 'a heroic pauperism', an ethical transfiguration of poverty, sacrifice, and a folkish realism.

Novalis, Tieck, Schelling and the Schlegel brothers, stretching their arms, as Milan Kundera said, 'to the outer reaches of non-being', delivered themselves intellectually to otherworldliness and death. Life, as Peruvian poet César Vallejo would have said, was in the mirror, and they were the original – death. Goethe, who at his most unforgiving dismissed them as 'sick' individuals, said sarcastically they were trying 'to represent more than nature had granted them'. Heinrich von Kleist, the great dramatist, though not medievalist and as unchristian as Shakespeare and Goethe, was also taken by the dark winds of passion: his *Penthesilea* was a hymn to death and insanity – Kleist actually, when his neurotic state was radicalised, ended his life by committing suicide. 'A desire for that life in death for which the centuries are but a moment' overwhelmed other Romantics, too, like the great nineteenth century Spanish poet Gustavo Adolfo Bécquer, or the Greek Romantic poet Pericles Yannopoulos. The latter killed himself spectacularly while riding a white horse in the midst of the raging sea.

Inspired by an almost religious regard, a reverence for 'nature' which was imputed with a mythical originality, the Romantics celebrated it as an 'organism', the spiritual substance of which, Schelling, the main philosopher of the Romantic circle, held, could not be understood by rational and analytical means but by intuition, perception and feeling. 'Rootless' Reason was placed under the heteronomy of the irrational. 'The world', Novalis, one of the first German Romantics, said, 'must be romanticised to bestow a high sense upon the common, a mysterious appearance upon the ordinary, the dignity of the unknown upon the well-known'.

Indeed, some of them developed an attitude with non-Christian, if not actively anti-Christian features – nature had something 'divine' or 'divinely willed'. Friedrich Schelling, the principal philosopher of German Romanticism, and also Johann Gottlieb Fichte and Arthur Schopenhauer, the man who Nietzsche said 'blundered in everything', influenced by a mysticism which had its roots in Boehme and Eckhart, began to develop a new kind of theology. The living world and its active moral order, Fichte, the German idealist philosopher, said, is itself God. We need no other God. Schopenhauer, for his part, decided that the universe is meaningless much as the individual is of no value. Blind, cruel and meaningless, life takes us only through extremes of pain and suffering about which we can do nothing, for everything is determined by the blind striving of Will.

Many of them did, however, engage in a robust criticism of industrialism, albeit from a conservative, aristocratic and even reactionary point of view. Robert Southey, the English 'Lake poet', saw in it a physical and moral evil in proportion to the wealth it created; Thomas Carlyle cried that 'men have grown mechanical in hand and in heart'; and Samuel Taylor Coleridge, the English poet and critic, described the philosophy of mechanism as the 'death' of 'everything that is most worthy of the human intellect'. Poet William Wordsworth and novelists Dickens, Kingsley and George Eliot were also involved in social criticism, and so was poet John Keats, who, committed to the Greek passion for beauty because, as Shelley said, 'he was a Greek', was, nevertheless, aware of the susceptibility of high Romanticism to mockery. Keats' preface of his *Endymion*, which retold the love of Goddess Selene for young Endymion, expressed with charming modesty his hope that he just had not dulled the brightness of Greece's beautiful mythology.

Objecting to Reason and the engine-driven new culture, they all rejected the theoretical, 'objective', non-evaluative, study of the non-human 'objective' reality as represented by science, and denounced the destructive powers of capitalism. But they also, all but the most radical of them, opposed the Enlightenment which they associated with atheism and the French revolution. Though profoundly religious, God, for them, was not, however, the Christian God: for Wordsworth God was 'a motion and a spirit that impels all things'; and for Coleridge 'one intellectual breeze at once the soul of each, and God of all'. Oscar Wilde, sceptical of Christianity and dismissive of the Bible – 'when I think of all the harm that book has done', he said, 'I despair of ever writing anything to equal it' – God was, as for Thales, Heraclitus or Democritus, 'part of every rock and bird and beast and hill, one with things that prey on us, and one with what we kill'.

Though they opposed, like the Radicals, the annunciation of Acquisitive Man, the Romantics failed, however, like them, to see a common future and create anything resembling a common action plan. 'In the failure of the two traditions to come to a point of junction', E.P. Thompson opined, 'something was lost. How much we cannot be sure, for we are among the losers'.

Thomas Carlyle called for balance, the satisfaction of both the inward and the outward claims of man. 'Undue cultivation of the inward leads to idle, visionary, impracticable courses', he said, and undue cultivation of the outward 'must in the long run, by destroying Moral Force, which is the parent of all other Force, prove not less certainly, and perhaps still more hopelessly, pernicious'. Carlyle, longing for a return to feudalism, was no friend of the 'masses', 'the great unwashed', just as Edmund Burke, the eighteenth century British political thinker, was hostile to the mass of men, this 'swinish multitude', and its revolutionaries. Hence Burke's call was for the reinstatement of the old style 'organic society' that was being broken by the new forces of capitalism, to ensure continuity in human affairs. His proposed partnership was to be 'not only between those who are living, but between those who are living, those who are dead, and those who are to be born'.

Burke's 'organic community', like that of the other medievalists was nevertheless inspired by the Middle Ages rather than Greece, whose history, Burke said, was 'but one tissue of rashness, folly, ingratitude, injustice, tumult, violence and tyranny'. The classical tradition carried no favours with the right wing opponents of the Enlightenment.

The Romantic attachment to the idea of an organic community had, however, another, and sinister side. The organic, in political theory, was represented by the Volk, which, by marginalising outsiders, was linked to authoritarianism. The whole idea emerged at the time when the industrial revolution was dissolving the old social order in favour of a new, anonymous one in which the individual needed, in order to survive, to feel a sense of belonging to a folk and its culture. It is the same need that today manifests itself so powerfully in football culture, the anti-EU backlash or the anti-globalisation movement against the creeping homogenisation of life. At the same time, capitalism needed a central political authority, and the Romantic rhetoric of distinct 'natural-organic' units, i.e. culturally identifiable nation-states, fitted the bill splendidly. This, Ernest Gellner, the social anthropologist, said, is how nationalism was born. Its irrational givens – nature, folkhood, blood and soil, and the cult of innate personality and natural nobility – were played against 'rootless' Reason.

Nationalism and religion fused particularly in the music of Richard Wagner, which 'unpatriotic' Goethe denounced as 'neo-German, religious-patriotic art'. The 'organic order of life' expected fulfilment of the individual's destiny as a result of that person's participation in the life of the whole. Rousseau's call for the submission of the individual to the 'General Will' – his model was Sparta rather than Athens – amplified the Romantics' understanding of the whole as did Carlyle's leading principle of a strong leader to be revered by the masses. Max Scheler, 'the Catholic Nietzsche', sought, likewise, a return to aristocratic values and the establishment of a new spiritual aristocracy to re-establish noble and heroic models of life through youth movements. Out of this Wagnerian attitude developed the organic doctrine of history with its natural laws which provided the intellectual basis for chauvinism and racism as full-fledged ideologies.

Mussolini, Hannah Arendt said, was one of the last heirs of this movement. Still, the unification of society, which the national socialists failed to achieve, is today being realised on a global scale by the market forces and the power of consumption. But ideology, a product of the Romantic age which, as Ionesco said, has not managed to abolish fear, pain or sadness as yet, has not given up the ghost. Even if postmodernism has officially proclaimed its end, it survives menacingly in the resurgent fundamentalism, Christian, Jewish and Islamic, and their political formations. It can be traced in nearly all -isms.

Influenced by the Germans, the British Romantics, in turn, exerted a powerful influence in nineteenth century France. Meanwhile, the 'I' had become more significant than the commonly shared human realities. The cult of 'personality', the natural nobility of the individual, whose eccentric or, even better, mad opinions were sufficient to turn him into a 'genius', became the Romantics' response to a class-dominated society and also to the socialists' class-based politics.

The intensity of the French Romantics as represented by François-René Chateaubriand, Lamartine, Charles Baudelaire, Arthur Rimbaud and Lautreamont was close to that of the existentialists of the twentieth century. Fyodor Dostoevsky, the Russian novelist, in the same tradition, in his *Notes from the Underground*, urged his readers to 'kick over all that rationalism at one blow, scatter it to the winds ... and live once more according to our own foolish will'. Even a stupid, non-rational desire, he said, may be better than anything else on earth 'because it preserves for us what is most precious and most important – that is our personality, our individuality'. Incidentally, Dostoevsky was sentenced to death in 1849 on account of his involvement with a group of Utopian socialists, the Petrashevsky group.

The revolt against rationalism, utilitarianism, positivism, scientism and the technocratic culture's march towards the 'perfect society' was carried on by the existentialists, the descendents of the Romantics. Defending civilisation against modernity's barbarism, 'the sclerosis of objectivity', technology and mechanistic systems which have proudly 'produced things that act like humans and humans that act like things', and objecting to the reduction of the unique human individual to an abstract and functional identity, they embraced a 'culture of feelings', notable also for its anti-intellectual bias. The individual, helpless in a world which, as Karl Jaspers said, progresses relentlessly to 'the annihilation of existence', had to find his own way to survival, i.e. to rely on his and her own personal truth.

With objectivity being the prerogative of the Christian, socialist, capitalist or scientific order, 'truth', Kierkegaard, the forerunner of existentialism, argued, 'is subjectivity'. Such a truth could possibly be ascertained in the journey into the centre of our being, in order to check, perhaps, if anybody is still in, or to the source of our happiness, just to get, perhaps, an estimate of its current value.

Kierkegaard's work, a grotesque Gothic monument, demonstrated a complete disregard for objectivity, and, in spite of his attacks on the sterile Lutheran Church and the childish versions of biblical faith, displayed an authoritarianism coloured with a Christian moralism. Of importance to him was only the inwardness of his morbid religiosity, an inwardness which was 'the relationship of the individual to himself before God', the self being unconstrained by Reason.

As religiosity has for most religious people nothing to do with their relationship with their own selves, his self-centred approach created a new school of thought, one which related everything to one's own self. Problems existed only insofar as the particular individual viewed them as problems. The ethical content of his philosophy demanded a choice between purity and impurity, the life of Christ or not – in his vague humanism, that was the way to 'become an individual'. This individual's search for authenticity and 'active beingmentation', which is what mystic Gurdjieff and all those aboard the big spaceship Karnak had embarked upon, not accompanied by an analysis of its ethics, left, however, a huge hole in his concept. Being true to yourself is good but not good enough if the norm by which you decide how to answer such a call is not set. As Hans Jonas, the German ethical philosopher formerly a student of Heidegger, said, the Führer cannot after all be absolved of his responsibility on the grounds that he was responding to the calls for an authentic existence.

Kierkegaard's theological approach was pursued by many prominent twentieth century thinkers, including the German theologians Paul Tillich, Karl Barth and Rudolf Bultmann, the Viennese-born Israeli theologian Martin Buber, and the German philosopher Karl Jaspers. The 'amoral Franco-German existentialism', which as an American evangelist decided, 'has made both (the French and the Germans) and their cultures so unpleasant', does not represent, however, a single school of thought. Among those who embraced it are many atheist thinkers including Jean-Paul Sartre, who took existentialism in a Marxist direction, Albert Camus, the French philosopher known for his concept of the 'absurd', Simone de Beauvoir, who placed existentialism in a social, gender-oriented, context, or Martin Heidegger, the 'existential pragmatist' who, though he joined the German National Socialist party in 1933, was later placed under the Gestapo's surveillance before eventually being sent to the Rhine to dig trenches.

Nietzsche's violent opposition to the Enlightenment's 'truths' and certainties, which claimed to be based on truth that is nothing less than 'the irrefutable errors of mankind', but which Nietzsche said were built 'on a movable foundation', 'running water', was developed further by postmodernist writers. Denying truth and objectivity, the latter declared the end of the social, of history and of man, in other words, the end of a culture in which, as Baudrillard put it, people believed in collective action, interpreted events in relation to a 'rational' metanarrative, and saw a connection between their petty affairs and the destiny of mankind. The 'truth', dismissive of 'values', antagonistic to the whole and shiny as a rotten potato, is only 'personal'. The contemporary epoch had come to consciousness, dissolving, in T.S. Eliot's elegant verse, 'the floors of memory... its divisions and precisions'. Yet the absolutism of uncertainty, which replaced the discredited absolutism of the age of certainty, if consistent to its own argument, cannot claim to speak on truth's behalf. It is just another voice in Babel.

Postmodernism 'freed' the 'Others', the marginals, from the European oppressive truths but it has not liberated them from either their prejudices or the tyranny of the market. Indeed, by refusing to provide a concept of the 'right' and the 'good' without which a free society cannot live or set the goals of the individual's ethical life, normless and shapeless, it has ended up pulchritudinously serving a pugnacious form of capitalism. The 'free' individual is, thus, delivered to the market with a fork as big as his greed can hold to snatch the delicacies, the new illusions, consumerism has graciously laid on the table. This is what underpins the soulless, materialistic, uninspiring and, even worse, destructive way of life of our time and also what feeds the resurgent religious fundamentalism.

Menacingly and also bizarrely, the attack on the values of the Greek heritage is also currently being carried out in its very name. At its forefront are the so-called Straussians, i.e., the American neoconservative acolytes of Leo Strauss, the German-Jewish philosopher who died in the US in 1973 isolated and dispirited as, according to his daughter Jenny, he could not get his books republished. Rediscovered some years later, he turned into the ideological father of American fundamentalism as personified by Paul Wolfowitz, the ideologist of president George W. Bush and failed president of the World Bank, William Kristol, publisher of the influential neoconservative *Weekly Standard*, and Richard Perle, former Defence Secretary Donald Rumsfeld's deputy.

Leo Strauss, who considered that American republicanism and classical Greece represented two systems in harmony with each other even during the MacCarthy era, had turned the theologico-political dimension of the Athens–Jerusalem conflict into the exclusive focus of his intellectual curiosity: a life in accordance with Reason or a life in accordance with Revelation. He chose Athens over Jerusalem and called for a return to the ancients but his reasoning for it must have sickened the dead Greeks in their graves. Only Plato, whose system inspired Strauss, would have raised a glass.

His starting point, as he wrote to his Nazi friend Karl Schmitt, the Crown Jurist of the Third Reich, was that 'mankind is intrinsically wicked' and 'has to be governed'. Such governance could only be established if people were united, 'and they can only be united against other people'. Rejecting the Enlightenment, liberal democracy, pluralism and relativism, he held that the best form of government is the one which provides for the natural selection of the *aristoi*. People have no rights, as the only natural right that exists is the right of the superior to rule over the inferior. The *aristoi*, the élite, has the right to manipulate the truth and resort to what Plato called 'noble lies', president George W. Bush's assertions about Iraq's weapons of mass destruction, necessary, as Shadia Drury, American professor and author of two books on Strauss, wrote sarcastically, to lead 'the stupid masses'.

Though it may be hard to imagine Donald Rumsfeld cuddling up in bed with a copy of Strauss' Xenophon's Socratic Discourse, Strauss' attraction to the American neoconservatives increased as time went on. Some things are, it seems, as inescapable as old age. What made him as red hot as Clint Eastwood in Dirty Harry was also his emphasis on the virtue of the individual rather than Justice as the firmament of a working democracy, and his belief that wealth reflects individual worth as much as poverty shows poverty of character. This is the moral justification of the free market democracy and president George W. Bush's moral philosophy, which, 'as practised by the ancient Greeks', Allen Bloom, Strauss' acolyte, wrote, achieved the 'highest form of civilisation'. The Straussians, mostly American Jews, together with the evangelists, further consider religion to be indispensable to a stable social order, for it provides its inner cohesiveness. Strauss' teachings evoked as much hostility as ridicule. Hannah Arendt, who knew him well, was one of the first to tell him that 'a political party advocating (his) views ... could have no place for a Jew like him'. Others dismissed him as a fascist, a racist, a 'Nazi-Jew'.

The universal Fury unleashed by the forces of destruction is represented, as in Dürer's Horsemen of the Apocalypse, not by angels of reconciliation and heralds of serene justice, but, as Foucault held, by the dishevelled warriors of a mad vengeance claiming to act on civilisation's behalf.

Meanwhile, opposition to the values of the Enlightenment has re-emerged from another quarter in the form of ancient wisdom, associated with hidden, mystical teachings. The New Age, which stormed the scene in the last quarter of the twentieth century, just like the Gnostics of the Hellenistic and Roman times, rejected the religious orthodoxies and the authority of the Church – hence His Holiness the Pope saw in it Christianity's greatest threat in the Third Millennium. For the mystics, the purpose of life, which needs to be rescued from thought, is the spiritualisation of matter, the full identification with the divine, the blending with the void. The *pax americana* has apparently created the conditions for our deliverance to a bleached obmutescence in the same way that the *pax augusta* had, according to Origen, the third century A.D. Alexandrian theologian, created the necessary preconditions for the spread of Christianity.

Should that be the case, a new chapter in the history of silence is about to begin.

Index